MORE PRAISE FOR 'BUSINESS FOR BEGINNERS'

"I have adopted your text 'Business For Beginners' as our in-class text for a number of entrepreneurial programs... It's a great read, and an easy reference, and a must for all small business and entrepreneur programs."
Ken Smith, Manager, Abbotsford Busir   ess Resource Centre

"The book is exactly as promised—a s   ng your own business! The easy-to-read s   ike anyone is able to start a business... Cc   "
Mary Ellen Kuehl, Trinity Western Ur

"... The CFDC has incorporated the newest edition of Frances McGuckin's book 'Business For Beginners' into our Business Plan Training course. We find the book to be especially helpful to clients who are first time entrepreneurs. The easy to read format and 'back to the basics approach' is just what we have been looking for in training material."
Susanna Lachance-Watson, Self Employment Coordinator, Community Futures Development Corporation

"... The material was thorough and covered all the basics when it comes to small business start-up... This book provides the perfect introduction to starting a small business. I am going to recommend it to my next self-employment class."
Tonya Furlong, SE Benefit Coordinator, Nipissing East Community Opportunities, Ontario

"The book has an excellent format... the language used makes the book very easy to read... the book can be read and understood by the various ethnic groups whose first language is not English... Please accept my congratulations on your efforts to contribute to the development of entrepreneurism in Canada."
Kofi Ohene-Asante, EASE Self Employment Program

"We are pleased to announce that the Entrepreneur Apprentice Resource Program will be using your book as required reading for our apprentices... Only after extensive research, we have found that its contents covered a full range of Canadian business operations and was well-received by our students."
Paul Berrettoni, Entrepreneur Apprentice Resource Program (EAR)

"As an observer of small business, it has long struck me that there was so little information available in easily readable form for the new entrepreneur. Then Fran McGuckin's book came on the scene offering a simple, step-by-step guide and I thought, Hallelujah, at last someone has offered a thorough course in business start-up that's understandable by the neophyte. I congratulate Fran, because 'Business For Beginners' fills the niche that no one seemed to want to fill."
Tony Wanless, Money and Small Business Writer, *The Province*

"Few books come close to 'Business For Beginners' in its simplicity and user-friendly style... If this book had been written 15 years ago, I know that I would not have lost the business I had. Congratulations and bravo to Frances..."
Allan Holender, Host, *The Homebiz Show*

"With the rapid rise in self-employment, 'Business For Beginners' is in the right place at the right time, providing practical, easy to read advice and guidance for start up companies. Well done Frances!"
Peter Thomson, Director, Venture Development Centre, British Columbia Institute of Technology

"It's a great book! You are to congratulated on having written such an informative and interesting book... It is a valuable contribution for both new business owners and as a small business information resource."
Doris Miedzinski, Office Manager, The Kiwanis Enterprise Centre

"I'm only half-way through your book and I have to honestly say that your book is one of the best, if not the best book on small business that I have read–and I have read a lot of them in my time. I have found that most other small biz books are too institutional, which in most cases creates confusion, not clarity. I think it would be safe for me to say that there is genius in your simplicity!"
Mike Phipps, Marketing, Delta Chamber of Commerce

Business For Beginners:

A Simple Step-by-Step Guide

To Start Your New Business

Business For Beginners:

A Simple Step-by-Step Guide

To Start Your New Business

by Frances McGuckin

Published by Eastleigh Publications,
a division of Eastleigh Management Services
1998

Copyright ©1997, 1998 by Frances McGuckin

First edition published in 1997 by Productive Publications

Second edition published September 1998 by
Eastleigh Publications, a division of Eastleigh Management Services
21944 - 6th Avenue
Langley, British Columbia
Canada, V2Z 1R6

Tel: 604-530-3601
Toll-free: 1-888-771-2771
Fax:604-530-6447

Web site: www.smallbizpro.com
e-mail: sales@smallbizpro.com

Canadian Cataloguing in Publication Data

McGuckin, Frances
        Business for beginners: a simple step-by-step guide to
start your new business

2nd ed., rev. and expanded.
ISBN 0-9684011-0-4

        1. New business enterprises--Canada. 2. Small business--
Canada--Management. I. Title

HD62.7M228 1998   658.1'1'0971   C98-900822-3

Project Manager: Heidi LeRossignol of Behind the Book Production Services
Editor: Ruth Wilson
Cover design: Anne Dunnett of Inklings Design Studio
Back cover photo: Bob Marlow of Marlow's Fine Photography
Text design: Michael Howell-Jones of Design F/X

Printed and bound in Canada by Webcom Limited

10 9 8 7 6 5 4 3 2

This guide is dedicated to all the new and hopeful entrepreneurs who are starting out on the road to self-employment. The road is not paved with gold, nor is there a pot of gold at the end of the rainbow. But there is the satisfaction of being your own boss and watching your dreams turn to reality, through learning and gaining knowledge, hard work, and perseverance. Good luck to each and every one of you.

CONTENTS

CHAPTER 8:
WHAT ARE YOU REQUIRED TO DO BY LAW...
AND HOW TO COMPLY 145

CHAPTER 9:
WHAT START-UP EXPENSES WILL YOU INCUR? 159

CHAPTER 10:
HOW DO YOU MARKET YOUR BUSINESS? 183

CHAPTER 11:
HOW DO YOU ORGANIZE YOUR ACCOUNTING
AND PAPERWORK? 211

CHAPTER 12:
YOUR HOME OFFICE – HEAVEN OR HELL? 243

CHAPTER 13:
WHAT WILL YOUR STORY BE? 257

SAMPLES

ACKNOWLEDGMENTS

The positive response to the first edition of *Business for Beginners* has spurred me on to preparing this second, revised and expanded edition. I extend my deepest thanks to the many colleges, institutions, self-employment programs, and readers who are using the book and who have given me many excellent testimonials, both written and verbal.

In this edition, I have expanded it in areas that have come to light from questions asked by participants during workshops and seminars. To all those wonderful and eager workshop participants—I thank you for your timely questions, support, enthusiasm, and feedback. I hope I have left no questions unanswered.

No author can write a book without the help of friends, caring people, and team work. Thank you to Jurgen Hesse, my editor and mentor of the first edition, who not only showed interest and had faith in this book; he taught me much in a short time.

A special thank you to Heidi LeRossignol of *Behind The Book Production Services*, who encouraged me to pursue this second edition, and worked tirelessly to meet a tight production deadline. To Ruth Wilson, thank you for a wonderful editing job, and thanks to all the people who helped in the production of this second edition.

Many thanks to Merle Campbell, lawyer, who very kindly reviewed and added information to the chapter on legal agreements. To my many friends and associates, thank you for your input and support. These include Ken Smith, Allan Holender, Sandra Warner, Leslie Good, and Zosia Ettenberg, with a very special thank you to Daniel Milaire, who gave input into the marketing section in Chapter 10.

To my husband Michael and daughter Katrina, how can I thank you for your continued patience and positive encouragement throughout the many months of writing, rewriting and editing, not just once, but twice in two years? You endured my prolonged absences as I buried myself in "the office," with "the book" surfacing only for nourishment, fresh air, and a comfortable bed. Your patience and understanding will always be appreciated.

To all my clients with whom I worked over the years, thank you. Without you, I could not have gained the necessary experience to finally put all this information down on paper and realize my childhood dream of writing and publishing a book.

INTRODUCTION

FROM DREAM TO REALITY

Starting your first business is a real challenge because everything is new and foreign to you. But now the decision is made: you *are* going to start your own business. You have dreamed of this moment for many months. Now you want to make your dream a reality. What an exciting idea! Your head is swimming with thoughts, creative ideas, and dollar signs.

But where do you start? What is the first step? What business is the right one for you? What will it cost? Where will you get the money from? Do you have a viable idea? How will you market your business? How much competition is out there? The questions continually revolve in your mind. You are probably eating and sleeping the thought of owning your own business, but in which direction do you take the first step?

Not everyone is a gifted entrepreneur, which is why there are more employees than employers. It takes a special type of personality to run a business. You may be the best interior designer in the province, but the worst business person. Yet the skills you need can be learned. They include good organizational powers, financial knowledge, business administration knowledge, sales and marketing skills, a sound emotional state of mind, and a practical, level head. A good sense of humour is also extremely helpful.

As owner of your own business, you will be responsible for a variety of jobs and need to have your finger on the pulse of them all. To achieve this successfully, you should be willing to acknowledge your areas of weakness and work to improve on them. You'll be wearing many hats at once, and you'll have to develop the ability to make sound decisions, many on the spur of the moment. Listen to the advice of people who have succeeded and follow it. This book will lead you through each step of start-up. It will warn you of the tricks, traps, and pitfalls that many people experience.

As we hurtle into the new millennium, small and home-based businesses are on the increase. It is estimated that by the year 2001, there will be 60 million home-based businesses in North America alone. At the same time, the world is becoming obsessed with mega stores, mergers, co-op ventures, and complex technological changes. Only the strong and well-planned small businesses will survive. With the emphasis on knowledge and education, if you want to be a successful entrepreneur, you can no longer fly by the seat of your pants.

You will have a long, hard road ahead of you, but if you take the right steps, one at a time, you will be successful. This book is designed to help you make those right steps and understand that the decision you have made is one of the biggest of your life. It is written in an easy-to-understand manner, and is aimed at helping the first-time entrepreneur become a success, rather than one of those depressing failure statistics.

It is indeed a wonderful feeling to be your own boss, but it's also scary. You are alone and master of your own destiny. This book is here to keep you company and answer those hundreds of questions that are keeping you awake at night. Once you have run your own business successfully, you will never want to be an employee again. Remember, it takes a good two to three years for the path to become really smooth, but each step taken wisely is a step in the right direction.

I wish you good luck, a successful venture, happiness, health and the excitement of a whole new world of knowledge opening up to you.

Chapter 1
Where do you start?

Always follow your dreams –
just make sure you know where you are going,
and what you are doing.

WHERE HAVE ALL THE GOOD JOBS GONE?

Something disturbing is happening to our economy. The word "job" is fast disappearing from our language—somewhat like many of our endangered species—particularly that rare animal called a nine-to-five, working for the man, secure job.

Where have all the jobs gone? Why have they disappeared? And if they have all gone, why do we have less quality time and more stress? I believe the problem is "progress." Progress, of course, encompasses technological advances, which has brought rapid changes to our lives and to the world. Not all these changes are for the best. In many ways, our quality of life has regressed as the world continues to speedily "progress."

A well-worn and tired word often used is "recession." Employers have used it as an excuse for the last 20 years to cut back, lay off, downsize, capsize, pint-size, and reorganize. It all means the same thing in plain English: "You're fired!" or "You're redundant." or "We aren't hiring."

The definition of the word job in many cases is evolving into "self employment." All around the world, people who can't find jobs are making their own to pay the bills and put food on the table. As we approach into the new millennium, self-employment, or self-job creation, is the fastest growing current and future world trend. Economists predict that by the year 2001, two out of three people will be self-employed in some manner. Already, millions of people are telecommuting, "moonlighting" in a second part-time business, or struggling in their first endeavour.

WHY START YOUR OWN BUSINESS?

While "how-to-start a business" courses are flourishing, very few new businesses can boast success. Ninety percent of small businesses fail within the first two years of start-up. Current bankruptcy statistics show a large increase in personal bankruptcies, a good percentage of them caused by small business failure. The new business that is thrown together on a hope and a dream without being researched thoroughly, or that started without enough working capital, could sadly become one of these statistics within six to 18 months.

Entrepreneurs who don't qualify for bank financing resort to using credit cards to start their business and to supply working capital. Dreams turn into financial nightmares. Not only does the business ultimately have to close down, the owners are then left with huge, high-interest consumer debts to pay off. And who do you think suffers? Not just the family, but the whole economy. These words are not written to disillusion you with dismal statistics, but to point out that the business world is becoming more competitive every day. The more you are aware of what you are up against, the better armed you will be. It is your task to make your first business a success, not a failure.

So with all these challenges facing aspiring entrepreneurs, why do so many people want to leave their "traditional" jobs? Here are the most common reasons—and the reality behind them.

1. More work, less pay

Workplace conditions have become unbearably stressful for many employees. They have been forced to accept wage freezes and only minor pay raises for the past 15 or more years. Many employees have had to take on increased workloads through layoffs, and have worked under these stressful conditions for long periods. Wages have not kept pace with the cost of living, with the average family having to adjust its spending habits to conform to meagre wages.

There comes a point for many when the scant pay cheque is not worth the job-related stress. Many people opt for self-employment with the vision of controlling their destiny and experiencing profitable returns. If your new business is well planned, this will be the case for you after a couple of years of hard work. If you don't plan properly, you will work even harder than a salaried position, and make less money.

2. Stress related illness and depression

"Stress leave" has become a new but common phrase in the workplace. More employees are now having to take stress leave, which has been recognized by doctors and employers as the business-related illness of the nineties. The incidence of heart attacks at an earlier age has often been linked to work pressures. Marriage failures are on the increase, one of the main reasons being financial problems caused by cutbacks and layoffs.

An unemployed person cannot help becoming depressed. I can relate, first-hand, to the feelings of worthlessness, futility at trying your hardest, and good old self-pity. Many people hope that owning their own business will solve the stress problem. Sorry, but being your own boss involves a high level of stress too. You have no pension, no employment insurance, and, in most cases, no future retirement plans—all good reasons for you to ensure that you set practical goals for your business and plan it out in extensive detail. Even a business heading in the right direction can be stressful at times, but the rewards are fulfilling.

3. Employer threats, not strokes

Employees are working under the constant threat of losing their jobs. People with secure positions are considered the lucky few. But is any job secure these days? Employees are no longer treated as well as they used to be. Verbal abuse, sexual harassment, and wages are common complaints in today's workforce.

Financial pressures of struggling businesses are passed on to the staff, who are not getting the rewards and pats on the back needed to sustain job motivation. Some corporations are becoming aware of these effects on employees and are taking steps to increase employee motivation, but many are not. Some workers have laboured under these types of conditions for over 15 years. The time eventually comes when one says "Enough! I'm quitting! I'll start my own business!"

4. Layoffs, downsizing, or no work

The inability to find work has created the largest surge in small business start-ups ever experienced in our economy, hence the high failure rate. People start businesses out of desperation, usually without enough cash flow and planning to ensure a successful, long-term venture. They will turn their hand to anything which promises the chance of making money, without first investigating it thoroughly.

Young people are faced with the bleak future of no work after all their education and training. Becoming an entrepreneur may be an exciting alternative to working for an employer for minimum wages when you have maximum qualifications. Young people have much to offer our economy with their new and innovative ideas, energy, and technological knowledge, and there are many programs that encourage our youth to seek self-employment as a job alternative. But with their enthusiasm for a new venture comes the chance that the wrong business will be chosen. Many young people feel that owning their own business means making heaps of money without doing heaps of work. It is crucial for young people to be fully business-educated before they make this important decision.

5. Incompetent employers

Talented workers with many years of experience in their jobs often realize that their employers are not particularly competent. Some get tired of working under these conditions, feeling that they have the experience and ability to strike out on their own. What is forgotten, however, is that being an expert at one thing does not ensure all-round business knowledge. Running your own business will definitely be a unique experience, but not necessarily a good one if you aren't prepared. When you are transported from a job with one area of responsibility—such as being a warehouse manager—to running all aspects of your own business, you will go from wearing one or two hats to wearing many. Quite a change of wardrobe.

6. Home-based business increase

People used to be almost ashamed to admit that they worked from home, but no longer. It is a well-accepted fact that this is the way most small business is—and will be—conducted. The thought of combining work and a quality family life is appealing to many. Unfortunately, the media promotes home-based businesses as a great tax write-off, without explaining the down side of operating from home. (See Chapter 12 for an indepth discussion on home-based businesses.)

7. Leaving the boss behind

No one enjoys being told what to do, let's be honest! When you are your own boss, you, and you alone, are responsible for all decisions. There is a certain pride in the words, "I have my own business," or, "I am going into business for myself." It is an exciting feeling, but many first-time entrepreneurs make terrible mistakes in the start-up stage. The image of being a business owner blinds them to the realities of running a business.

As much as you may not enjoy being told what to do, at least you had direction in your old job. As an entrepreneur, you are the one who makes all the decisions. This requires massive self-motivation and self-confidence—what a responsibility! Who shoulders the blame when things go wrong? You, of course. That's a heavy load to place upon yourself, so let's hope you are not a procrastinator, and that you have confidence in your business acumen.

Why do you want to start a business?

Some of the reasons for starting a business aren't very sound. People starting up out of desperation risk making hasty decisions. They may have spent many years working for one employer, feeling stressed, unmotivated, and depressed, viewing self-employment as a solution to all their problems. Almost any opportunity to escape their current situation seems like a great opportunity. But firstly, they find themselves needing an immediate income replacement when they are often tired and worked out. What is really needed is a good long rest with time to research their new venture thoroughly. If you are in a similar situation, *please* proceed with caution.

Some people are just not suited to self-employment. They may not be used to decision-making after decades of working for an employer who did it all for them. They have not been exposed to the business world from the entrepreneurial side and do not realize what it takes to run a successful business. They find themselves with no time to take the necessary courses to round out their knowledge and fill in the missing gaps. The two most important steps, preparing a proper business plan and researching the market thoroughly, are not taken. They may have what appears to be a great idea, or perhaps they are presented with what seems like a wonderful money-making proposal, and jump in with both feet without checking the depth of the water first.

Let's face it, there's no easy way to make money. Business means hard work, diligence, patience, and careful planning. That doesn't mean you shouldn't start your own business, but it does mean you must think about what lies ahead. If the business that interests you does not meet the criteria as set out in this guide, or if you have negative feelings about a prospective business, walk away from it. People tend not to listen to their intuition; remember that intuition was given to us for a good reason. The older you get, the more you learn to rely on it. Call it your better judgment, your sixth sense, or your inner self: peel away your conscious thoughts and listen to it before making any important decisions. Most important of all, consult professionals for advice.

DO YOU HAVE WHAT IT TAKES?

It takes a dedicated person to handle the successful start-up and running of a business, but it's well worth the effort. The rewards of doing it yourself are bountiful. You will gain self-confidence, knowledge, and emotional satisfaction. If you love what you are doing, and you do it well, you will be motivated to persist and strive for your future goals. Not only will you have grown, you accomplished this success by yourself.

An entrepreneur is described in the dictionary as a "business person," "financial executive," or "capitalist." These days, we tend to associate the word more with a person striking out on his or her own, usually equating the word with a successful venture. A successful entrepreneur is not a particular type of person, but someone with a combination of well-rounded talents that enables the business to progress positively. Some people thrive on the challenge, and some have a natural aptitude for business. Others study hard, take courses, and read extensively, learning as they progress. A true entrepreneur will have a passion for business and an unquenchable desire to learn, absorb, explore, and grow.

Exercise #1 lists 20 questions which are designed to give you some insight into the desirable qualities an entrepreneur needs or should develop. Answer them honestly now, before reading on.

EXERCISE #1
ENTREPRENEURIAL TRAITS CHECKLIST

	Yes	No
1. Are you a decision-maker or a procrastinator? Can you make quick decisions and feel comfortable?	❑	❑
2. Do you relate well to people on all levels?	❑	❑
3. Can you join in a conversation in a room full of strangers and feel at ease?	❑	❑
4. Can you pick up the phone and ask a direct question in an uncomfortable situation?	❑	❑
5. Can you direct others to carry out your orders without being too aggressive or overbearing?	❑	❑
6. Can you start a project and follow it through, or do you get sidetracked easily?	❑	❑
7. Can you express yourself well so that people are interested in what you are saying ?	❑	❑
8. Do you like yourself and who you are?	❑	❑
9. Do you start each day in a positive manner?	❑	❑
10. Can you maintain a positive attitude even in adverse situations?	❑	❑
11. Do you have technical skills in the area in which you are interested, and are you willing to expand on these skills?	❑	❑

	Yes	No
12. Do you read the financial and business sections of the newspaper on a regular basis and keep up with current affairs?	☐	☐
13. Can you cold-call or sell yourself over the phone?	☐	☐
14. Do you have a sound financial knowledge of how a business operates and know the difference between gross and net profits?	☐	☐
15. Can you express yourself well in writing?	☐	☐
16. Can you take the initiative and work without direction?	☐	☐
17. Are you willing to work long, hard hours?	☐	☐
18. Can you work without getting easily distracted?	☐	☐
19. Do you understand cash flow, assets, liabilities, equity, income, depreciation, goodwill, cost of sales and working capital?	☐	☐
20. Do you keep legible notes, and pay attention to details?	☐	☐

Ideally you have been able to answer "yes" to at least 15 of these questions. You need a variety of skills so you can control a multifaceted operation by yourself. If you answered "no" to any questions, ask yourself how you could improve in these areas, and make a note of them below, or at the end of the book.

_____

_____

_____

_____

_____

_____

SIX SKILLS FOR SUCCESS

The traits defined in the questions in the checklist above can be categorized into six skills which are essential to an entrepreneur's success. You may not have developed all of these skills, but like most things in life, you can learn by reading, practice, and determination.

1. People skills

People make or break your business. You make or break your business, because *you* are your business. The way you deal with people will determine much of your success. How many times have you decided not to return to a store because the cashier, clerk, or manager was rude to you? How many times have you been impressed by a business person going out of his or her way to help you?

Good manners, politeness, and attentiveness to your customers' needs are what will ensure repeat business. Customers need to feel they are important to you. The same principles apply to dealing with your trade suppliers, employees, business contacts, and even the competition. Never burn your bridges by treating people badly, and respect those with whom you deal. Treat each person with the same respect you would expect to receive.

Recently, I dealt with a large department store when I frantically needed a replacement computer part. The part was promised the next day, and the next, and the next. I phoned the store about twenty-five times within four days, and every time different people gave me a different story. Each phone call meant a lengthy period of being placed on hold. My blood pressure rose rapidly as my patience level quickly diminished. No one seemed to care—until an irate call to the manager finally elicited some action. Needless to say, that's the last time the store will see the colour of my money. Why? I was made to feel as if I didn't matter, and as a customer, *everyone* matters.

Part of the package of people skills is a good sense of humour. It's an important survival tool, as is a smile. A smile or a little joke in a tense situation can do wonders in turning a problem around. Keeping a positive outlook on a daily basis will maintain your motivation level. Allowing depression, apprehension, insecurity, and doubts to affect your thoughts will lower your production level and make goals seem inaccessible.

While it is hard to smile when things aren't going right, remember that no one wants to talk to a negative person or a pessimist. If you maintain a positive outlook, you will transmit this to the people you deal with. They will want to be associated with you and do business with you.

2. Personal skills

A healthy self-esteem is necessary for you to tackle each day positively and productively. As an entrepreneur, you will spend a great deal of time working alone, so listen to your heart but consult your head before making a decision.

You will have to keep yourself motivated, staying on track with your plans and keeping well organized. These qualities rarely come from people who do not like themselves. If you have problems in this area, read some self-help books, take courses, or talk to a counsellor. Hypnotherapy can be a wonderful tool to remove many of these mental blocks and allow you to work more positively. You will need all these positive skills to communicate with others and to market your business. Remember, you are selling yourself to your clients, not just your product or service.

3. Financial skills

There is no way around it! You have to be financially knowledgeable in the business world. Otherwise, how can you understand the overall concept of doing business and the meaning of profitability? You don't want to learn the hard way, by making serious mistakes. Your entrepreneurial knowledge should include basic accounting, organizational and administrative skills, an understanding of all tax laws, federal and provincial requirements, and an in-depth knowledge of the business that you are about to undertake. (See Chapter 3 for more on financial statements.)

Sounds like a lot to learn, and it is. But take heart: you can learn everything you need to know. No one was born a business hot-shot, and there are an abundance of courses available offering business management training. Usually you can take them to fit your schedule, part time, full time, during the day, or in the evening.

4. Technical skills

Please don't start or purchase a business that requires technical skills you don't have or cannot learn quickly. Start in an area where you can utilize your talents. They may need expanding through evening courses or additional reading, but at least you will have a basis with which to start. Never cease your education in your area of expertise, and remember to keep up with the changing technology within your chosen field.

Attend seminars, workshops, trade shows, and conferences to add to your knowledge and keep a leading edge on your competitors. Don't make the mistake that many entrepreneurs do of becoming so engrossed in working *at* their business, they forget to work *on* their business. This is a critical lesson to learn, so learn it well.

Your customers will come to you looking to you as being the expert, and that is what you have to be. Think about the various services you use yourself. When you look in the Yellow Pages for a plumber or an electrician for example, you assume the companies advertised there are run by professional and skilled people. As a consumer, you put your trust in them. Your customers put the same trust in your skills, and you should never let them down. Be the expert, be the professional, or don't be in business.

5. Communication skills

Now is the time to sharpen your communication skills if they have become a little rusty. You may need to communicate with lawyers, accountants, bank managers, loan companies, or venture capitalists. You may have to negotiate leases, contracts, work with building inspectors, municipal officers, government and various tax officials, suppliers, advertising agencies, employees, and more. You need to be able to get your message and needs communicated clearly to all these people. Some you meet will be difficult to deal with, so good communication skills will reduce the chance of being misunderstood. Both verbal and written communication skills are essential tools for success. Your messages require clear and precise language.

People are judged by their written skills, or the lack of them, more often than you would think. Are you adept at composing business letters and written information which reads easily and is direct, polite, and informative? If not, refer to any one of the many helpful books available in the reference library which will help you tone up your communication skills. Even better, take a course on writing business letters.

Have you ever listened to a talk show host or sales person who constantly punctuates their conversation with "ers" and "ums"? Your immediate perception of those people is likely that they lack knowledge, self-esteem, or communication skills. Remember that when you communicate with others, your competence will be judged the same way— by your ability to get your message across clearly and professionally.

The ability to communicate effectively at a variety of levels, in a variety of manners, to a variety of people, is a skill few people possess naturally. One of the best ways to build your confidence is to join Toastmasters International. There you can learn how to get your message across in a professional manner. What you learn at Toastmasters International can be applied to a telephone conversation, a sales pitch, or to a room full of people. Many prominent business people owe a good part of their success to this highly effective organization.

6. Marketing skills

To round off your entrepreneurial skills, you will need to learn how to market your business. Without a sound knowledge of marketing, you will not have any customers. Marketing is explained in depth in Chapter 10, but in a nutshell, it is the ability to communicate to your potential customers and inform them of your products or services. Marketing is not putting an advertisement in the local paper or flyers in the mail. The most effective forms of marketing involve one-on-one communication skills and knowing how to define and target your market.

Once again, you may have to take a marketing course to learn what will work for your business. You will have to study your competitors and decide if their marketing techniques will work for you. You will have to read books, talk to others in a similar field, and observe how other types of businesses successfully market their products or service. No one has the magical marketing answer: usually, effective marketing is a combination of many techniques that can change from time to time. Your job will be to define which will work best for you.

DO YOU HAVE THE MANAGEMENT SKILLS?

You've taken a look at entrepreneurial skills. What about basic business management skills? Do you have what it takes? Exercise #2 highlights some important areas which require strengths and competent management. Complete it now.

EXERCISE #2

MANAGEMENT SKILLS CHECKLIST

	Yes	No
1. Could I cope with pressures and deadlines on a constant basis?	☐	☐
2. Could I keep the pressures of business away from my family life?	☐	☐
3. Could I fire an incompetent employee?	☐	☐
4. Could I maintain strict credit control?	☐	☐
5. Could I refuse credit to a good but slow-paying client?	☐	☐
6. Could I pick up the phone and ask for payment of a late account?	☐	☐
7. Could I maintain control of my daily, weekly and monthly finances?	☐	☐
8. Do I understand financial statements, and how my business is taxed?	☐	☐
9. Do I know the break-even point of my business?	☐	☐
10. Could I delegate responsibilities to others?	☐	☐

If you can't answer "yes" to all these questions, then you need to analyse why. Make a note below of the areas that will need some concentrated improvement, or at the end of the book.

_____

_____

_____

These last two questionnaires will help you define your areas of weakness on which you should work. Some of these areas will be covered in more detail in this book. You want the very best for your new business, so make yourself the best manager you possibly can.

WHY DO BUSINESSES FAIL?

There are seven main reasons why the majority of businesses fail:

1. No planning and poor management

2. Poor cash flow/undercapitalized

3. Poor location

4. Inadequate marketing plans

5. Competition not researched

6. Wrong choice of business

7. Business grows too quickly

Any one of the above reasons can cause your business to fail, but combine two or more and your business is in hot water. But if you do your homework, none of them should apply to you. Let's look at each in turn.

1. No planning and poor management

Statistics cite that over 80 percent of businesses start without a business plan. Perhaps this is why over 80 percent of businesses fail. Just as an architect must work to blueprints, so must your business. If a business plan is not in place, then poor management is bound to follow.

An understanding of what constitutes sound business management is crucial for success. Look around your town as you drive past the smaller stores. How many of these have closed down after three to nine months, only to be replaced by a new business? To prevent failure, there are some important, basic guidelines you should follow:

a) Provide the right service or product at the right time, in the right location, at the right price.

b) Ensure profit margins are calculated to support overhead, and pay all salaries and personal commitments.

c) Ensure the business provides a steady income year-round and does not rely solely on seasonal trading. Have a "plan B" in place for quieter months.

d) Keep inventories carefully selected to allow a regular turnaround.

e) Keep accounting records up to date and consult them regularly to monitor progress.

f) Monitor marketing strategies carefully for results and compare your return on investment.

g) Be aware of changes in consumer trends, technology, and the changing economy.

h) Make time each day to follow up, market your business, and keep on top of paperwork.

i) Monitor accounts receivable at least weekly, keeping in touch with slow-paying clients to ensure promised cheques are received.

The term "management" covers many areas, from financial planning, sales and advertising methods, correct buying of inventory, control of overhead costs, staff control, administration, and awareness of changing markets, competitors, and trends. Can you cope with all this? Ask yourself whether you are ready.

2. Poor cash flow/undercapitalized

"Cash flow" describes the movement and flow of money within a business. Opinions vary about how much money you need to start and maintain a business in the first year. The very minimum you will need is enough to support the business and personal commitments for the first three months or longer. This is the barest necessity, based on a business that has a guaranteed and immediate cash flow. A much more sensible rule of thumb is to have a financial reserve that will cover all your costs and expenses for at least the first nine months.

The average business is started with the minimum of capital, often borrowed from family, banks, through credit cards, or high interest loans.

Some people remortgage their home, a step which should be taken with great caution, because if the business fails, the home could be lost and the marriage really put to the test.

Know where your financing will come from, what the terms of repayment are, and whether the business can afford the repayments during the first year or two. If you can't afford to borrow—then don't. Rethink your business plan before making any final decisions.

3. Poor location

For retail businesses in particular, location is a key factor for success. Is it practical to have a hairdressing salon in an industrial area? Or a consignment store in a business centre mall? Or a restaurant tucked into a small, out-of-the way strip mall visited mainly by seniors? Despite this self-evident logic, people often locate their business in the wrong areas for the wrong reasons. They make their choice based on cheap rent (and why is it so cheap?), or because the size or layout of the building suits their purpose. Heavy advertising costs are then incurred to entice customers to the location. Walk-by traffic is vital to a retail location. Studies show that the average consumer will not travel more than three blocks out of his or her way, particularly if the same product can be purchased at a closer location.

4. Inadequate marketing plan

With the abundance of mega-malls, chain stores, and small businesses opening, your business must fill a need and a niche in the marketplace. A marketing plan is an integral part of your business plan. It should be clear not just in your head, but also on paper, showing how you are going to market your business. This information can be documented only after thorough market research has been completed. With small and home-based businesses, marketing is usually cited as one of the largest hurdles faced by the owners. (Marketing is covered in more depth in Chapter 10.)

5. Competition not researched

If there are 40 restaurants in your town, is it an astute decision to open another one? If there are four well-established camera and photo developing stores, why would you open another? Only so much business can be generated in one geographical area. Too many stores offering the same service eats into one another's profits. Each will struggle to make a living, offering profit-draining specials to entice consumers. Ensure you study and know your town or marketing area intimately before purchasing or opening your business. Your local municipality or chamber of commerce has a wealth of information on this subject which can help you.

Ask yourself: what more can you offer than your competitors? Product saturation and competition go hand-in-hand. Researching your competition is a must. Can you compete with large chain stores or well-established smaller outlets? What can you offer that is different? Chapter 4 details how to outwit your competition in more depth.

And don't limit yourself to the current competition: think about the future. What would happen to your business if a large store selling your product or service cheaper opened up within a few blocks of you? There are no regulations prohibiting businesses offering similar services from opening up near each other.

6. Wrong choice of business

A business proposal can seem very attractive to an inexperienced and excited buyer. Many unprofitable businesses have been presented in a profitable light through professional presentation, skilled wording, and a good sales pitch. A professional portfolio often glosses over the real reasons for the business sale—lack of profits.

Some people think they can take a business and do better than the last person. If it's your first business purchase, don't be so sure that you can create miracles. Remember: no matter how attractive the business may appear, you have to love what you are doing and be the expert. Consulting an accountant will probably save you from making the wrong decision, so don't be cheap. Don't fall for promises of a quick return for little outlay and minimal work. These promises are found in many advertisements, and they belong in the fiction section.

7. Business grows too quickly

Business growth doesn't sound like it should be a reason for business failure, but it is often the case. If a business is started with minimum cash flow, particularly one involving a large inventory, rapid growth can create all kinds of problems. Sudden growth may mean that your location is no longer suitable, and moving a business is costly. Additional inventory requirements, staffing, machinery or equipment upgrading— all must be paid for with profits. There is always a lead time between the necessity for extra cash, and the eventual cash flow back into the business from increased sales. Sudden growth puts extra demands on your management abilities as you cope with the changes.

WHAT TYPE OF BUSINESSES ARE AVAILABLE?

There are so many types of businesses that research can become confusing, but as you will find out, very few will fit your personal criteria. The business has to be compatible with your personality and abilities. If you don't like cold-calling, opt for an established business with regular clientele. If you are uncomfortable selling to friends and family, don't enter into a multilevel situation. If working seven days a week is not for you, avoid retail.

Let's look at the various and most common types of businesses available. They come in all shapes and sizes:

1. Multilevel and network marketing

2. Franchising

3. Manufacturing

4. Distribution

5. Retail

6. Service

1. Multilevel and network marketing

Multilevel and network marketing is attractive to many first-time entrepreneurs, and it is certainly an increasingly popular way to do business. In many cases, the start-up costs are quite low, the business can be operated from home, and you can start on a part-time basis.

Over the years, I have watched many friends and associates drift in and out of various multilevel businesses. Very few of these people have ever made it to the top. Most continued to dabble in the business part time, ending up with inventory they could not sell, and ultimately gave the products away to friends at below cost or as gifts.

Statistics reveal that approximately 0.6 percent of people make it to the top level, 20 percent earn a reasonable part-time or supplementary income, and the balance of people drop out after trying this type of business for a short time.

Don't get me wrong. If you have the right personality, drive, ambition, and time to devote to the business, you can be successful. But it is important to ask yourself if you have the personality to sell, sell, sell. You must have total confidence in the products you are selling. You have to be prepared to market those products at every opportunity, always looking for people to either expand your down-line, (your own distributorship) or to sell to. All of this can even affect your social life: instead of enjoying a social event, you may see a room full of potential clients instead. You may even find friends avoid you if you constantly grind away at them.

If you are outgoing, an extrovert, and a person with a lot of business, social, and networking contacts, multilevel could be for you. Most multilevel companies require that you attend training sessions, motivational seminars, and "bring a friend" weekly sales sessions, often held at hotels in the evenings. Their products are often distributed through in-home parties, so be prepared to work nights and weekends.

Ask yourself these questions before jumping into multilevel:

1. Can I feel comfortable approaching friends and family for sales?

2. Am I confident enough in the products to sign up friends and family as my down-line?

3. Will my family life suffer through constant evening and weekend commitments?

4. Am I able to attend out-of-town and out-of-country seminars?

5. Can I close deals quickly?

6. Do I have enough money to cover me through training and start-up?

7. Is the company secure? Does it have a good reputation?

8. Who are the principals of the company? What is their track record?

Multilevel and networking companies come and go. You need to find one with a solid history. There are many disreputable companies distributing through this system. You become a distributor for their products and should be aware of what is involved. The real money from multilevel business is earned when you sign up other distributors under you (your down-line), who in turn sign up distributors under them. At that point, you start receiving commissions based on their sales.

To start up, you will probably have to spend quite a few dollars on sample kits and sales aids such as brochures, videos, company magazines, and promotional items. Then you need a sample inventory; you can't sell products without it. Some sample kits can cost up to $2,000, especially with jewellery lines. When ordering your products, you will need credit card facilities and will be charged shipping and handling costs, approximately four percent of the total dollar value of the order.

If you have been signed up by an enthusiastic and aggressive up-line (the person who signed you up), you may have to cope with being asked to attend regular seminars, sign up more people, and make more sales, so that your up-line can progress further up the ladder. These pressure tactics don't suit many people, so be sure to get to know your potential up-line and his or her goals and strategies before you sign with them. Most team managers are extremely supportive and helpful.

Research the company thoroughly. Find out the history of top management. Does the corporate management structure change regularly? How long has the business been around? Does it have a good reputation? Are the products of good quality, and does the company back its products with acceptable warranties? Talk to others who have been in the same company for a while and listen carefully to their feedback.

A few years ago, I was talked into trying a multilevel venture part time. The products were excellent, and I proudly sold some to my neighbours. Unfortunately, after three years, the product needed repairing, as did my own. The company was out of business—and I was embarrassed to have sold goods to a friend and neighbour when they couldn't be maintained or repaired.

Many companies restrict how and where you can sell their products. Some want you to market only through home parties and will not allow you to sell through trade shows and community trade events. These marketing restrictions can severely reduce your sales avenues, so be sure you are aware of these restrictions before making a final decision.

Multilevel marketing is like any other self-employed business. You incur start-up costs of printing and stationery, advertising, inventory and sales aids, promotional materials, gifts, transportation expenses, telephone system upgrading, and probably a cellular phone. Talk to a few people who have succeeded in the business and review start-up costs with them, including the continuing costs of remaining successful.

2. Franchising

It seems that everyone is franchising everything these days, from a cup of coffee to house cleaning services. As with multilevel companies, franchisers come and go. Those with a solid reputation who have perfected their business strategies over the years will be asking a fair price for a franchise. Traditionally, established franchise business failures are significantly less than independent businesses, because they have designed effective marketing strategies and administration systems. This is what the purchaser is paying for, along with the good name of the company.

Be wary of new franchising companies who cannot show an adequate track record. Investing in some of these businesses will be as risky as starting your own. If you are thinking of investing in a franchise business which is riding a current popular trend, be careful. Your market research will indicate whether the trend is predicted to be short-lived or long-term. Definitely consult your accountant before making a decision.

Well-established and profitable franchises are expensive, but there are many reasons for this:

1. They have spent the time and money on in-depth marketing research

2. They have perfected their marketing and advertising methods

3. Locations are researched for viability

4. They have built their reputation and are trusted by the consumers

5. Profit margins and operating expenses have been established and refined

When you purchase a franchise, be aware that you must abide by their rules. Uniformity is what makes franchises a success. They have designed an operational plan and formula that works, and they don't like people going against the system. Although you are an independent, you are controlled by the head office. If you have a strong and creative entrepreneurial spirit, you may find a franchise too restrictive and regulated.

You pay a certain amount for goodwill on purchase, plus a percentage of profits or sales volumes each year. You may have to purchase their own brand or recommended supplies and raw materials, paying more than if you shopped around for better prices. A good franchise is an expensive proposition, but in most cases, a profitable business is the end result.

3. Manufacturing

If you want to purchase a manufacturing business, you need to understand what manufacturing is. As a manufacturer, you are responsible for the end product and its safety in the marketplace. Manufacturing businesses require a larger financial stake, in-depth market research, and a solid business plan.

Unless the business is extremely easy to learn, think carefully about manufacturing. Most vendors will provide a training period after purchase, but their expertise usually comes from many years in the industry. Are they going to take the time and teach you all the tricks of the trade? As an owner of a manufacturing business, you need to have many of those management skills mentioned earlier. Organizational skills are a must, as is a sound financial and production background. You may purchase a business with dependable, well-trained employees already in place, but you cannot rely solely on your employees—they are transient. You have to rely on your own experience and good judgment.

During you market research, check local, North American, and overseas markets producing similar products. Current Canadian consumer statistics show that consumers want the best value for their dollar. They are not loyal to one supplier anymore, only to their bank account. In some cases, Canadian-made goods cannot match the prices of internationally produced goods because of our higher salaries and living standards.

It takes years to establish a new name in an industry, so if you are starting from scratch, you need enough working capital to maintain the new business for up to two years or until regular profits roll in. There are various types of government-funded programs available for manufacturing businesses, and these can be found in the publication *Overview of Government Assistance Programs for Small Business*, available from the Canada Business Service Centres.

If you are buying an existing business, talk to the key employees if possible. Ascertain their long-term goals with the company and listen to any complaints or suggestions about the current operation. Employees are the backbone of every business and usually know the inside story that you would not hear from the vendor.

If you plan to export a product or import raw materials from out of the country, you have to learn about the various methods and costs of shipping, customs documentation, and letters of credit. Products have to be costed to allow for fluctuations in currencies, particularly if dealing with the United States and Mexico. A Vancouver distribution company almost went bankrupt when the Canadian dollar dropped sharply in a short time. The company had not diversified its inventory lines with enough local product, with 70 percent of the inventory imported from the U.S. The drop in the dollar made the products so much more expensive to land that the wholesale cost of the product nearly equalled the sales price.

If you are considering starting a manufacturing business, allow enough time and money in your budget to talk to various government agencies and consultants in that area. A business plan prepared by a professional can cost thousands of dollars. Do not consider manufacturing if you are undercapitalized. Be sure that you have the personnel resources to cover all areas of production, distribution, sales, and accounting. You will need an experienced team, working together, to make your business succeed.

A well-run manufacturing concern can make healthy profits for the owners, as well as increase the value of the goodwill over time.

4. Distribution

Distribution (or wholesaling) is an excellent field, provided you can find profitable product lines to distribute. A distributor acts as a link between the manufacturer and retail outlets. It helps to know about the product lines you are distributing, and many manufacturers will help enhance your product knowledge.

The size and variety of lines you distribute will dictate the type and size of the premises you will need. If you are dealing in larger items, your warehouse facility will have to accommodate your product efficiently. The warehouse may need dock-loading facilities, shelving, forklifts, and special equipment for moving materials. You will also need an efficient shipping and receiving system with dependable and honest employees in charge.

Research your product lines carefully. Has the product been available for a number of years? Does it have a good reputation? Does the manufacturer supply and honour product warranties? If distributing a new product line, how large is the market? Is it a gimmick? Has the market been saturated with similar items? Are the products of good quality? Are the prices competitive?

If you are purchasing an existing business, the retail client base should already be established. You will need to look at the financial statements to see whether the client base needs expanding. You also need to know the current payment terms, how slowly clients pay, and whether there are bad credit risks. If you are starting your own distribution business, you first must source out potential clients and see what interest is shown in your product lines. It's no use distributing products that move slowly; they take up valuable warehouse space.

A good business plan will help you determine if there will be a high enough profit margin in your product line to cover all overhead. In distribution, an average gross profit margin (i.e. profit after the sale, less the cost of the product) should range up to 45 percent of selling price, and no less than 20 percent. This allows room in your profits to cover the cost of warehouse space, vehicle and equipment maintenance, marketing and promotion costs, and all other normal overhead expenses. If you are starting out small with just a few products, calculate how much you must sell each month to break even. Ensure that you will have enough interested retail clients in place to cover those costs before making a firm commitment to carry that line.

5. Retail

If you are interested in retail, choose carefully because the competition will be fierce. Many small retail businesses hardly make an acceptable living. Retail outlets are not only competing with each other, they are competing with large chain stores, retail warehouses, multilevel, and mail-order sales. With the recent increase in "mega-malls" in most towns and cities, a small retail outlet is quite a gamble. In one British Columbia town recently, two large mega-complexes were approved for building within a couple of weeks of each other. They are situated only a few miles apart, with each offering a multitude of movie theatres, restaurants, and similar retail outlets. Many smaller businesses in the town and other malls may well be affected by this enormous amount of competition, and some will surely fail.

Prime retail locations are expensive. If a store is located in a large shopping mall, rents can be disproportionately high, with advertising funds paid to the mall property managers each month. You have to sell a lot of doughnuts to pay a $2,000 or $3,000 monthly rent.

If you do decide on a retail business, choose one in which you have a reasonable knowledge of the products you are selling. Customers are always looking for quality, service, and the cheapest price in town. They ask store personnel for advice, and expect thorough product knowledge and after-sales service from them. Many customers have been lost to the competition because sales staff are not knowledgeable about products.

The retail industry is certainly one where your people skills will have to be in fine shape. You need a lot of patience to deal with a variety of people. You will face teenagers, seniors, immigrants, tourists with language difficulties, parents with screaming children, and some rather disagreeable customers who will seem to enjoy giving sales people a difficult time.

There are some factors specific to retail that you should consider as you research your potential business:

a) Inventory

Your inventory selection is what will make your store. A large inventory is usually necessary to attract customers and obtain better price breaks from your suppliers. It's not unusual for a small retail store to carry a minimum of $60,000 worth of inventory. This means you need a large investment, and you will have large amounts of cash tied up in your inventory. Poor selection of inventory can mean that slow-moving products will eventually have to be sold at a discount. Select your lines carefully to facilitate a quick turnaround. Try to find out how many times a year your inventory should "turn" or sell by your industry's standards. You can then monitor your inventory turnover and watch for the slow-moving products.

Always keep up to date with economic trends, as consumer trends vary with the economic climate. As the nation seems to be working harder and getting poorer, vary your inventory lines to appeal to a broad cross-section of consumers. Unless you specialize in strictly high-end products, maintain an inventory that appeals to the pockets of lower and middle-income brackets.

b) Hours

Retail outlets are often open seven days a week, many offering extended evening hours. You cannot work seven days a week as well as ordering supplies, restocking shelves, banking, paying accounts, preparing wages, and doing the accounting all by yourself. You need help. First, determine the hours you can manage to work on a regular schedule without over-extending yourself, then decide for which work you are better suited, and then look around for additional staff to fill in the gaps. However, when you first start, you probably won't be able to afford extra staff, so be prepared for long and tedious work days.

c) Advertising and sales promotions

To keep your store's name in the public eye, you will need to advertise regularly, run promotional specials, clearance sales, and special events. Advertising dollars can be eaten up quickly if ineffective media are used.

Profit margins are much lower on sale and clearance items. The dollar volume may increase, but the profit margins decrease. Learn your product costs intimately and calculate how much you can reduce a sale item before losing money.

Many retail stores waste huge amounts of dollars advertising ineffectually. When you are planning your marketing, study how similar stores advertise in your area and note the effectiveness of their advertising and how it appeals to you as a consumer. Visit the stores both before and during an advertised sale, noting whether traffic has increased or not.

d) Consumer spending cycles

Retail outlets are extremely vulnerable to consumer spending cycles. Depending on the type of store, your sales can be affected by weather, post-Christmas financial woes, summer vacation periods, back to school rush, current economic climate, and after-sale quiet periods. Learn the spending cycles that will both increase and decrease your sales volume so you can plan your cash flow and marketing strategies.

e) Overhead and profit margins

Unless the business is family-operated, part of your profits are immediately going into other people's pockets, the biggest portion to your staff and the landlord. Family members obviously need to be paid, but at least the money stays in the family. Standing overhead costs—that is, overhead costs that do not decrease whether or not you make a sale—must still be met. Advertising, rent, telephones, power, and wages can eat up a good percentage of profits.

If you are purchasing an existing store, study the financial statements carefully, particularly the overhead costs. Be sure there is enough room for the business to pay yourself an acceptable wage. If you are starting a new store, carefully plot your break-even point (the amount of sales you must make each month to cover the bills), calculate how much you must sell, and determine how you are going to achieve this figure. (See Chapter 9 for how to calculate your break-even point.)

Because of competition from large department stores, bulk warehouses and other outlets, you have to learn your pricing structure and review it regularly. There aren't many businesses that can boast total exclusivity of product lines; even specialty stores have their competition. If you are a smaller store, your buying power is much weaker. You can only corner a certain percentage of the market and no more, unless you have developed a unique product or marketing angle.

Be sure that your normal retail prices are in line with those of the competition; at the same time, they must be high enough to support your overhead costs. Carefully monitor your sales and discounted prices, as it is easy to fall into the trap of offering continuous sales that realize very little profits. It is the profits that pay for the overhead.

Consider all these factors as you think about opening or purchasing a retail store. Use the services of your accountant to review the financial statements thoroughly, ensuring that they are up to date. For example, a store with financial statements six months old could be trying to cover up a recent decrease in sales and profits. You want the most current information, preferably for the last two years, so your accountant can compare sales fluctuations and cost variances. Because the economy is changing so rapidly, what was once a healthy store could be suffering severe financial losses: financial statements will reveal the true picture.

6. Service

What is a service business? Quite simply, a business which performs a service in return for a fee. Service industries include financial consulting, accounting and bookkeeping, home repairs, gardening, all the trades such as electricians and plumbers, vehicle repairs, computer-related services, telecommunications services, medical professions, and so on. In a service industry, clients pay for your expertise and knowledge to help them with their problem.

If you want to start a service business, you must know your area thoroughly and be extremely competent. Once you advertise your service, and open the doors for business, you are representing yourself as a professional in your field. Unless you belong to an accredited association—mandatory for doctors, lawyers and accountants—the consumer has little recourse if you offer wrong advice, except to sue you.

Clients come to a new business expecting service, and you'd better be prepared to offer just that plus a little bit more at a reasonable price. Be sure to offer a guarantee with your service. Clients can be demanding, expecting 100 percent performance and value for their dollar. If you can't perform to that standard, you shouldn't open your doors until you can.

Service businesses don't require as much capital to start up as other businesses, which is why so many people are starting out on their own, tapping into their experience and whatever talents they have. Businesses such as a bookkeeping service can be started for well below $10,000. A mobile mechanic can use his van and tools to get started. But remember, it takes more than the tools of your trade to open a service business. Your competence is the lifeline of the business.

Likely, you've experienced dissatisfaction with a service business at some time. We often read about home renovators performing substandard work, or mechanics who don't fix the vehicle's problem adequately, or a bookkeeper who operates without proper accounting knowledge. In a service business in particular, you have to be the expert. Imagine what could happen if a gas appliance was not installed properly? An improperly wired house could cause a devastating house fire, and a brake failure may cause someone's death.

Remember, your clients should receive the same professional expertise that you would expect to receive yourself. Service business owners are taking the lives, property, and welfare of their clients into their own hands. Before you open your doors to customers, consider taking out liability insurance. This will protect you from unforeseen disasters. Serious errors can lead to lengthy and costly legal battles, causing irreparable damage to the business name.

Three of the major factors in running a service business are punctuality, reliability, and follow up. Be on time for appointments with clients and call if you are unavoidably detained, then always follow up after working for a client, asking if everything is to his or her satisfaction. This one phone call will earn you many brownie points, and will give you the opportunity to fix any problems before the unsatisfied client starts complaining to others.

There are many benefits to operating a service business. You can operate out of a home office, allowing you more flexibility with your time. You can schedule your work to sneak in the occasional round of golf or an extended weekend. You can operate with a cellular and residential telephone line, a simple accounting system, and use the spare bedroom as your office. It may be just what you are looking for. (See Chapter 12 for information on operating a home office.)

WHICH BUSINESS IS RIGHT FOR YOU?

The choice can only be yours, and no one can make that decision for you. I hope that the information in this chapter enables you to narrow down your choices. Consider the following factors as you are trying to decide which area to pursue:

1. Suitability of your skills

Your personality is an essential part of any business. Don't choose a business in which you will not feel comfortable actively promoting and operating. Choose an area of expertise in which you can use all your past experience and skills, or an area in which you can upgrade your knowledge until you are an expert. If you have a problem dealing with people, perhaps you shouldn't start a business at all.

2. Financial limitations

First, decide on your budget for the business investment, start-up capital, and operating capital. If you have less than $10,000, you may have to consider a service business, multilevel or network marketing, or perhaps a partnership with an associate. If your finances are in good shape, look at other options—retail, franchising, wholesale, or manufacturing, for example.

3. Time and stress factors

All new businesses will take up a lot of your time, particularly in the start-up period and the first two years. If you are not willing to work seven days a week, don't even think about retail. If your family life is important to you, try to find a business that will not impose unnecessary stress on your relationship. A home-based business is ideal for this situation, or one that requires only a five-day working week.

4. Future goals

If you have plenty of drive, are ambitious, and like to set high goals, look for a business that can be expanded or diversified, or purchased and expanded. Service, manufacturing, and distribution businesses all have this potential. Retail expansion on the other hand, can be an expensive proposition. Know what your goals are two, five, and ten years down the road. Without goals, you have no direction for your business.

Even if you are not too ambitious, set goals for the business and write them down, reviewing them regularly. What will your business look like next year, and in five tears? How many people will you employ then? What does your dream house look like? Goals will help motivate you when the going gets a little rough. They are also an excellent indicator of your progress.

5. Listen to professional advice

Consult professionals. This point can't be stressed enough. Most people make the mistake of not wanting to spend the money yet, ultimately, it costs them because of poor decision-making. Engage the help of an accountant or business consultant when you have formulated an idea or when you find a business which really interests you. Don't make a final decision without the help of professionals to guide you. Use a lawyer for all legal work and to review all contracts.

If you don't know how to find professional advice, ask friends in business who they use, and if they were happy with their accountant, lawyer, or consultant. Be careful with referrals though–what works for one person may not be the best for another. Also consider your budget, as many professionals charge an expensive hourly rate. Their time is worth the money, but you still have to work within your budget. Contact your nearest Business Development Bank of Canada, as they work hand-in-hand with various professionals and may be able to refer you to a consultant. They have a CASE counselling service, which is affordable for new entrepreneurs. There are legal and accountants' referral services in most provinces.

Because you will be working closely with your chosen professionals, try to find people with whom you are comfortable. Don't ever be scared to ask questions. Remember the old saying, "A question is only a dumb question until you find out the answer." Prepare a list of questions before you meet each time, and write down all the answers. A good professional will fill in all the other gaps and tell you what you need to know.

Chapter 2

How do you find the right business?

Sir, do I have a deal for you!
Anonymous

WHY DO BUSINESSES SELL?

Whether you are entertaining the thought of buying an existing business or investing in a "business opportunity" that appeals to you, you will be paying for someone else's creation. Many first-time entrepreneurs start with a low-cost business opportunity, only to find the exercise extremely expensive. However, if you do your homework thoroughly, you should be able to make an astute decision.

Buying an existing business is a road that should not be travelled alone. This is probably one of the biggest steps you will take in your life and it should be done with the help of professionals. Don't rush into any venture with blinders on. Take the time to digest "the ten golden rules of buying a business" found later in this chapter, and follow those rules step by step. They will help guide you through each important stage.

Established businesses sell for a variety of reasons, the most common discussed here:

1. Business runs out of money

Most small businesses are short of money when they first open. If not enough thought and planning was put into the start-up and costs exceed expectations, or sales did not meet expected goals, the bank account quickly depletes, and the owners become desperate to sell. Most are happy just to pay off their debts with the sale proceeds and will appear eager to persuade you that their business is the best thing since the invention of the cellular telephone and computers combined.

This situation could be an excellent opportunity to buy a business at a fair price; perhaps all the business needs is a competent manager to turn it around. But do your homework. It's no use buying someone else's troubles if they can't be remedied.

2. Illness, death, or family problems

There are many legitimate reasons to sell a business. A business owner may become ill and unable to continue working. This is common with smaller businesses that do not have the staff or family members to continue the operation. Statistics cite that 75 percent of small businesses close after the principal owner dies or becomes seriously ill. Some businesses cause too much stress on the family relationship, and the decision has to be made between keeping it or maintaining the health of the family. If it is being sold because of family pressures, try to find out why the work created these pressures in the first place. If the business is that stressful, do you really want to take on someone else's problems?

3. Business burnout

Getting tired of doing the same old thing can apply to running a business, not just a nine-to-five job. After many years of repetitive work, some people get plain tired and need a change. Many burn out after a few years because they have tried to do it all themselves, or the business has been floundering or not meeting expectations. Wanting a total lifestyle change is also a common reason for a business sale. This is often the case with people in their forties and fifties.

If the business has supported the owner adequately for many years, there is no reason why it should not be a worthwhile proposition. There is nothing wrong with a person wanting to explore new avenues, and this is a valid reason for selling. In many cases, these businesses have a well-established clientele and reputation. All the start-up costs have been absorbed, and the business should have a solid financial history you can explore.

4. Increased competition

Perhaps one of the most obvious reasons for selling a business is the ever-increasing competition. For a small business, it is hard to keep abreast of the competition. The battle never seems to end. For many smaller and well-established retail businesses, the addition of a large supermarket or shopping mall is often their ultimate demise. Even if the vendor doesn't admit to this reason, it should be obvious to you if you research the area and the competition thoroughly. If this appears to be the main reason for selling, pass this one by, because you will only inherit someone else's failing business.

WHAT IS A BUSINESS OPPORTUNITY?

Just what is a business opportunity? Usually, it is a business concept, a multilevel or network marketing group, distributorship opportunity, vending route, janitorial contract, franchise, or a computer-related or mail-order business that can be operated from home. What is being offered with these businesses is usually an idea which may work, depending on your business or sales abilities. It is up to you to establish an area or your clientele. You are usually provided with the tools, such as the vending machines, the inventory, or the samples and the business opportunity. For this, you will pay a price—the rest is up to you.

Many of these businesses will present you with an idea that is made to sound so exciting and profitable, you can't wait to sink your teeth into it. Caution, caution, caution! Do not proceed or pass go without sound, professional accounting advice. Remember: you are usually buying an unestablished business using someone else's ideas, for which you may be paying too much. You are starting from scratch, and those promises of big money usually don't pan out.

Warning! You must be especially diligent about so-called business opportunities that offer huge, quick returns. There are people who are ready to take your money and run, or sell you a business that is either non-profitable, not quite legal, or makes money for no one but the vendors. Ask your friends and associates whether they know of anyone who has experienced a bad business venture lately. You have to research not only the market, but the business, the business owners, and the history of the products they are selling. Before making any final decisions, consult with a lawyer and have an appropriate agreement for sale drawn up. If problems arise between you and the vendor, your agreement will become a valuable document in court.

Take a look in your newspaper under the Business Opportunities section on a Saturday, and read the tempting offers of easy money. Here are just some advertisements, taken from a Vancouver newspaper in one weekend edition:

"Amazing! No competition! Possible $1,500 income weekly. Part time, minimum investment."

"Awesome Internet Business. Home based, no computer or exp. necessary. Huge profit potential."

"Canadian 1-900 numbers. Your phone profit potential is unlimited."

"Earn $1,000 a day as information broker. Explosive growth franchise."

"Entrepreneurs wanted. Not MLM. Earn $500 profit per sale."

"From home earn $2,000, $3,000, $4,000 mo. Best home based business in country!"

"Home based revolution! Work from home. $427 billion dollar industry."

"HOT! HOT! HOT! $6,000 per month realistic with home business for 90's. Min. Inv. $1,800."

"Join 1000's others, earn $750 next weekend."

"Retire in three years! Incredible income, low start up costs, huge market!"

"Tired of being broke? Want to make a million? No tricks, no gimmicks."

"This unique program enables you to earn $5,000 weekly plus! Home based business of the 90's."

"$100,000 year potential, Computer earns you money 24 hours a day!"

This is how advertisers reel in unsuspecting victims. The lure of easy money is the most effective method of advertising a business venture. Advertisers prey on people's desire for quick, easy cash with a minimum investment. Home-based businesses are usually their target market. When you read a list of golden opportunities such as this, it is hard for the eager not to get excited with these wonderful promises. But if all these types of businesses were legitimate and as easy as they sound, then we would all be rich in a few short months, retired in three years, and rolling in money thereafter. Legitimate business does not work that way. Any type of business requires serious dedication.

Here are two different cases of what appeared to be legitimate business sales. In both instances, the vendors' intentions were to cheat the purchasers. The vendors were friendly, convincing, well rehearsed but dishonest people who could fool almost anybody into believing their stories.

The Case of the Crooked Bookkeeper

Jan operated a small accounting company which, although struggling, was slowly growing and earning her an excellent reputation in town. To minimize her costs, she shared an office with a secretarial service. Her goal was to get her monthly workload more stable so that she could hire a part-time bookkeeper and spend more of her time marketing the business.

She read of a bookkeeping business for sale in the local paper and called the number. After talking with Valerie, the owner, Jan became quite excited. Valerie operated a business out of her home and said she grossed about $25,000 a year. She was selling the business for $12,000.

Jan calculated that she could buy the business and have it paid off in nearly a year. "It's perfect!" she told her husband. Eagerly, she met with Valerie to find out more. Valerie told Jan that she had a family, and that her work was taking up too much family time. Her teenage children needed her more than ever now, particularly with the peer pressure they were facing. They needed their mom. She said she really had enough of bookkeeping and would find something else to do part-time. If Jan had thought a little longer, the story really did not make all that much sense. Valerie could have hired help with the bookkeeping and operated the business part time.

Valerie showed Jan a list of clients, marked only by numbers (to protect her client list until the business was sold, she informed Jan). Each client's number had an annual dollar volume marked next to it. The list looked reasonable to Jan, and the annual volume appeared to total nearly $26,000. Valerie said she would introduce the clients to Jan and would work with her for a month to help achieve a smooth transition.

Jan did the right thing. She went to a lawyer and had an agreement for sale drawn up before paying any deposit. The lawyer drafted the document and went through it with Jan. Part of the agreement included a competition clause, which stated that Valerie was not allowed to start up another bookkeeping service within a five mile radius of Jan for a period of five years. Valerie was very reluctant to sign the agreement, holding up the sale for a few days.

By chance, the woman with whom Jan was sharing an office overheard from a friend of hers, who knew someone who knew Valerie (commonly called the grapevine) that Valerie was in fact keeping the best clients for herself, fully intending to continue bookkeeping at home. She was selling off her tax clients, who were mostly once-a-year accounts, plus the clients who were slow to pay or difficult to work with.

Jan did not buy the business. It cost her $500 in legal fees, but she saved herself $12,000. Over the years, she built up an excellent little business without buying someone else's castoffs. Had Jan purchased the business, she probably would have never found out about Valerie's deception and would have paid good money for bad clients.

The Case of the Repeat, Repeat, Repeat Sale

The nineties have bred a slick generation of con artists. Recently, a couple, whom we'll call David and Katie, wanted to purchase a home-based business for David, who had been laid off from a middle management position. Tired of working for employers, he wanted to be his own boss. Worn out from a decade of high-stress jobs, David and Katie decided to look for something that would not involve full-time work to start.

Looking in the Businesses for Sale section in the newspaper, they came across an advertisement for a part-time mail-order business for sale, which netted $5,000 a month, and was priced at $10,000. Now Katie was quick with figures, and she could see that after two or three months, this investment would pay for itself. They wouldn't have to take out a loan, their line of credit would cover the investment nicely, and it would be so nice for David to be able to work from home. Katie quickly picked up the phone and made an appointment with the vendor, Mr. Slick.

Mr. Slick operated out of an impressive packaged office, although his own office held little more than a few files and his mobile telephone. Katie mentally noted the sparseness of the office, comparing it with the other offices in the complex. Mr. Slick was smooth, polite, and courteous with a constant fixed smile. He explained the concept of his mail-order business, which, he said, he had operated with a partner for five years. They had written a series of books, marketing them directly though the mail. Why were they selling? Because they were tired of packaging thousands of books, and they were now working on another business. It all sounded fairly reasonable to Katie, although she did have an uncomfortable feeling that something was not quite right.

Mr. Slick offered Katie and David full training along with the exclusive rights to market one of the books. He would do all set-up work, including registering the business, looking after the business licence, and placing advertisements in the newspapers. If Katie and David did not receive a specified amount of orders within the first month, he would refund their deposit. The balance of the deal was payable after the required number of books had been ordered.

Katie was smart. She had a full legal agreement prepared by her lawyer with exclusivity, misrepresentation, and competition clauses included. Mr. Slick stated that he did not understand all this legal "mumbo jumbo" and insisted on a basic agreement, eliminating the important clauses. Katie insisted on certain clauses remaining in the agreement, and finally, after many days of negotiating, Katie and David signed, paying a large deposit.

True to his word, Mr. Slick registered their new business for them, and that was when things started to fall apart. Katie had been working extremely hard preparing the necessary printing, stationery, and an information package that went with the book. She visited the local printer to have quotations prepared. Someone was looking out for David and Katie that day. By chance, another person in the same town, had been sold the same book a month earlier, and had gone to the same printer with the same book, to get quotes.

We will call the other purchasers Simon and Sally. The printer gave them Katie and David's telephone number, they met, and showed Simon and Sally the same book. They too had purchased the book with exclusive rights from the same Mr. Slick for even more money. They had paid him a large deposit up front and were marketing the product.

Simon went to the library and checked the national Canadian newspapers, discovering that three more people were advertising the same book, using the same promotional voice tape supplied by Mr. Slick for ordering purposes. After contacting these people, the two couples discovered a person who claimed to have started this same business in the United States in 1989. He advertised regularly in an Ontario newspaper. He stated that someone in Canada had copied his book and marketing tape, word for word, but could never locate who it was. The book had also been sold, with exclusive rights for Canada, a year previously to another person who was advertising, and yet another person in the next suburb to the two couples was *also* selling the same book. The list of victims eventually became quite long.

These young men were in the business of selling businesses. When they ran short of cash, they just sold their book, sometimes with exclusive rights, to a new, unsuspecting person. The two couples reported the case to the commercial crime section of the police, who were not interested in the case. They filed actions in Small Claims Court, discovering there was another silent partner involved. They sued him too.

At mediation, the judge noted that their contracts included a clause for private mediation, and nearly didn't allow the case to go ahead. After a long, drawn-out battle, Mr. Slick left town before the final court hearing. His silent partner was held responsible for the crime of allowing multiple sales of the business, but to date, no one has been able to collect a penny from either partner. None of the other victims bothered to take legal action. They were embarrassed, being prepared to lose their $4,000 to $10,000, chalking it up to experience.

THE TEN GOLDEN RULES OF BUYING A BUSINESS

The two case studies above demonstrate how easy it is to be conned into investing in a bad business opportunity, even when you think you have covered the bases. There is no easy answer to avoiding these situations, but the following rules will help you make a sound decision. If there are words that you don't understand, please turn to the accounting definitions in Chapter 3.

Rule #1: Spend $10 and have a company name search prepared

Is the business properly registered? Are the owners really who they say they are? What is the corporate structure? In the "repeat sale" case it was discovered after a name search that Mr. Slick not only used many other first names, he also had another silent partner listed on the business registration. This silent partner had never been previously mentioned. You can have the business name, structure, and owners searched by calling the corporate registry in your province as listed in the appendix.

Rule #2: If in doubt, check them out

If you have any doubts about the person with whom you are dealing, play super sleuth. Write down the person's licence plate number. Check his or her personal telephone number with the telephone company and see under what name he or she is registered. If the person claims to own property, do a title search. Mr. Slick said he owned property, but a title search disclosed that he did not. Ensure you have the person's home address, not just the business address. Be wary of personal references unless they come from a reputable source. Mr. Slick used shady friends who gave glowing references, including his silent partner who did not tell the purchasers he was involved in the business.

Rule #3: Check the vendor's credentials

Checking credentials is particularly important if you are considering investing money in a new venture or a partnership. People seeking your venture capital will often tell you anything to get their hands on your money. Some become quite desperate. They may have a good idea, but not the expertise to carry it through to fruition. Ask for a resume and a list of previous employers, and check any references or contacts.

If you are purchasing a business, research the reputation of the business in the marketplace. Ask the clients if they are happy with the products

41

or the service provided by the vendor. Ask the vendor for references. If you can find out the name of their bank, it might provide a reference. Ask for the names of the main suppliers and call them. Ask them how they paid their accounts and how they would rate their credit. If you are a member of a credit bureau, have a credit check performed on the company. Call the Better Business Bureau to see if there have been any complaints against the business.

One couple invested in a new business with two others. They left the "business stuff" to the other partners, who were supposedly more conversant with "legal mumbo-jumbo." After a year of operation, the business was thriving and earning a good reputation in the town. They invested more money into equipment and fixtures. To cut a long and sad story short, to save money, they did not have a lawyer thoroughly check the lease agreement. It was left to the other partner.

The building was suddenly foreclosed on. It turned out their lease had only been a sublease, and the payments were not being made. They lost the business along with all the equipment and improvements. They had borrowed against their mortgage to start the business, and were left with nothing, except more legal bills. (See Chapter 5 for more information about legal matters.)

Rule #4: Take a thorough inventory of the premises

If you are interested in a business that is already located in a building, visit the premises and ask questions. Note the overall appearance of the premises. If retail, is it clean, cheery, well decorated, and a comfortable place to do business? Is the staff friendly? How are the products displayed? Do prices seem competitive? Is the inventory sufficient and up to date? Talk to the staff and find out everything you can. Are the employees happy in their work? Will they stay on after a change of ownership? What are their areas of expertise? Is the location really suitable for the type of products or service being sold? What needs improving? Are these costly improvements? Ask to see the lease or talk to the landlord. When will the rent increase? How long is the lease signed for, and what are the options for renewal?

If you are out of your depth in a manufacturing or distribution environment, take someone with you who can help you assess the operation.

You need to be sure that equipment is in good working order and that the internal operation is efficient.

Rule #5: Perform a physical inventory of the assets

If a list of assets (equipment and inventory) for sale is available with the business, take the list with you on your field trip. Physically check each asset, ensuring that what is needed for the full operation of the business is on the list. Note model and serial numbers of larger pieces of equipment. You can phone around later to see whether what you are buying is being sold to you at a fair market value. Find out what type of regular repairs and maintenance the equipment requires and when it last broke down or was serviced.

If you are purchasing an inventory with the business, ask to see it. Make sure there are no outdated, old, or unsalable items included. If there is old or obviously useless stock, you should make a deal to either purchase it at a very low cost, or have its book value deleted from the final inventory purchase price. It is then the vendor's responsibility to dispose of these items.

Two partners were interested in buying an equipment store which carried a large inventory worth nearly $100,000. Much of the inventory was rebuilt stock or looked as if it had been around since the Dark Ages. Their knowledge of this equipment was basic, so under their accountant's advice, they spent three weeks physically checking the inventory, finally arriving at a price reduction after a thorough physical check.

What they didn't do was take along someone who had expertise with that type of equipment. After the first year of operation, they realized they had still paid far too much for the inventory. Much of it was useless and finally junked. Of the remaining inventory, large, expensive pieces sat on the floor without moving all year. These pieces had to be reduced almost to cost to regain some of their cash flow, so they could stock faster-moving items.

Rule #6: Discuss all information with your accountant

Most people prepare some type of a business plan to help sell their business. These plans can range from a couple of roughly typed pages to glossy, eye-catching, professionally prepared packages which can boggle your mind with facts and figures. All businesses for sale should submit financial statements, preferably for at least two years. These can vary from self-prepared statements (be wary of these) to those prepared by a professional accountant.

It's easy for your accountant to review the proposal and statements to get a good feel for the business being presented. He or she will also prepare a list of questions to be asked, or will ask those questions for you. Accountants can read the whole history of a business in financial statements. (If the statements have been prepared by the owners, ask them to have their own accountant review them or, preferably, prepare a proper set of statements. Some statements prepared in-house are worthless.)

People can be extremely creative with their accounting, and you need to know that the statements have been prepared by a reputable company. Your accountant will contact the accountant who prepared the statements, and will know the right questions to ask. As an example, if just one supplier account for $3,000 is not entered in the books, the profits will be overstated by $3,000.

Rule #7: Have a proper agreement for sale prepared

Don't purchase any existing business without having an agreement for sale prepared. This agreement will protect both the vendor and you, as demonstrated in our case studies above. Without such a document, you have no recourse when trouble arises. (This subject is covered in more depth in Chapter 5.)

Rule #8: Visit your local municipal office

You need to check that the company has not at any time infringed on or broken any local by-laws. You should check pending or possible future by-laws which could be detrimental to the business. For example, there could be planned changes to zoning regulations or even traffic route changes. Traffic changes can adversely affect a retail business. New road construction may involve cutting off easy access to the store, sending customers to a more accessible location.

If the business is a manufacturing facility, ensure that there are no possible environmental problems or proposed by-law changes that could affect the current location. While you are there, check to see if there is any pending new construction within the surrounding area. You don't need a new competitor opening a sparkling new store a few months down the road.

If the business you are considering can be operated from home, you should become familiar with the home-based by-laws in your municipality. Most restrict retail sales, manufacturing, the type of business, traffic generation, office size, and building usage. Many home-based businesses have been closed down due to by-law infractions.

Rule #9: Research your competition and the market

No matter how well the business appears to be doing physically and on paper, presume that the competition is still fierce. Find out who your competitors are, what type of products they sell, and what their pricing structures are. What does this business offer that is better than that of the competitors? Is your business a market that will attract more and more competitors, and if so, how will this affect you?

Some large chain stores are currently suffering because even larger warehouse-type stores are opening up nearby. They eventually starve out the competition. Ultimately, no one wins except the consumer. Both stores have to offer cheaper prices, better service, and loss leaders (goods sold at or below cost) to tempt the consumers. Both stores' profits and the employees working conditions suffer.

Research the current market for consumer trends. In 1995, many retail stores experienced up to a 20 percent drop in consumer spending. Since then, consumer bankruptcies have dramatically increased because people are generally getting poorer. The business you are thinking of purchasing may be seriously affected by consumer spending trends, continued downturns in the economy, environmental issues, or advanced technology. The business may have performed adequately to date, or may show a slight drop in sales over the previous year or two. No matter what the vendor tells you, a thorough market research will indicate current and future trends in your area of business.

No matter what you do to promote your business, if it is going out of style, there isn't much you can do to reverse those trends. A classic example of a short-lived trend is the sports card stores. They opened by the dozens and have decreased to a rare few. One also wonders just how many coffee shops and Internet cafés a town can support. This latest trend has already taken some casualties with it. Think about how many cups of coffee you have to sell to pay for the rent each month. (Chapter 4 deals with market research and strategies in depth.)

Rule #10: Don't start a business on a shoestring

Purchasing or starting a business on a shoestring budget or completely borrowed capital is usually a formula for disaster. You should prepare a business plan that includes projections and cash-flow forecasts. Your business has to meet loan payments one month after you open your doors. Allow time for take-over or start-up, a period when revenues may drop or be slow, and expenses are usually higher than normal. If you ruin your credit rating by defaulting on loan payments, it will take years to repair. You should have a minimum of six months' working capital available with a new venture.

HOW DO YOU ASSESS A POTENTIAL BUSINESS?

When you are interested in a business idea, you will usually be presented with an overview of the business by the vendor. This is called a business proposal. They come in many shapes and sizes, and you will have to wade through a lot of information to find out whether this business is right for you. What you really want are answers to these questions:

1. Is this business profitable?

2. Does it earn enough to pay you a decent wage?

3. Are sales increasing or decreasing?

4. Do you have the experience to take over this business and maintain it profitably?

5. Are you paying too much for this business?

6. Are the assets really worth the asking price?

7. Is the goodwill portion worth the asking price?

8. Could this business be expanded?

9. What mistakes did the owners make that you should avoid?

10. What is the life expectancy of this business?

11. If a franchise, who is making the money, the franchiser or you?

12. Are the projections stated attainable or realistic?

You may look at many different proposals before getting excited about one in particular. You can't afford to consult your accountant about every one, so you have to learn to analyze them yourself. Then you can weed out those of no interest and pass the others on to your accountant.

A well-presented business proposal should contain the following information:

1. History and detailed operation of the business

2. Profile of the company owners

3. Profiles of key employees, if any

4. Summary of current and future markets

5. Details of all relevant competitors

6. Details of property leases, description of location and its benefits

7. Full description of the business assets for sale, including any training period and any other services offered with the business

8. Asking price of the business

9. Payment terms required

10. Financial statements for the previous two years

11. Projected income based on past performance and future goals

12. Letters of reference from clients or suppliers

Many proposals will not contain all this information, so it's up to you to ask the vendor the right questions to fill in the gaps. Don't be mislead by projections. They are just one person's idea of how the business may perform in the next one or two years. Anyone can create a wonderful picture by placing figures on a sheet of paper. Projections are only as good as the substantiated reasoning behind them. They must be based on past history, current performance, as well as the current and future market trends.

TWELVE IMPORTANT QUESTIONS TO ASK

1. Is this business profitable?

A business's profitability can only be determined by looking at the financial statements. If possible, obtain two years' statements and analyze them with your accountant. They will show the growth of the business, the operating expenses, the wages paid to the owners, and any profits or losses. How the business has been operated will also be reflected in the figures. Your accountant will show you any areas of concern and explain the different expenses.

2. Does it make enough to pay you a good wage?

The financial statements will show all wages paid by the business. These wages should be broken down into various categories such as manufacturing, sales, office, and management wages. You will have to first decide which role you and your family or partner will play in the business. Then look at the wages paid out each year on the financial statements. This will give you an idea of how much the business overhead can support. Take into account the profits (if any) after expenses. They can be used as additional wages for yourself, as long as your wage requirement does not negatively affect the operating cash flow of the business.

3. Are sales seasonal, increasing, or decreasing?

If the vendor is astute and keen to sell, he or she will supply you with a month-by-month breakdown of sales over the last two years. This will give you a picture of any seasonal fluctuations or varying sales trends. Combined annual figures do not give you this information. If sales are decreasing, you want to know why and when. If sales are increasing, ask what marketing methods are being used and which are the most successful.

As an example, suppose a seasonal garden supply business for sale showed annual sales of $150,000. The business needed $10,000 a month to cover all operating costs, including wages. The $150,000 seemed a satisfactory amount of sales, but when the month-by-month sales for the last year were made available, this is what they revealed:

January	$ 5,000
February	$ 6,000
March	$ 9,000
April	$15,000
May	$29,000
June	$27,000
July	$13,000
August	$11,000
September	$11,000
October	$13,000
November	$ 7,000
December	$ 4,000

For five months of the year, the business did not generate enough sales to cover overhead. Spring was the best season, tapering down over summer, with August being slow. A little burst occurred in October as people prepared their gardens for winter, then virtually nothing again until March. With this type of business, only careful cash-flow management would enable the business to survive the quiet months.

4. Do you have the experience to maintain the business profitably?

A new business is a challenge. Question the vendor about his or her role in the business. Make sure that you have the experience and knowledge to take over this role and fill his or her shoes adequately. As the new owner, you will be responsible for the success of this venture. If you can't do it, then can you afford to employ someone who will? Don't tackle a business where there will be gaps in the key areas of management, namely sales, operations, and administration.

Two partners who purchased a mechanical business thought they were well suited. One had some technical experience, although this was gained mainly from tinkering and a short night school course, while the other partner was meticulous at paperwork. He had operated his own small business for many years.

When they took over the store, things didn't go quite as planned. The larger operation required a vast knowledge of different components, and the paperwork, sales, and marketing was more than a full-time job. Extra trained help was needed to keep the business operational. The first year experienced a dramatic loss due to increased wages. Combined with the business being seasonal, the financial losses were horrendous, with extra financing being required to carry the business into the second year.

5. Are you paying too much for this business?

Most businesses are advertised for sale at a much higher price than the vendor expects to receive. A thorough analysis of the figures by your accountant helps you arrive at a realistic price. When you buy a business, you are buying the assets, goodwill, and a job for yourself. The final price should reflect a fair value for all three of these areas.

6. Are the assets really worth what is being asked?

The assets of a business consist of equipment, buildings, furniture, fittings, and inventory. Assets are usually sold at the book value as listed on the financial statements, although some vendors will insist on a higher price. The vendor has already benefitted from the taxation advantage of the depreciation. No matter what a piece of equipment is worth when appraised, it is really worth no more than its book value at the time of sale. This is how banks usually evaluate assets on loan applications. Some vendors and purchasers arrive at an agreed purchase price somewhere between book and market values. If you purchase an incorporated business on a share basis, the asset value remains at book value.

People inevitably end up buying worthless inventory or overpriced equipment. As a new purchaser, you may not be aware of what sells and what does not. You don't want to purchase inventory which will not turn over quickly, as this depletes your operating capital. If in doubt, it's a wise move to contract a company to evaluate your inventory for you. They may also be able to appraise your equipment.

For example, a client once showed me the evaluation of the equipment for sale with the business. There was one piece of equipment valued at $6,500. When the financial figures were requested, this piece of equipment turned out to be quite old, having a book value of only $2,300. The purchaser then offered the book value price for the equipment, based on these figures, saving herself $4,200. If you are unsure of the value of the equipment, take the make and model number and phone around for some independent evaluations before paying the asking price.

7. Is the goodwill portion worth what is being asked?

Goodwill is an intangible item. It is a value that the vendor determines through the growth of the business over the years. It is difficult to decide whether the goodwill amount is within reason. If you are purchasing a franchise, the goodwill portion is a set amount: you are paying for the name and the national advertising. If you want the business, you have to pay what is asked.

In a non-franchise business, the goodwill is often calculated, (as a rule of thumb), as the sum of money you can earn as a wage from the business within a one-year period, as well as the money that could be earned by investing the profits. If the vendor is drawing a wage of $40,000 a year from the business, or $65,000 a year including his or her spouse, then the goodwill portion could be as high as $65,000. If the business is still making a profit after these wages are drawn, then the goodwill may be worth even more. If it is losing money after these wages are being drawn, then the goodwill amount should be reduced. This is definitely an area in which your accountant should be consulted.

8. Could this business be expanded?

Always keep in mind that diversification is the key to growth, and growth is the key to success. Are there other areas in which the business could expand? If it is a bedding store, could other product lines be introduced? If purchasing a service industry, could you branch out into other areas? If you purchase a seasonal business, how could you bring an income into the business during quiet times? If the business cannot be expanded or diversified, what else can you do to build it up?

9. What mistakes did the owners make that you should avoid?

Your accountant will highlight any areas of concern in the financial statements. The balance sheet may show too much inventory, a growing bank overdraft or loans, and perhaps too many outstanding accounts receivable. Government taxes, or employee withholdings may be unpaid. The statement of income and expenditure will highlight any areas of over-spending, such as wages or advertising. The profit margins after cost of sales may not be as high as you have been told. These questions should be asked of the vendor by either you or your accountant. From there, you have to decide whether you could run the business without making the same mistakes. What would you change? What can be changed? What will take time to change?

10. What is the life expectancy of this business?

Consumer trends are constantly changing. Some businesses do not continue to grow because "the times, they are a-changing." Over the years, technology has replaced menial tasks. Typewriters and word processors have been replaced by computers. Computer programs can do the work of many designers. Shopping channels on television, the Internet, and mail-order catalogues have replaced traditional shopping habits to a degree. Large chain stores make competition tough for small retail outlets.

Your business must have built-in longevity to survive. For example, you might choose one that caters to the basic needs of humans or animals. The pet market is growing in popularity. The service industry performs tasks that many of us can't or don't want to do, such as house painting, yard work, or carpet cleaning. The work of the farrier who shoes horses is one of the few professions that has hardly been touched by technology. A good farrier can earn $85 an hour or more, with material costs well under $10.

Research the history of the industry that interests you. Study the consumer trends and be reasonably certain that your business will still be a business, performing profitably in the next five to ten years.

11. Who is making the money—the franchiser or you?

If you are interested in a franchise, remember that they are governed by the rules of the head office, and each franchisee must abide by these rules. The business must conform with the guidelines as set out, so if you don't like being told what to do, franchising may not be for you.

While studying a franchise proposal, look carefully at the monthly and annual costs you expect to incur on behalf of the franchise. Because the franchise is advertised nationally, you will have to pay a percentage of gross sales into an advertising fund. Many franchises require an annual fee toward operational costs. These costs may increase over the years, based on sales. If purchasing an existing franchise, those numbers will already be in place. Study just how much of your profits will be eaten up in franchise fees and compare this amount to the wages you can make from the business.

At the same time, you will be paying a franchise fee, or goodwill, if you purchase the business. This amount usually ranges in the tens of thousands of dollars. Take all this into consideration before making a decision. In some cases, the franchise makes more money than the operators can expect to make. Think about how much ice cream, or how many doughnuts, you would have to sell to cover all your operating costs.

12. Are the projections stated attainable or realistic?

Projections should be based on past and present performance, taking into account the economy, future expansion plans, and sales and marketing strategies. Many projections I've seen are impressive, but very few live up to their claims. When looking at projected sales and expenses, don't take them at face value. Remember, they are merely one person's thoughts on what the business could do under certain given conditions. It makes more sense to study the financial statements closely and see how the business has performed in the past. If you see financial statements that show a loss, but projections that reflect a great profit in the coming year or two, ask what magic formula the business will be using to achieve these figures and market that formula yourself—you'll get rich a lot quicker!

Follow these guidelines as set out above, and you will make an informed decision. Be prepared to pay for a well-established, profitable business. It is worth it, because you will have an immediate guaranteed income. Take into account the hard work someone else has put into the business. He or she has experienced the mistakes and the learning curves. There are times when being cheap and frugal does not pay.

As you review your intended business, make sure you ask and answer the questions in Exercise #3.

EXERCISE #3
BUSINESS REVIEW CHECKLIST

	Yes	No
I've searched the company name and had it validated.	☐	☐
I've validated the vendor's personal credentials.	☐	☐
I've validated business and trade references.	☐	☐
I've researched the business location, the lease and employees.	☐	☐
I've evaluated the assets and inventory and they are satisfactory.	☐	☐

	Yes	No
I've discussed the business proposal with my accountant.	☐	☐
My lawyer has prepared the agreement for sale.	☐	☐
The municipal approval and research is completed.	☐	☐
I've researched the competition and market.	☐	☐
I have sufficient funds available to start and operate a business.	☐	☐

EXERCISE #3a:

BUSINESS ANALYSIS CHECKLIST

	Yes	No
This business is definitely a profitable concern.	☐	☐
This business can pay me a satisfactory wage.	☐	☐
The sales figures are steady and not declining.	☐	☐
I can operate the business competently.	☐	☐
My accountant agrees that the price is satisfactory.	☐	☐
The assets are fairly evaluated.	☐	☐
The goodwill is fairly priced.	☐	☐
This business could be diversified or expanded.	☐	☐
I am aware of mistakes made by the previous owner.	☐	☐
This business has a definite long-term life.	☐	☐
This franchise does make acceptable profits.	☐	☐
The projected returns are realistic and attainable.	☐	☐

Chapter 3

What is a financial statement?

*Your biggest asset is realizing that you are a liability if you don't
know the meaning of these words.*

As you start to browse through financial statements, you may feel like
you are reading a foreign language. Accounting has a language all of its
own, and it leaves the average person in the dark. On asking many business owners whether they really understood their financial statements
prepared by their accountants at year-end, less that 10 percent admitted
they understood what a financial statement is, or what it was telling
them.

Yet year after year, they pay their accountant hundreds, if not thousands
of dollars to prepare this table of figures written in a strange language
which they never ask to be deciphered. Not only that, the average business
owner files this expensive document away where it does nothing but
yellow with age. Then they grind their teeth as they reluctantly write
out their accountant's cheque, and carry on.

In my business, I have never let clients leave the office until they have
received a thorough, line-by-line understanding of what the statements
contain. It may take a few cups of coffee, but clients have the right to
expect proper service. You cannot operate a business without understanding what is happening to it.

Financial statements are a written history of how your business has
performed during a set period of time. They can be prepared monthly,

quarterly, half-yearly, or annually. Most small businesses have a financial statement prepared annually for tax purposes only. Not enough owners monitor their businesses regularly by studying their financial figures. They are too busy running the business to operate it effectively. This is one main reason why so many businesses tend to fail. Problem areas develop, but no one takes the time to find out why. The statements will show you sales fluctuations, profit margin increases or decreases, cost increases, overhead fluctuations, and changes in net profit. They will tell you whether you are further in debt or have too much cash tied up in inventory or receivables.

I realize that some of those big accounting words are starting to appear in this text so, to make it easier, I've defined many of them in this chapter. And take heart: understanding financial statements is probably the hardest chapter to digest in this book, so hang in there; the reading gets easier once you finish this section.

DEFINITION OF A FINANCIAL STATEMENT

A financial statement is a snapshot taken of your business at a given time. Usually this picture is taken at a month-end. It will tell you what the business owns, what it owes, your capital and equity in the business, what the sales were, what it cost to make those sales, what the business overhead was, and how much profit (or loss) the business made.

A financial statement follows a set format, consisting of the following sections:

1. Notice to reader or review engagement report

2. Balance sheet

3. Statement of retained earnings (if incorporated)

4. Statement of income and expenses

5. Notes to financial statements

6. Statement of changes in financial position

1. Notice to reader or review engagement report

A financial statement consists of many pages of valuable information. The first page is a notice to reader or a review engagement. This is a statement from the accountant to the business owner telling you which method was used to prepare the figures.

A notice to reader often states that the accountant has prepared the information provided from the records of the business, but "has not reviewed, audited, or otherwise attempted to verify the accuracy or completeness of such information or determine whether these statements contain departures from generally accepted accounting principles." Some even state that "these statements are for internal use of management and for income tax purposes only. Accordingly, readers are cautioned that these statements may not be appropriate for their purposes."

If you read such a disclaimer, be warned that the accountant has little faith in the bookkeeping or the information provided. This is written in cases where, in particular, the owners may have prepared the monthly bookkeeping themselves (and may not be experts at the job), or perhaps a mediocre bookkeeping service was used. In these instances, the accountant cannot be sure whether the entries are accurate. The bank accounts may be reconciled and all information processed, but the correct allocation of the information may not have been made or, possibly, information is missing. If a person prepares books but does not have an accounting background, serious mistakes will occur without a doubt.

For your own peace of mind, find out how the books were prepared and by whom. What are his or her credentials? Contact the accountant who prepared the year-end, and ask his or her opinion on the accuracy of the financial statements. Accountants often unearth some horror stories in bookkeeping. One wrong entry can change a loss situation into a profitable one, and vice versa.

On most statements, you will find the words "unaudited" on each page. This simply means that the accountant has not performed a full audit of the books. Audited statements are usually required for nonprofit organizations or businesses that have gone public on the stock exchange. They are very costly and not needed for the average business.

If a review engagement report has been prepared, you can feel more confident about the accuracy of the statements. To complete this process, the accountant must perform thorough checks and cross-checks, with nearly 30 pages of directions to follow. These statements cost more money to be prepared and will be more accurate than a notice to reader statement. (It still pays to contact the accountant who prepared the statements to verify the accuracy of the books and records from which the statements were prepared.)

2. Balance sheet

The balance sheet is a picture of the financial position of the business at a given date, usually at month-end. This statement shows, at that time, what the company owns and owes. It also shows how much equity or capital is in the company, as well as how much money the company is making or losing. This information is expressed in terms of the company's assets, liabilities, and equity.

3. Statement of retained earnings

This page of the financial statements is prepared only for incorporated businesses. It is an ongoing record of the profits or losses that the business has incurred since inception. The figures show the opening balance for the period, adds or subtracts the period's profits or losses, and reflects a new closing balance of profits or losses to the date of the statement. These figures are a similar calculation as seen in the equity section of an unincorporated business.

4. Statement of income and expenditure

A statement of income and expenditure is just that. It shows all sales and other income the business has generated, less all expenses. The "bottom line" shows how much profit or loss the company has made during a given period, usually one year. An example is included in this chapter.

5. Notes to financial statements

The notes to the statements provide details in areas such as how the inventory was costed, when the business was incorporated, the rates of depreciation used, the terms of loans and shareholder loans, and any other information the tax department or banks may need to see.

6. Statement of changes in financial position

A statement of changes in financial position is usually only prepared for an incorporated business. Most people look at it and scratch their heads, but banks like to read this type of information. It details where the money came from during the year (profits or loans) and how the money was used (to finance a loss, pay back loans, or purchase assets). It also shows the working capital of the business and whether it has increased or decreased during the year.

LEARN TO LIKE FINANCIAL STATEMENTS

Running a business is really not much different than running your own household. Your home and contents are your assets. Your mortgage and unpaid bills are your liabilities. The difference between the value of your assets, minus the total of your debts, is called your equity. We all know what the equity in our home means. Your pay cheque is your income and pays the home expenses such as food, clothing, utilities, and all other expenses. The money you have left over (if any) is your profit.

This is why it is important to respect financial statements, and establishing their authenticity is one of the most important steps to take. If the statements have been prepared by the owners, it is not unfair to ask that they have the statements reviewed by an accountant and for a formal financial statement be prepared. They should be the main selling tool of any business, so don't take them lightly. Be sure of their accuracy because you will be making many of your business decisions based on these figures.

Would you buy a used vehicle without having a mechanic do a thorough check? Would you buy an expensive jewel without having it appraised? Would you buy a business without establishing the accuracy of the financial figures? Of course not.

ACCOUNTING TERMS AND DEFINITIONS

Here is an explanation and some examples of all those confusing words you will encounter during your business career, and as you read this book. They are listed in the same order as those in a typical financial statement. Turn to the end of this chapter to see an example of a financial statement for Jason's Garden Service.

Balance sheet terms

Assets: Everything the business owns, including bank accounts, inventory, accounts receivable, equipment, buildings, vehicles, computers, deposits and investments. Assets are broken down on the balance sheet into current assets and fixed assets.

Current assets: A current asset is any asset the company owns, which could be turned into cash within 12 months. These are listed in the order of the most current of the current assets, which is cash in the bank accounts.

Cash at bank: The balance of all the company bank accounts at the time the statements are prepared. Each account must be reconciled (balanced) with the bank statement or bank book, to the penny. When you read the statements, all the different bank accounts will be grouped together as one total under this heading. If an account is in an overdraft, it will show farther down as a liability.

Accounts receivable: The outstanding money from sales not yet collected. This amount is balanced with a list of money due to the company, client by client. This list is called a receivables list or an aged analysis. An aged analysis is simply a list of money owed the company by each client. The age of the debt is separated into current, 30, 60 , 90 days and over. This list should be prepared monthly and used as a reference to help you with debt collection.

Prepaid expenses and deposits: A total of all deposits in trust a business has made, such as the last month's rent on a lease or a deposit on hydro service. Any insurance policies would be a prepaid expense. A policy may have been taken out for a whole year in July, for example, with the year-end being December. Only half of the insurance cost is an expense for this financial year. The balance belongs as an expense to the next financial year and is called a prepaid expense. Prepaid expenses also include service contracts such as security monitoring or photocopier maintenance, vehicle and shop insurance, and property taxes. Your accountant will calculate these figures for you.

Inventory: The total of all materials or products you purchased for resale, but are unsold to date. This can include manufacturing raw materials, goods purchased for distribution, or finished, but unsold retail products. The inventory is always taken when a statement is prepared and should be valued at the actual cost of the product. Old, dated, or slow-moving products can be devalued in price at year-end and are included in this figure. Stationery on hand is not considered inventory as it is not resold to your clients.

Work in progress: Partially completed contracts not yet billed to the client. The value of the work to date is estimated and classified as work in progress instead of being called accounts receivable.

Fixed assets: An asset owned and utilized by the company. Fixed assets are usually equipment or similar items with a singular value of more than $200. Smaller items, for example a chain saw or an office chair, are considered overhead expenses. Fixed assets are listed at the actual purchase cost, not appraised value. A bank does not consider appraised values when reviewing the assets of a business. Fixed assets include items such as furniture and fittings, computers, cellular phones, buildings, vehicles, manufacturing equipment, land, machinery, telephone systems, and leasehold improvements. A leasehold improvement is an addition such as new carpeting, lighting, or renovations to a building. These assets will remain in the building if the company closes or moves. (See "depreciation and amortization" below to see what happens then.)

Accumulated capital cost allowance, depreciation, and amortization: Capital cost allowance (CCA) is the allowance made for depreciation on a capital expenditure, such as equipment. Each type of fixed asset has a defined rate of depreciation as set down by the taxation department. For example, vehicles depreciate at a rate of 30 percent a year, furniture at 20 percent a year. Each year, your accountant will depreciate your assets for you, so don't worry about learning how to do it yourself. This allows the business a write off or expense amount for the wear and tear on the assets.

Amortization is an allowance for wear and tear on some fixed assets. Leasehold improvements are a good example. If you signed a five-year lease and spent $10,000 on improving the building, your accountant would depreciate these leasehold improvements over five years, or at the rate of $2,000 a year. The balance sheet shows the amount of depreciation taken since the assets were purchased, over a period of years. The annual amount of depreciation will show as an expense on the statement of income and expenditure.

Net book value: The difference between the purchase price of an asset less accumulated depreciation. If equipment is shown at a value of $40,000 and accumulated depreciation is $34,400, with the net book value of $5,600, these figures tell you that the equipment is old and has been in the company for a long time. When you are looking at the purchase price of equipment, it should be worth no more than the listed net book value.

Incorporation fees: Fees paid to incorporate your company. The cost of incorporating a company is usually shown as an asset on the balance sheet, although sometimes, they are shown as an expense on the statement of income and expenditure. Please don't query the logic; that's the way it is.

Goodwill: The intangible cost of the value of the business. If a person has purchased the business before you, they would have paid a certain amount for goodwill, considered an asset. Goodwill can be amortized or depreciated over a period of years. The amount of goodwill you pay will be higher than that shown on the books if the business has made a profit. Franchises charge a franchise fee on purchase: another word for goodwill.

Total assets: The total of current and fixed assets, shown on the right hand side of the page. The two amounts added together reflect the book value of all the company assets on the date the financial statement was prepared.

If you read a balance sheet which shows little cash in the bank and only a few outstanding receivables, with large equipment purchases or inventory, this will tell you that the business is probably having a cash-flow problem. There has been too much money spent in these areas, and the business is likely having trouble paying its bills, which you would see in the liabilities section which follows.

Liabilities: The debts owed by the company at the time the balance sheet is prepared. These are broken down into current liabilities and long-term liabilities.

Current liabilities: Any debt owed by the company which is due and payable within one year. Current liabilities include any bank overdraft or short-term loans, supplier accounts (accounts payable), federal and provincial taxes payable, and employee payroll deductions due to Revenue Canada, and Workers' Compensation.

Long-term liabilities: Any type of loan payable over a number of years. This may include loans on equipment, bank loans, mortgages, loans from friends, and shareholders' loans. The principal portion due for each loan within one year will show up under current liabilities. The balance due will show up under long-term liabilities. Your accountant will make all these calculations for you at year-end.

Equity: In a proprietorship, equity consists of the capital put into the company by the owner, minus any money taken out, plus or minus profits or losses. In an incorporated company, equity consists of the shares issued, plus or minus profits and losses.

The balance sheet is called just that because "the total assets will equal the total of the liabilities plus the equity." This is called the "balance sheet equation." As an example, here is a simple transaction:

John put $20,000 into his carpet company to start a business. He was a sole proprietor, and used $10,000 of his own money as well as borrowing $10,000 from the bank.

His asset will be called: Cash in bank	$ 20,000	ASSET =
His liability will be called: Bank loan	$ 10,000	LIABILITY +
His equity will be called: Capital	$ 10,000	EQUITY +

> Equation: Assets = Liabilities + Equity

If John were incorporated, the balance sheet entries would look like this:

Cash at bank	$ 20,000	ASSET =
Bank loan	$ 10,000	LIABILITY +
Shareholder loan	$ 10,000	LIABILITY +

Equation: Assets = Liabilities + Equity

Cash flow: The term commonly used to describe the movement of money through the business. It describes the financial situation, dependent on how the term is used. A business with "poor cash flow" is probably having trouble paying the bills. Too much money may be tied up in accounts receivable or inventory. "Planning your cash flow" means projecting when and how the money will come into the business and where and when it will be spent.

Working capital: The amount of cash flow a business has available to work with. It is usually calculated when a financial statement is prepared. A bank will always look at the working capital of a business when considering loan applications. It is calculated by taking the amount of current assets and subtracting the amount of current liabilities. The difference is the working capital. The theory is that if you turned all your current assets into cash and paid off all your current bills, a healthy company should have some cash left over. In most cases, the equation seems to work the other way. For example, if you look at the balance sheet for Jason's Garden Service in this chapter, you will see that Jason still has some working capital available.

Current assets:	$ 21,895
Less current liabilities:	17,546
Working capital:	$ 4,349

Statement of income and expenditure terms

A statement of income and expenditure is a graphic picture of how a business is operating over a given period. It is usually broken down into

66

three or four sections. Using a furniture store as our example, the structure of a statement of income and expenditure is defined in detail below.

Income (sales or revenue): The total of all revenue sources from a business. This is mainly derived from sales but also includes interest earned from bank accounts, commissions, and from other miscellaneous sources. It does not include funds loaned to the company, only monies earned. The income section would show as below:

Revenue: By furniture sales: $ 125,000

Cost of sales: The actual costs incurred to generate sales made. Each business will have different sales costs that can be broken down even further into cost of sales, then direct costs. For example, if a business deals with inventory, the cost of sales section would look like this:

Cost of sales:
Opening inventory:	$12,000	(Furniture in stock at beginning of period)
Purchases	50,000	(All the furniture purchased for the period)
Freight in	1,000	(Freight costs to deliver furniture to store)
Customs & duty	5,000	(Import customs and brokerage charges)
	68,000	
Less closing inventory	(9,000)	(Cost price of unsold stock on hand at end of period)
Total cost of sales:	59,000	

Gross profit: (53%)   66,000 (Cost of sales subtracted from sales)

The gross profit is calculated by dividing the $66,000 into the $125,000 as a percentage. This is the gross profit on retail price, not cost price.

Direct costs: Cost of sales applicable to selling the product. These are often split out from other overhead costs to help analyze all the expenses applicable to selling the products, before normal overhead.

Direct costs:
Wages–sales staff	$25,000	(All wages paid to sales staff)
Discounts	1,000	(Discounts given on sales)
Damaged goods	500	(Written-off damaged furniture)
Delivery expense	3,000	(Delivery costs to clients)
	29,500	

Gross profit: (29%)   36,500 (Direct costs subtracted from gross profit)

Overhead expenses: Costs incurred whether or not sales are made. Expenses such as rent, telephone lines, and insurance will not change, even when sales increase or decrease. Some overhead expenses will increase or decrease depending on sales volume, such as advertising, office stationery, and long-distance phone calls. They are usually listed in alphabetical order:

Overhead expenses:

Accounting fees	5 00	(Cost to prepare statement)
Advertising	2,000	(Newspapers, flyers, magazine advertising)
Bad debts	200	(Uncollectible unpaid accounts)
Bank charges	500	(Monthly bank, Visa & MasterCard fees)
CPP & EI expense	2,800	(Employer portion of CPP and EI)
Depreciation	2,500	(Allowance for wear and tear of assets)
Fees, licences, dues	300	(Licences, dues to organizations)
Interest, loans	1,500	(All loan interest for period)
Legal fees	400	(All legal fees, excluding incorporation)
Management salaries	15,000	(Salaries paid to shareholders, incorporated company)
Office stationery	1,500	(All printing, coffee, and office supplies)
Office salaries	7,000	(Clerical wages)
Promotion	1,200	(Client gifts, incentives, open houses, etc.)
Rent & taxes	5,000	(Monthly rent and property taxes)
Repairs & maintenance	700	(Store repairs, general maintenance)
Shop supplies	500	(Odds and ends, small tools)
Telephone & fax	800	(Phone rental, long distance, fax, pager, cellular)
Utilities	1,200	(Light, heat and water)
Workers' Compensation	800	(Workers' compensation payable)
Total overhead	44,400	

Net profit/loss: (7,900) Loss

How to analyze a statement of income and expenditure

This example shows that something is wrong with the operation of this business. The gross profit margins are healthy at $66,000 or 53 percent after cost of sales, but when sales staff wages and operational costs are deducted, there is no profit left. The total wages are $47,000, or 37.6 percent of costs. The cost of sales is 47 percent, the two amounting to 84 percent of sales. This leaves only 16 percent of sales, or $20,000 to cover all other overhead costs. This store is employing four people—

two sales staff, the owner, and a bookkeeper. The figures indicate that either the wages are too high or the sales volume too low. Perhaps hours should be cut, or a sales incentive scheme put into place to encourage more volume.

The other overhead costs do not appear to be too far out of line. Advertising is necessary, and it is usually a rule of thumb that five to seven percent of sales should be allocated to advertising. The figure of $2,000 is only 1.6 percent. Perhaps more targeted advertising would increase the sales volume. Other overhead costs could be trimmed slightly, but the main problem appears to be high wages that are not supported by enough sales.

HOW TO UNDERSTAND A FINANCIAL STATEMENT IN ONE EASY LESSON (I HOPE): JASON'S GARDEN SERVICE

Jason started a landscape supply delivery service. He borrowed money from the bank and from his father, also putting in money of his own. He bought two dump trucks and hired a delivery driver. Renting a small office in the country town where he lived, he hired a receptionist-bookkeeper, Stella, to take care of the office. Jason was all set to make a good deal of money.

After six months, he decided it was time to see where he was going. He didn't like working with figures, preferring just to drive the truck and deliver to customers. His accountant went through his financial statement with Jason, which is shown in Sample #1 on pages 71 and 72.

WHERE DID JASON GO WRONG?

Jason wanted too much, too soon, without thinking enough about what he was doing. Excited by the thought of having his own business, he wanted to maintain a certain image, and this cost him dearly.

What the balance sheet tells us

In the current assets, Jason still has money in the bank, because he put in $22,000 of his own capital. In a normal cash-on-delivery business such as this, he should not be carrying too many accounts. One-tenth of his sales for six months are tied up in accounts receivable of $3,551. Jason is a little too generous with his credit. This is a mistake that many new entrepreneurs make, so Jason is not alone.

He delivers bark mulch, sand, and garden supplies, and has been keeping a stock pile of product in his yard for convenience, yet there are plenty of suppliers close by to draw from. He has $6,245 tied up in product, which could be used to pay off some of his accounts. He could be buying his product as needed and free up more of his money.

His fixed assets are two trucks worth $65,000, with a little more in office equipment and furniture. The accountant has not yet made an allowance for depreciation for six months. He will make this calculation at the end of the year. However, a half-year's depreciation would reduce his profits by nearly $10,000. His total assets for the six months are valued at $88,295.

Jason's current liabilities consist of $10,520 owed to trade suppliers, probably mostly for inventory. He owes some provincial sales tax, but is due for a rebate on his GST when he files. This has arisen from the purchase of the two dump trucks and other start-up costs. He is due to pay back his bank loan at the rate of $12,000 principal in one year, plus the monthly interest. He also owes his father $28,000, and the total of the bank loan is $44,000. His total debt load is $77,546, not including the money the business owes him for his capital.

Jason's equity is getting eaten up quickly. Being a proprietorship, his equity is calculated by taking the money Jason put in (capital), less any money he takes out (draws), plus or minus any profits. In this case, the loss of $9,960 is deducted from his equity, which has now shrunk to $10,749 in only six months.

Jason's working capital position is still safe for now. Working capital is calculated by taking his current assets, minus his current liabilities. His current assets are $21,895 and current liabilities $17,546. He has a surplus of $4,349. However, Jason has only taken $1,291 out of the business in six months. This does not equate to a good monthly pay cheque.

SAMPLE #1:

FINANCIAL STATEMENTS

JASON'S GARDEN SERVICE
BALANCE SHEET
FROM JANUARY 1, 19XX - JUNE 30, 19XX
(Unaudited)

ASSETS

Current assets:

Cash at bank	11,019	
Accounts receivable	3,551	
Inventories	6,245	
Prepayments & deposits	1,080	21,895

Fixed assets:

Automotive - trucks	65,000	
Office equipment	550	
Office furniture	850	66,400
Total assets:		**$ 88,295**

LIABILITIES

Current liabilities:

Accounts payable	10,520	
PST payable	315	
GST/HST payable	(5,289)	
Current portion bank loan	12,000	17,546

Long term liabilities:

Bank loan	32,000	
Loan, R. Davies	28,000	60,000
	77,546	

EQUITY

Contributed capital for period	22,000	
Proprietor draws for period	1,291	
	20,709	
Loss for period:	(9,960)	10,749
Total liabilities and equity:		**$ 88,295**

JASON'S GARDEN SERVICE
STATEMENT OF INCOME AND EXPENDITURE
JANUARY 1, 19XX - JUNE 30, 19XX
(Unaudited)

Revenue:

By product sales & delivery		$ 32,705
Cost of sales:		
Opening inventory	0	
Material purchases	19,150	
Wages, driver	7,200	
	26,650	
Less closing inventory	(6,245)	20,405
Gross profit: (37.6%)		**12,300**
Overhead expenditure:		
Accounting fees	500	
Advertising	2,200	
Bank charges	120	
Discounts	790	
Fees, licences	100	
Insurance, shop	480	
Loan interest	2,390	
Office stationery	1,270	
Office wages	2,800	
Rent	2,100	
Telephone	1,280	
Truck fuel	2,960	
Truck R&M	1,820	
Truck insurance	3,000	
Worker's compensation	450	22,260
Profit/(loss) for period:		**$ (9,960) Loss**

What the statement of income and expenditure tells us

Jason's sales were $32,705 for six months. He made a good sales start, but went wild on his overhead. He had to make a decision—either hire a driver so he could do some marketing and attend to the day-to-day matters and delivery, or try to do it all himself. By hiring a driver, he has spent $7,200, or 22 percent of his sales on wage costs. Jason would have done better to purchase just one truck, drive it himself, and get some part-time or commissioned sales help to market the company. He now has the expense of running two trucks, and he has to pay a regular wage to his driver.

If Jason did the deliveries himself, his gross profit would have increased to nearly 60 percent, leaving more money to support his overhead. Starting up a business always requires more working capital than taking one over because you have to become established in the marketplace.

His accounting, advertising, and bank charges are all in line for a new business. His discounts may appear high, but to Jason they were necessary in securing new accounts. What is really hurting his business is the loan interest of $2,390. He has to find $400 a month for loan interest, whether or not he is making money, plus repay the principal portion of $1,000 a month.

Jason spent a fair amount on office stationery, ordering large quantities to start with because the prices were lower for larger quantities. For such a small business, he could have reduced this expense by using standard forms and invoices from the stationers. He also had expensive letterhead stationery printed, and he has used only a few dozen sheets.

Such a business could have been run out of an office in the home, using a cellular telephone or paging service. He could have learned to write up the books himself or used a bookkeeping service once a month. This would have reduced his costs from $6,900 to probably no more than $2,000.

Jason had elaborate signs painted on his trucks. He could have used magnetic signs until the business made more money to support this cost. He will have to do some serious thinking if he wants to survive another six months. With half of his equity gone, he is basically operating on borrowed funds, a very precarious financial situation.

Jason is an example of an entrepreneur who did everything wrong, although such cases are more common that you might think. Perhaps he will listen to his accountant's advice, study his financial statement, and work on the areas where he is losing money.

If he is smart, he will have another financial statement prepared in three months and compare the results with the first six months. Perhaps by then he will have sold his second truck, laid off Stella and the driver, moved the office to his home, bought a cellular phone or a pager, paid down his bank loan with the truck proceeds, stopped extending such generous credit and discounts, hired a part-time bookkeeper, stopped stock-piling product, and started eating the leftovers for lunch at home.

If he made all these changes immediately, in the next six months he would make approximately $17,000 profit and then show a six-month profit of between $7,000 to $8,000. If you are looking to stay a business for a long time, try not to emulate Jason's mistakes.

The five-minute financial test in Exercise #4 will help you get a feel for some basic accounting terminology. The answers can be found on the following page, so complete the excerise and no peeking.

EXERCISE #4

THE FIVE-MINUTE FINANCIAL TEST

1. A computer system is classified as _____

2. An unpaid bill for stationery is called _____

3. A five-year bank loan is called a _____

4. The difference between sales and cost of sales is called

   _____

5. Annual profits are added to the _____
   of an incorporated company.

6. In a proprietorship, a loss is _____
   from equity.

7. Purchases, freight in, and duty are all part of

   _____

8. Advertising, telephone, and shop supplies are called

   _____

9. In an incorporated company, the money contributed by
   shareholder is called _____

10. In a proprietorship, money contributed by the owner is called

    _____

11. Working capital is calculated by subtracting
    _____ from _____

12. Unpaid sales invoices by clients are called _____

13. The taxes charged on sales invoices are called_____

14. The annual allowance made for the wear and tear of assets is
    called _____

15. Net book value is the cost of an asset less _____

    _____

ANSWERS:

1. An asset
2. Accounts payable
3. Long-term liability
4. Gross profit
5. Retained earnings
6. Deducted
7. Cost of sales
8. Overhead expenses
9. Shareholder's loan
10. Capital
11. Current assets from current liabilities
12. Accounts receivable
13. Current liabilities
14. Depreciation
15. Accumulated capital cost allowance

Chapter 4

How do you research the market?

Some people just dream about becoming rich –
others go out there and make it happen.

DOES YOUR IDEA HAVE MARKET POTENTIAL?

Now is the time to take your dreams and ideas and discover whether it is practical to turn them into a full-fledged business. How many times have you heard people say "I have a great money-making idea!" "This is going to be a winner!" "I'm going into business to market this wonderful invention, everyone's going to buy one." The dollar signs blind reality as they head off on a fruitless venture with this great gizmo clutched in their hands.

At some point in our lives, many of us have thought of an invention or idea which could make money. The successful ones are those who take their golden idea and research the market thoroughly. The key to a successful and innovative idea is to identify a niche and a need in the marketplace. Remember those two words—need and niche—because they are what successful marketing is all about. Many people make the mistake of wanting a huge slice of the pie. The key is to take a small slice, become an expert in that area, and to discover whether there is a need for your business. The next step is to learn how to successfully market your business.

Sometime in the seventies, I had a wonderful idea for a little plug-in device which would keep a half cup of cold coffee warm. A little warming plate seemed like a great idea and would sell by the millions. Think about all the office workers and their coffee always going cold. That is as far as the idea went.

Lo and behold, some time in the late 1980s the same invention appeared on the store shelves just the way I had imagined it. Someone else had the same wonderful idea; obviously he or she did their market research and followed it through to fruition, hoping to make some money as well. And many sincere congratulations to that person. You may not see little coffee warming plates on every desk, certainly not the millions which had been envisaged, but they do exist—and someone else made it happen.

Unfortunately, researching a new business, its products, and the competition are the vital areas in which many people fall down. Excited by the thought of owning their own business, the research process is often cut short by the desire to get started quickly. This is not a good idea. You have to do your homework, and that can be a long and tedious process. It many take weeks, or even months, depending on the type of business you are researching. But the efforts are worth it in the long run. Your new business will have greater longevity and success if you know your product and the market intimately.

Business in the new millennium is going to be tough. Even now, as so many people are contemplating starting a business, or have already started one, many are finding the going tough. Those who keep up with technology and effective marketing techniques will come out the winners. Those who cater toward the future trends will have an excellent starting point. Those who drift into something in an unorganized manner will drop out quickly.

Consider how our lives and the world are changing as you contemplate what your business should be. The one commodity the average person is extremely short of is time. Another one is computer knowledge. How can you cater to these people? What could you do to service all these people working from their homes? The top ten home-based businesses in North America are nearly all related to services that small business people need, such as business and financial consulting, computer services, marketing and advertising, graphics, writing, and sales.

As a person who works long hours in a home office, here are some ideas I believe could be viable. I personally could use all of these services if the company was prepared to come to my home, so for what it's worth, here is my Top Ten Businesses of the Future.

1. Computer and equipment servicing, repairs, and cleaning

2. Computer program training

3. Office services for filing, data entry, running errands

4. Vehicle oil changes and minor (if not major) repairs

5. Shopping service

6. Nutritious and tasty meal delivery service

7. Gopher (i.e. running children to after-school activities)

8. Hairdressing and beauty needs

9. House organizer (clean closets and cupboards)

10. Personal fitness coach

As this list no doubt tells you, I, and many thousands of other people, don't have time for these mundane chores anymore. Think how you could simplify the stress in home-based workers' lives if you came to them and serviced their car, delivered healthy meals occasionally, made them fit and beautiful, or did all the tedious running around which detracts from valuable, productive work time. Don't discount the fact that home-based businesses are the current and future trend–you could be passing up a potentially profitable business.

It was enlightening to receive a telephone call recently from a woman who is thinking of opening an in-home shopping service. I will be her first client, as I waste at least four hours every three weeks performing the mundane task of a major supermarket shopping spree. A client of mine who is a mechanic provides a service of repairing vehicles at his customers' homes. He is making a healthy living, with very little overhead, except his truck filled with tools and parts.

WHAT DO YOU RESEARCH?

So where do you start the research process? There are a few key areas that should be researched thoroughly with your new business venture.

You are not just starting or buying a business, you are buying an entity which sells products or a service, with the hopes of generating enough profit to pay you a decent wage and build a healthy goodwill factor over time. You need to be very sure that when those doors are opened, your business will generate the profits that you have projected. If you have completed your research thoroughly, you can feel much more confident your goals will be met.

Your research will explore the following areas:

1. The current and future market

2. The export market

3. National and local markets

4. Product knowledge

5. The competition

1. The current and future market

Remember that you will need a business that will withstand the ever-changing market trends. As technology changes, new businesses are born. Look at the new businesses evolving over the last few years, such as Web-page design, Internet mail-order, 1-900 sales, and coffee shops. The large electronic warehouses have really only evolved and blossomed in the last few years. Who would have thought that entire stores would be devoted to compact discs? In the last few years, coffee shops have become all the rage. One young man I know is currently researching supplying healthy vegetarian lunches to businesses and large corporations for the employees. The market is never constant and always changing. Who ever heard of a Californian wrap until recently?

There are many factors to consider during your research. The extent of your study will be determined by whether you intend to trade locally, nationally, or internationally. You need to find the answers to these questions:

1. Will the product or service be wanted or needed within the next five to ten years?

2. What is the past history of this type of business?

3. Is the industry growing, has it levelled off, or is it decreasing?

4. Is there export potential?

5. Are imported products cheaper and of comparable quality?

6. Is this a short-lived business subject to consumer trends?

7. Could this business be diversified?

8. What does this business offer that others don't?

9. Is this business seasonal or are sales constant year-round?

10. Is there enough cash-flow to maintain a sufficient inventory?

a) Identifying consumer trends

Because the market changes so rapidly, you should study the trends over the last decade and think and read about the potential future ones. What factors influence consumer trends? There are many, and the more conversant you are with our changing world, the better you can plan a business with a long life.

Here are some important trends to consider as you prepare your market research. Can your business accommodate or withstand any of these trends?

- The ageing population as the baby boomers progress slowly to old age

- More medical facilities and long-term care needed

- The environment—chemicals, global warming, pollution, conservation, recycling, endangered species

- Large swing towards self-employment and home-based offices

- Lack of time to perform basic chores—shopping, house cleaning etc.

- Healthier diets—natural foods, less fat, vegetarian meals

- Exercise and fitness

- Housing—multi unit dwelling, downsizing of homes and number of children

- Technology—communications, Internet, computer-reliance

- Increased desire and necessity for knowledge and education

- Immigration—changing populations

- Youth—fewer job opportunities

- Media influences

- Need to be entertained

- Less income as job markets change

- Downsizing of businesses

- The Internet–bringing the world into the average home

- Trend towards alternative medicines and remedies

- International economies—their changing structure and currency values

2. The export market

If you are considering manufacturing, think about exporting your products; there are many initiatives and government grants available. The federal government is keen to boost export sales and a sound idea and business plan may qualify for one of the many programs offered. There are many resources offered to you for research. Marketing internationally requires knowledge in many areas such as the following:

- Current and future market trends

- Customs procedures, regulations, and paperwork

- Transportation choices and costs

- Financial transactions in foreign countries

- Methods of distribution

- Locating distributors, manufacturing representatives, buyers and sales agents

- Packaging and labelling requirements

A worthwhile investment in time and money would be a visit to an international trade show. You will be exposed to the most current information available, be able to study your competition indepth, and research your business potential first-hand. Without knowing the latest information about the world market, you could be reinventing the wheel.

Listed here are some of the federal programs available to businesses who wish to export, or who are already involved in export activities. Your local Canada Business Service Centre offers publications available at a minimal cost, which details all provincial and federal programs. When you are researching your business, read about all the programs applicable to your type of business. You could possibly manage to obtain financial help for your research and business operating costs. (Keep in mind that all government programs are subject to change.)

a) Market Intelligence Service

The Market Intelligence Service (MIS) is a government-operated informational service designed to assist entrepreneurs, manufacturers, and small-to medium-sized enterprises in researching the area of domestic and export manufacturing within Canada. Information is provided to increase your awareness of import marketing trends for Canada and the United States. There is a variety of statistics and information available, including areas such as:

- Foreign exporters to Canada

- Canadian exports by country of origin and destination

- Imports by country of origin and state or province of entry

- Analyses of specific products

- Canadian and U.S. market reports and information

- Tariffs

- Canadian importers

The information is provided on request, and previously published reports can be ordered from a regional office of Industry Canada. For more information, call the Market Intelligence Service, Industry Canada at

(613) 954-5031, or fax requests to (613) 954-1894, toll-free 1-800-328-6189, or visit their Web site on the Internet through the Strategis Web page (see Appendix 1).

b) New Exports to Border States

The New Export to Borders States (NEBS) program is aimed at teaching small-to medium-sized businesses everything needed to export into the United States. It is described as an intensive course with first-hand exposure to nearby marketplaces in a U.S. border state. Your business is eligible unless it's already regularly exporting. If you are considering diversification or exporting your product, this is an excellent program. It explains all border procedures and programs available to exporters, and includes visits to a U.S. border or nearest Canadian consulate. You will be briefed on U.S. border requirements and have one-on-one interviews with a Canadian consulate trade officer, potential customers, agents, or distributors. The program also includes a talk by a U.S. manufacturer's representative, sales agent, distributor, or buyer. You will be given a tour of a related trade show or trade mart as well as visits to local wholesalers or retailers.

The program cost is negligible and lasts one to three days, plus your personal expenses. For more information, contact the Department of Foreign Affairs and International Trade office in your province.

c) New Exporters Training & Counselling Program

The New Exporters Training & Counselling Program (NEXPRO) is designed to mentor businesses that have export potential but lack the knowledge and experience to proceed. The program consists of a combination of group mentoring and one-on-one counselling. It helps entrepreneurs develop and implement their business export plan and increase their exporting knowledge. There is a cost involved, but the investment is well worthwhile for a business with definite potential. Contact your nearest Business Development Bank of Canada. Telephone numbers are in Appendix 1 at the back of this book.

d) Other programs

There are many other programs available, and these can be found in the valuable publication *Overview of Government Assistance Programs For*

Small Businesses, available from an office of the Canada Service Centre. Orders can be placed using your telephone and Visa card. Many are designed for specific industries, trades, professions, and businesses of varying size and structure.

3. National and local markets

You can learn a great deal about the national market by studying which goods are imported into Canada. This information is available through the Marketing Intelligence Service (see above). You should also consult other statistical agencies, such as Statistics Canada, and spend time researching on the Internet. (See Appendix 1 for useful Internet Web sites.) If you have the budget for it, marketing consultants can help you with current information and market trends.

If your business is strictly local, your municipal office will have some very helpful information, as will your chamber of commerce. You can do some of the leg work yourself by physically taking a tour of your town and gathering the following information.

- The number of competitors successfully trading in your area

- The accessibility of your potential location

- Where shoppers are in abundance and shopping actively

- The quiet shopping areas and what type of stores trade there

- How your competitors advertise in the local paper

- What competition is listed in the local Yellow Pages
  (Visit these locations to see whether they are still open for business)

- Leasing costs of suitable vacant buildings with parking accessibility

- Applicable local by-laws and applications for new commercial building permits

Once again, visit as many trade shows as possible and gather all the information you can from your competitors. You may have a wonderful business idea but be behind on advances made within your area of interest. You will come home with your head teaming with new ideas, plus have the opportunity to speak to others in your field of work. From them, you can glean some information about how they started, how the consumer market is currently reacting to this type of business, and see how they market their businesses.

Another tip is to read the businesses for sale classifieds, and call businesses similar to yours. Try to find out why they are selling, whether their business is successful, and how long they have been in business. Join associations and groups specific to your business interests. You will receive up-to-date information from the industry across Canada and the United States. This information will help you to gauge whether your timing is right in the market.

4. Product knowledge

As stressed in Chapter 1, you have to be the expert before you even start your business. The old saying "we learn by our mistakes" will not do your business reputation any good if it applies to your lack of expertise. You have to know your products or service inside out. You may love a business for the product lines, but will your customers love the products too? When problems arise with a product, or when a customer asks technical questions, are you knowledgeable enough to resolve these problems and answer their questions competently and confidently?

One way to increase your product knowledge is to contact the manufacturers or a local distributor. They are usually happy to send you product information and answer your questions. Some of the questions you should research about your product lines (or service) are these:

- How long have these products been on the market?

- Are they seasonal, and when do most sell?

- How often are these products upgraded or changed?

- Could you be caught unexpectedly with obsolete inventory?

- What do the manufacturers' warranties cover?

- Are replacement parts readily available?

- Are the products competitively priced?

- Are they C.S.A. (Canadian Standards Association) approved?

- Are buying trends increasing or decreasing?

- Are the products high, medium, or low in quality?

- How do the products compare to the competition?

- What age groups do these products appeal to ?

- What is the life expectancy of the products?

- Could the products become obsolete due to changing technology?

After these questions are answered, you may find that the business is not viable after all. The product pricing may be too high compared to the competition, or you may discover that over the previous five years, overall demand for the products is declining due to technological changes and shifts in consumer buying trends. In another five years, the demand could become substantially less. The products may appear high in quality on sight, but you may discover that they are poorly made and not something that you would feel confident selling. Perhaps the manufacturer's guarantees are inadequate, or replacement parts are priced exorbitantly and hard to secure.

5. The competition

Competition is an ugly word, but competitors are a fact of life. If your business can't compete with other stores or services, don't start this business. You have to have some sort of an edge. You may have an excellent product, but if everyone else is selling a similar commodity, just how much of the market can you expect to capture? You will have to get to know everything there is to know about your competition and keep up to date with their marketing strategies.

The best way to research your competition is to locate those you consider the largest threat to your potential business. Then it is time to take a field trip, armed with a small note pad and sharp pencil. Select at least two or three large competitors and at least three similar in size to your business. To really acquire a feel for how the competition deals with its customers, you will have to pretend to be interested in purchasing a product, preferably one that will require the help and knowledge of a salesperson. You should now be familiar with your own products or service, so your fact-finding mission will be to find answers to the following questions.

- What appeals to you most or stands out on entering the premises?

- How large an inventory do they carry?

- How are the products displayed and are the displays eye-catching?

- How many customers are in the store, browsing or buying?

- What attracted the customers who are purchasing products?

- Do the staff appear to be helping customers in a friendly manner?

- Are their prices in line with your industry?

- Are your prices competitive with theirs?

- Did you wait long to be helped?

- Was the salesperson helping you knowledgeable about the product?

- Were they willing to bargain or undercut other competitors?

- By how much were they willing to reduce an advertised price?

- What do they offer that you could not?

- What could you offer that they could not?

- Do they have brochures or promotional literature available about their products?

- Do they offer any special services, such as free delivery?

- Would they replace a faulty product immediately?

- Which areas could do with some improvement, and could you improve in these areas?

- What is the age group of the customers?

• What is their return policy?

• Do they offer credit terms or credit card facilities?

• What means of promotion do they use? (e.g. coupons, flyers, free samples)?

If you are not able to research some of your main competitors due to physical distance, telephone them instead, or ask for information to be mailed to you. Ask as many questions as possible on the list above. You should then be able to build a profile of each main competitor and know how they advertise, why customers shop there, what their pricing and service policies are, what areas need improving, and how successfully you can compete with them. At the same time, you will probably glean some further ideas for promoting or improving your own business. Your strength will lie in knowing and assessing your competitors' strengths and weaknesses.

WHERE DO YOU FIND RESEARCH MATERIAL?

Knowing where and how to locate your research material can save you valuable time. There are more information services available than you will probably need, and much of it is free. Listed below are some invaluable resource centres, along with the type of information available.

1. Canada Business Service Centres

Canada Business Service Centres (CBSC) are located across Canada, and the main offices are listed in Appendix 1. There are over 20 federal departments currently involved in this program, and these include CBSC's Industry Canada, the Federal Office for Regional Development Quebec, the Atlantic Canada Opportunities Agency, and the Western Economic Diversification.

Information is provided about all government services, programs, and regulations in a variety of ways. For example, the Business Information System (BIS) is a large database supplying current information that is immediately passed on to the customer. The fax-on-demand service can be accessed and is available 24 hours a day, seven days a week.

Many publications are available free of charge or for minimal cost and can be ordered over the telephone. Other forms of published materials include videos, CD-Rom products, external databases, directories, and how-to manuals. Information officers will also refer your queries to the necessary agency, and some branches have an automated system to provide immediate answers to frequently asked questions.

There is a Web site available that will access a large database of information (see Appendix 1), plus pathfinder documents which briefly describe requested programs. Make a call or visit to your local centre a priority.

2. Business Development Bank of Canada

As mentioned earlier, the Business Development Bank of Canada offers many services for entrepreneurs. There are a variety of programs, including business counselling, venture capital and term loans, export assistance, management training, strategic planning, business training, young entrepreneur mentor and financing programs, and student business loans. Make it a point to call your local branch to see if they can help you. All the current branches are listed in Appendix 1.

3. Statistics Canada

If you need business and trade statistics, Statistics Canada is the place to call. Their telephone number can be found under the federal government pages of your telephone directory. They can provide statistics from all over Canada, and although some may not be right up to date, they should give good you a good indication of what you need to know. Information is also available on their Internet site; the Web site address can be found in Appendix 1.

4. Yellow Pages

The Yellow Pages are a wonderful source of information. You can research both the local market and your competition by studying the competitors' advertisements. From there you can determine how your competition advertises and what services they offer. You can call the competitors as a potential customer, asking questions about products or have product information mailed to you. New ideas many come to light by studying their advertisements.

You can assess how many competitors are in your trading area and perhaps get some indication of their size. You can also find out how many businesses have failed by calling the listings. Out of 11 car detailing businesses called in a local community, only four were still operational after one year. This is a definite indication that there is a problem with that type of business—or the operators.

5. Chamber of commerce

Your local chamber of commerce is in business to help businesses, both new and established. Their job is to help and encourage new businesses with resource information. In Langley, B.C., the chamber of commerce responds to well over 125 calls a month from new and hopeful entrepreneurs. They supply business start-up kits, which include a resource guide, business plan and cash-flow information, business registration forms, and one-on-one consulting services. Each chamber will offer different information. Once you become a member, you have access to mailing lists, networking opportunities, group medical plans, monthly newsletters, meetings, and special events.

6. Municipal offices

Municipal offices can supply you with statistical information, traffic counts, potential rezoning plans, new building applications, by-laws, and certain business information. To familiarize yourself with your municipality, take a trip to their offices and see which information will be relevant to your business.

7. The Internet

The benefits of using the Internet are endless. As a research tool, nothing beats sitting in the comfort of your own home as you travel your country and the globe collecting information. It seems that if you are not on-line these days, you are falling behind the times. Information from all government agencies is available, as well as from competitors, libraries, and businesses in other countries. You can download the information and print it out without moving from your chair. Many informative small-business Web sites can be found in Appendix 1.

8. Trade shows and seminars

As mentioned previously, make it a point to catch a few trade shows during the research stage. You will be inundated with the most up-to-date information relevant to your industry, allowing you to make much more informed decisions on the future potential of your business. There are also entrepreneurial trade shows that demonstrate new products and franchises available. This is an opportunity to see if there are any new competitors entering the market and also gives you a chance to review promising new businesses.

If there are any seminars being held which could help you with your business in any way, try to attend them. Not only will you learn new skills, you will have an opportunity to network with other entrepreneurs, and you may be able to do some future business with them. Keep in mind you should not just be researching your business, you should be learning about other areas of operating a business, such as hiring staff, customer service, updating computer information, and management skills.

9. Publications

Various publications are available for research purposes. Use your library, the Internet, newspapers, flyers, magazines, directories, trade and financial papers to glean every ounce of information you may need. Make a point of subscribing to journals and newspapers specifically aimed at your area of interest.

Chapter 5

Why do you need a legal agreement?

But he seemed so nice and sincere—
besides, we shook hands on the deal!
Anonymous

SHOULD YOU HAVE A LEGAL AGREEMENT?

Yes, yes, and yes again. Please don't invest in any type of business without a legal agreement. A legal agreement is a comprehensive document that protects both you and the vendor in case of unforeseen circumstances. A verbal agreement or a handshake isn't good enough when it comes to business. Many people have lost money on a smile and a handshake. It is human nature to want to trust people, a trait we hope will not disappear from society—but get everything in writing anyway.

Some vendors tend to make verbal promises and offers they have no intention of keeping. They tend to play down the negative side of the business (and rest assured, there is a positive and negative side to all businesses) as well as forgetting to mention important factors you should know. If you consider statements, offers, and promises important to your purchase, ensure that these points are all documented in the agreement, no matter how trivial they may seem to you at the time, and no matter how sincere the vendor appears to be.

For example, if a vendor promises to train you full time for a month, get it in writing. If he or she suggests a certain sales volume, put that in writing too. Then, if you are doing everything right and the business fails to meet certain expectations, you have a signed document and legal recourse. Even if you are purchasing a franchise from a reputable company, have their legal agreement checked by your lawyer, preferably one who is conversant with franchise agreements.

A legal agreement sets out the full terms of the purchase, all the goods and services to be purchased, payment conditions, and all other conditions. It covers areas which you, as a layperson, would not even think to consider. Some vendors will write up their own agreements, expecting you to sign eagerly on the dotted line. If a vendor has an agreement prepared by his or her own lawyer, ask your lawyer to review it. It doesn't matter how small the business is, or how few dollars are involved, have an agreement prepared. No one can afford to lose money these days, particularly if a deal turns sour.

WHY DO YOU NEED A LAWYER?

Whether you are investing in a small, home-based distributorship, multilevel or network marketing business, or purchasing an existing business, seeking a lawyer's advice should be a standard procedure. How often do you read all that fine print on contracts and leases, and how much of it do you really understand? To most people, it is just a bunch of words in a strange language, yet contracts are signed all the time without a proper comprehension of the content of the documents.

You have heard the old saying "sign your life away," and this is what inevitably happens in countless situations. A young man was recently excited by a new business he saw at an entrepreneur's show. The business, its potential profits and ease of making quick money were described in glowing terms. What was not told to the young man was the large investment of money and warehouse space that would be needed to make the business work, and that the training was performed over the phone along with a couple of generic manuals containing information that could mostly be found in the library.

He signed on the dotted line and paid thousands of dollars for this concept. He was locked in, signed, sealed, and delivered the paltry goods. The head office was based in the United States, so legal recourse would have been costly, and he would probably have lost his case anyway, because he had agreed to the written terms. It was an expensive lesson for him. A lawyer would have investigated the company for him and advised him accordingly.

Below is a discussion of some areas which a lawyer will thoroughly investigate and advise you on before letting you enter into an agreement. These subject areas are particularly important if you are buying an established incorporated business or any business with assets being a part of the purchase price.

1. Searches

A lawyer can perform company searches of the business you are interested in. A search will discover whether any underlying problems exist, and entails the following:

- A search and review of the company minute books (if an incorporated business).

- A check with municipal authorities regarding taxes, zoning and licensing.

- Searches through special registries (depending on the nature of the business) and with the various taxation and government agencies, such as Revenue Canada, Workers' Compensation Board, Waste Management Branch and GST/HST office.

- Searches to check that there are no infringements of registered patent trademarks or copyrights plus ensure that there are no infringements on any laws, statutes, or other regulations.

2. Tax considerations

Taxes have an important bearing on the purchase of an existing company. These are the areas which a lawyer will investigate on your behalf:

- **Assets**: If the company being purchased has assets and the assets are a large portion of the purchase price, you must know the tax position of those various assets and whether they have already been depreciated.

- **Tax history**: There should be representations and warranties regarding any previous troubles with the tax authorities. There may be tax benefits and previous losses to be considered in the purchase price.

- **Taxes payable**: When a business is sold, taxes are usually payable on the sale of the property and assets. These include provincial sales taxes and the goods and services tax (GST/HST).

- **Other**: Other tax issues might include whether the vendor or the purchaser are filing taxes and remittances for that particular year, or on any land, or on a particular asset that is being transferred for sale.

3. Incorporated businesses

If you are purchasing an incorporated business, your lawyer will review the history of the business in depth. When you purchase such a business, you are usually purchasing the shares of the company at a certain value. When you enter into a share purchase agreement, you purchase the assets and the liabilities of the business at book value. Your lawyer will research the following areas:

- Representations and warranties regarding the shares

- Representations whether it is a reporting company or not

- Where it is registered and where it does business

- When and where the last annual report was filed (If it has been two years since the last annual report has been filed, the Escheat Act allows the government to seize the assets of the company.)

- How many authorized or common shares it has issued, and how many of the shares are validly issued and outstanding

- Whether the vendor has authority under the terms of the memorandum and articles of the company to sell shares or capitals, and who the directors and officers of the company may be

4. Competition

How would you feel if, after purchasing your business, nine months later the vendor opened a similar business one block from you?

Remember, the vendor has already operated a business before and knows how to do just that. You don't know what will happen to the vendor's personal financial situation in the future. The vendor could be forced into opening another business to survive, and will, nine times out of ten, start a business in which he or she already has knowledge, expertise, and business contacts.

A competition clause in your legal agreement can prevent the vendor from doing this. Usually, the clause states that the vendor will not participate, set up, or operate a business similar to the one you have purchased within the next five to ten years and within a given geographical boundary (typically a five-or ten-mile radius). It is a comfort to have this clause in your agreement and should be standard in most agreements.

5. Exclusivity

If your potential business involves an exclusive product line or type of service, be sure to include an exclusivity clause in your agreement to prevent the vendor from selling the same products, rights, or services to other people at a later date. Any exclusive product or service immediately makes the business more financially viable to the purchaser. If these exclusive rights are encroached upon in any way, the business will obviously be affected negatively.

6. Records and documentation

Certain items belong to, and should remain with, the business after the sale; specifically, all company records and documentation. These records should include client lists, sales, marketing, and costing information, accounting records, files, working papers, supplier information, lists of information sources, correspondence, and all usual business records required for day-to-day operation. There have been cases of vendors selling a business and keeping copies of records of clients' names, addresses, and telephone numbers to use in the future.

Unfortunately, nothing prevents the vendor from taking copies of records, and computers make it easy. However, this sensitive area should be covered in your agreement.

7. Licences and rights

Your lawyer will see to it that any licences, area rights, or other business rights, designs, or trademarks that are being purchased with the business are covered in the agreement. If you are buying a business with a specified marketing or operating area, such as a dealership, make sure your area is clearly identified in an appendix and included in the agreement. In one case, a new dealership did not honour the promises of certain rights written in their agreement with a distributor. The agreement was not clearly worded and the disappointed distributor ultimately had no recourse. The case would have had to be left up to the judge's discretion, but the legal costs involved were not worth taking such a chance. You may want a clause written into the agreement regarding the existence of various licences, permits, and operating authorities required for carrying on the business.

8. Insurance

It is the responsibility of the vendor to keep the assets of the business insured until you have purchased the business. If there is any damage to the assets before you take possession, it should be the vendor's responsibility to make good on damages. It should be stipulated who is responsible for maintaining the insurance on the assets and whether the purchaser of the business has an obligation to continue and maintain certain insurance policies.

9. Other considerations

There are many areas to be considered in a buy-sell agreement, and each business will have different requirements. Here are some areas that may apply to your purchase:

1. Employees: If you are purchasing a business with employees already in place, obtain a vendor's statement as to how many employees there are and whether they have a collective agreement. What are their obligations to long-term employees who may require extensive periods of notice if they were terminated. You need to know how these projected future expenses are being accommodated within the buy-sell agreement. Another fact to consider is unpaid vacation pay at the date of take over and other monetary concerns such as existing sales bonus plans or incentive schemes for the employees.

2. Company debts: Your lawyer should research the company's debts or contractual obligations.

3. Financial assistance: If the vendor is offering financial assistance in the form of a loan to the purchaser, two issues could be relevant:

a) the relevant provincial legislation does not allow financial assistance if the loan would render the company insolvent;

b) short term loans may constitute a criminal rate of interest if the various fees total more than 60 percent a year.

4. Support documentation: It is useful to enclose a list of documents to be transferred at the time of closing, especially if there are corporate records or business licences or non-competition agreements, resignations of the previous directors of the company, and transfers of title. Appendixes to the agreement may include a list of property being transferred, leases, licences, types of insurance coverage, important contracts held by the company, as well as audited or unaudited financial statements.

5. General provisions: At the end of the agreement, there should be a section of general provisions. This section should include a statement that vendor's and purchaser's liability remain in force after the agreement has been closed. This clause is inserted for protection in the future.

Another provision should state that "this agreement contains the whole agreement between the vendor and the purchaser, and this supersedes all other previous agreements; there are no representations other than those contained in this agreement, and the purchasers or vendors have relied on these representations."

WHAT IF LEGAL PROBLEMS ARISE?

Once your agreement is signed and dated, and the date of takeover has been reached, the business is yours. If for any reason a serious problem with the agreement arises after signing that cannot be resolved between you and the vendor, you will have to ask your lawyer for advice. If the agreement has been broken in any way and a settlement cannot be reached, it will be up to the courts to make a ruling based on the contents of the agreement and the events that occurred. This will be a time-consuming issue which may very well affect your business operation.

It has been proven conclusively that the person with the most detailed documentation has a better chance of winning his or her court case. When you go into a court room, the judge can only base an opinion on the paperwork and evidence presented. The case is built around evidence—not hearsay (i.e. any statements quoted by a third party). For statements to be admitted as evidence, the person must be called as a witness. Written statements from people are not acceptable. Tapes are often not admitted as evidence. What *is* considered is documented evidence. As you explore your new venture, keep a log and diary of events, phone calls, meetings, and statements made by vendors and their associates. If the need arises, these people can be called to the stand to testify. Your documented information will allow for thorough questioning.

If the business is affected adversely, keep detailed notes, documentation, and records of all events applicable to the case until it is heard in court. Compensation may be awarded for loss of profits. It's a comfort to have an agreement prepared in the first place, because you will have written proof that the contract has been broken. Without an agreement, you do not have grounds for a court case.

WHAT DO THOSE LEGAL TERMS MEAN?

As in the world of accounting, the legal profession has its own jargon. To help you out, here is a glossary of common legal terminology found in buy-sell agreements for businesses:

Assign: To give someone else your property or rights under a contract

Assurance: A positive declaration

Authorize: To commission or allow

Case: A disagreement settled in court

Covenant: An oath, promise, pledge, or vow

Consideration: Payment for something given, such as money, services, or promises

Contract: An agreement between two people which can be enforced

Deed: A document in which an owner transfers ownership of an asset

Default: Failure to act or meet one's obligations

Encumbrance: An impediment, usually a loan or mortgage on a property

Hereafter: In the future

Herein: In this place

Hereinafter: Below

Heretofore: Formerly, once

Herewith: With this

Indemnify: Exempt from a penalty, or to compensate

Lien: A hold on another person's property until an outstanding debt is paid

Memorandum: Notes or records made for future business use

Misrepresent: Falsify or distort facts

Statute: A written law

Vendor: Seller

Vested: Placing of the right to

Warranties: Agreements, guarantees, pledges, or assurances

Sample #2 on the following pages shows an example of a buy-sell agreement for the sale of a gift shop.

SAMPLE #2

A SIMPLE BUY-SELL AGREEMENT

THIS AGREEMENT made the *Twenty-ninth* Day of *July, 19XX*

BETWEEN:

Peter James Turnbull Businessman, of *9291 - 295th Street, Vancouver* in the municipality of *Vancouver,* in the Province of British Columbia.

(Hereinafter called the "Vendor")
OF THE FIRST PART

AND:

Sarah Elizabeth Scott, Businesswoman, of *19775 - 26th Avenue, Burnaby* in the municipality of *Burnaby ,* in the Province of British Columbia.

(Hereinafter called the "Purchaser")
OF THE SECOND PART

WHEREAS:

a. The Vendor carries on the business of selling retail gifts to the general public under the business name "Artsy and Crafty," (hereinafter called the "Business") and operates the said business in Willowdale Mall, in Burnaby, in the Province of British Columbia, and in connection therewith owns certain records, supplies, and other assets at the aforesaid address.

b. The Vendor has agreed to sell the Business as a going concern and to sell the said assets and the Purchaser has agreed to buy the same on the terms and conditions hereinafter set forth;

PURCHASE AND SALE

1. Subject to the terms and conditions of this Agreement and based on the warranties and representations herein contained, the Vendor agrees to sell and the Purchaser agrees to purchase all the property, rights, undertakings and assets as listed in Appendix A (except as hereinafter provided), belonging to or used in the Business, as a going concern, including but without limiting the foregoing:

(a) The goodwill of the Business, together with all trademarks, designs, licences, Authorities and other rights used in connection with the Business, and all records, documentation, correspondence, and other property related to the Business.

(b) The Vendor agrees to provide one month's full-time training to the Purchaser at no extra cost.

(c) The Vendor agrees to bear the cost of having the lease changed into the Purchaser's name.

(All of which property, undertakings, and assets are hereinafter called the "Assets")

VENDOR'S REPRESENTATIONS

2. The Vendor represents, warrants, and agrees that:

(a) The Vendor has the power, authority, and capacity to enter into this Agreement and to carry out the transactions contemplated hereby, all of which have been duly and validly authorized;

(b) The completion of the transactions contemplated hereby will not constitute a breach by the Vendor of any statute, by-law, or regulation or of any contract or Agreement to which the Vendor is a party or by which it is bound or which would result in the creation of any lien, encumbrance, or other charge on any of the Assets.

(c) The Vendor has good and marketable title to the Assets, free and clear of all liens, mortgages, encumbrances, equities or claims of every kind and nature whatsoever.

(d) The vendor is not in default and has received no notice of default of any term or condition of any statute, by-law, or regulation to its Business.

(e) The Vendor has no indebtedness to any person, firm, or corporation which might, by operation of law or other else, hereafter constitute a lien, charge, or encumbrance upon any of the Assets.

PURCHASE PRICE AND PAYMENT

3. The Purchase price payable by the Purchaser to the Vendor for the Assets (the "Purchase Price") will be One Hundred and Twenty-Five Thousand Dollars ($125,000.00).

4. The Purchase Price shall be paid as follows:

(a) Twenty-five Thousand Dollars ($25,000.00) shall be paid directly to the Vendor's solicitor upon execution of this Agreement, as a deposit in Trust.

(b) Fifty Thousand Dollars ($50,000.00) shall be paid to the Vendor's solicitor on the date of occupation, which shall be no later than August 1, XXXX.

(c) Fifty Thousand Dollars ($50,000.00) shall be paid to the Vendor's solicitor in trust in monthly installments of $2,083.33 for a period of Twenty-Four (24) months, plus interest of Nine Percent (9%) per annum, payable in one cheque each year on the Thirty-First of August, 19XX and 19XX. These payments will be made by way of postdated cheques to the Vendor no later than August 31, 19XX.

5. Upon Execution of this Agreement, the Purchaser shall deliver to the Vendor:

(a) A certified cheque or bank draft in the amount of Twenty-Five Thousand Dollars ($25,000.00).

(b) A certified cheque or bank draft in the amount of Fifty Thousand Dollars ($50,000.00), dated August 1, 19XX, to be held in trust by the Vendor's solicitor.

(c) Twenty-four (24) postdated cheques in the amount of Two Thousand and Eighty-Three Dollars and Thirty-Three cents ($2,083.33), the first cheque to be dated August 31, 19XX, and every month thereafter, to be held in trust until the Execution of this Agreement by the Vendor's solicitor.

(d) A Promissory Note for the annual interest, which will be Four Thousand Five Hundred Dollars ($4,500.00), due August 31, 19XX, and Two Thousand Two Hundred and Fifty Dollars ($2,250.00) due August 31, 19XX.

VENDOR'S COVENANTS

6. The Vendor will:

(a) Take or cause to be taken all proper steps, actions and proceedings on its part to enable it to vest a good marketable title in the Purchaser to the Assets, free and clear of all liens, mortgages, encumbrances, equities, or claims of every nature and kind whatsoever and shall deliver, upon date of execution, such bills of sale, transfer, assignments, and consents (including consents by Creditors of the Vendor under, or other evidence in compliance with, the Sale of Goods in Bulk Act, if required), and consents to transfer of licences, leases, contracts, and rights as the solicitor for the Purchaser may require;

(b) To deliver possession of the Assets to the Purchaser on execution of this Agreement;

(c) From the date of execution of this Agreement to the date of removal, maintain in force policies of insurance heretofore maintained, and obtain and maintain such additional policies of insurance as may be required to insure the Assets, in the amount against such perils as are customary in other similar businesses;

(d) from the date of execution of this Agreement to the date of removal, take good care of the Assets and to take all reasonable care to protect and safeguard all Assets;

(e) Execute and do all such further acts, deeds, things, and assurances as may be requisite in the opinion of the solicitors for the Purchaser for more perfectly and absolutely assigning, transferring, assuring to, and vesting in the Purchasers titles to the Assets, free and clear of all liens, mortgages, encumbrances, equities, and claims of any nature and kind whatsoever;

(f) Not from the date of execution of this Agreement to date of removal, sell, consume, or dispose of or transfer possession of any of the Assets;

(g) Not from the date of execution of this Agreement, and for a further period of Five (5) years, start or operate a business involved in the wholesale or retail selling of arts, crafts, and similar items, within a Ten (10) mile–Sixteen (16) kilometre–radius of the Willowdale Mall in Burnaby, British Columbia.

PURCHASER'S CONDITIONS

7. Notwithstanding anything herein contained, the obligation of the Purchaser to complete the purchase hereunder shall be subject to the following conditions:

(a) The representations and warranties of the Vendor contained in this Agreement shall be true on and as of the date of execution.

(b) All of the covenants and Agreements of the Vendor to be performed on or before the date of execution pursuant to the terms and conditions of this Agreement shall have been duly performed.

(c) No substantial loss or destruction of or damage to any of the Assets shall have occurred on or before the date of execution.

(d) The Purchaser shall have received from her solicitor an opinion to the effect that a good and valid title to the will vest is vested in the Purchaser, free and clear of all liens, encumbrances, equities, or claims of every nature or kind whatsoever.

The foregoing conditions are for the sole and exclusive benefit of the Purchaser and may be waived in whole or in part by the Purchaser.

VENDOR'S CONDITIONS

8. The obligation of the Vendor to complete the sale under this Agreement shall be subject to the condition that on the date of execution the Purchaser pay to the Vendor all monies due to be paid to the Vendor under this Agreement.

POST-EXECUTION AGREEMENT

9. If the Purchaser shall fail to make all or any part of any payment to be made pursuant to paragraphs 5 (a), (b), and (c) herein, and such default shall continue for a period of seven (7) days, the Vendor may, by notice in writing to the Purchaser, declare the full balance owing under paragraphs 5 (a), (b), and (c) immediately due and payable.

10. If the Purchaser shall fail to pay the balance owing, as demanded in writing by the Vendor pursuant to paragraph 9 herein, and such further default shall continue for a further period of seven (7) days, then the Vendor's solicitor is hereby authorized by each party hereto to take all necessary steps to recover the promised funds.

GENERAL PROVISIONS

11. All transactions in the Business, on or after the date of execution, shall be for the account of the Purchaser.

12. The Assets shall be at the risk of the Vendor up to the date of execution of this Agreement and shall be at the risk of the Purchaser on or after the date of execution of this Agreement.

13. All representations, warranties, covenants, and Agreements of the parties contained herein shall survive the execution date of this Agreement and the payment of the Purchase Price.

14. The Vendor shall indemnify and save the Purchaser harmless from all loss, damage, cost, actions, and suits arising out of or in connection with any breach of misrepresentation, warranty, covenant, agreement, or condition contained in this Agreement.

15. If prior to the date of execution of this Agreement, there shall have been any loss or damage to any of the Assets, and the Vendor shall be

entitled to receive monies as a result of such damage or loss, the Purchase Price shall be reduced by an amount equal to that portion of the Purchase Price allocated to the asset totally destroyed, or if the asset is only damaged or partially destroyed, the reduction in the Purchase Price shall equal the amount of the insurance paid to the Vendor with respect hereto.

16. Time shall be of essence in this Agreement.

17. The purchase and sale of Assets herein contemplated shall take effect as of and no later than the opening of business on the *Twenty-ninth* Day of *July* , 19XX.

18. Any notice required or permitted to be given hereunder may be effectively given by prepaid post addressed to the Vendor at:

> 9291-295th Street, Vancouver, British Columbia V3P 2Y6

and prepaid post addressed to the Purchaser at:

> 19775-26th Avenue, Burnaby, British Columbia V7A 4P5

And if given aforesaid, any notice shall be deemed to have been given seventy-two (72) hours following such posting.

19. This Agreement shall enure to the benefit of and be binding upon the respective successors and assigns of the parties hereto, PROVIDED THAT this Agreement shall not be assigned by the Purchaser without the Vendor's consent, which consent shall not be unreasonably withheld.

20. Both the Vendor's liabilities and the Purchaser's liabilities as contained herein shall remain in force after the execution of this agreement.

21. This Agreement contains the whole Agreement between the Vendor and the Purchaser, and this Agreement supersedes all other previous Agreements. Both the Vendor and the Purchaser state that there are no representations other than those contained in this Agreement.

IN WITNESS WHEREOF the parties hereto have hereunto set their hands and seals on the day and year first above written.

SIGNED, SEALED AND DELIVERED   )

by the Vendor in the presence of:)

Mary Jane Whitehead
NAME   )

)

5751 Central Road, Richmond, B.C)

ADDRESS)   *Peter James Turnbull*

)

Housewife)

OCCUPATION)

SIGNED, SEALED AND DELIVERED)

by the Purchaser in the presence of:)

)

Russell Brian Smithers)

NAME)

19834 Oak Street, Vancouver, B.C.) *Sarah Elizabeth Scott*

ADDRESS)

)

Businessman)

OCCUPATION)

APPENDIX "A":

LISTING OF ASSETS, ARTSY AND CRAFTY GIFT SHOP

ITEM	PURCHASE PRICE
2 - Electronic Cash Registers, "Cashall" brand	4,200.00
6 - 6 foot counters with shelves underneath	2,700.00
300 feet glass wall shelving	2,500.00
Crystal chandelier	800.00
Persian display rug	750.00
Carpets, lighting fixtures	4,100.00
1 - Coldasair refrigerator	400.00
1 - Quickcook Microwave oven	250.00
1 - Coffee pot, cups and cutlery, miscellaneous plates	50.00
1 - Kitchen table with four chairs	100.00
12 - Brass display stands, various sizes	1,200.00
1 - lateral four drawer filing cabinet	400.00
1 - Selectronics Pentium Computer, hard drive, keyboard,	
1 - laser printer, 15" monitor, all software included	2,400.00
1 - Computer desk, adding machine &	
Miscellaneous stationery	750.00
Inventory as listed on Appendix "B" at cost (to be adjusted at date of takeover by Purchasers)	65,400.00
1 - Month's full time training by Vendor	.00
Goodwill	39,000.00
TOTAL PURCHASE PRICE:	$ 125,000.00

Note: This is a sample agreement and should be used only as a guideline to demonstrate which areas a legal agreement should cover. Consult a lawyer when having your legal agreement prepared, and follow all the advice given. Don't forget to take any leases to your lawyer for review and a detailed explanation. A lease is a legal contract which many people don't understand. Because you are committing to a financial obligation for a period of years, understand your obligations once a lease is signed. They can be tricky to get out of, should you need to.

Chapter 6

Where and how do you borrow money?

Never borrow money from a friend,
unless it's the only way you know to end your friendship.

CAN YOU AFFORD TO BORROW?

The lifeline of any business is money. You can't get away from this fact.
Yet many entrepreneurs have no idea where their cash will be coming from
to start their business. Let's be honest: it's too easy to use credit indiscriminately. But what happens if loans or credit cards can't be repaid? In the
majority of cases, projected repayment plans are not met in the first year or
two. Financial problems are the main reason for small businesses closing
their doors within the first 6 to 12 months. If you take a positive approach
and plan your cash requirements, there will be more room to maneuver if
the unforeseen happens.

Starting a business does take a lot money, as well as a reserve of extra cash
or working capital. You have to plan how much you need to start up and
operate for the first 12 months at least. How is this achieved? Once you
have found a potential business and know the costs involved, you need to
prepare a business plan. No bank, lending institution, or venture capitalist
will even open their doors to you unless you have a sound business plan in
place.

Without a business plan, the lenders immediately judge you as being poor
management material because you have not planned your business on paper.
They interpret this to mean that there has been no thought put into the
business, so it probably won't work. Your business plan is your foot in the

door to obtain finance, so make sure it shines. You will know how much you need to borrow, and whether you can afford to borrow, once the business plan has been prepared. It will indicate your break-even point and whether the business can afford to pay you enough wages to support your personal commitments. Many people prepare their plans realizing in the process that their idea needs some major reworking or further research. It is far better to realize this in the planning stages than after the business is up and running.

WHAT IS A BUSINESS PLAN?

A business plan is a map of your future business, detailing all aspects of the business to both you and potential lenders or investors. A comprehensive business plan should cover all the areas listed below. It can range in presentation from a few typed pages to a bound book in full colour. The length and detail of the plan will depend on how much money you need and how large your potential business will be.

1. Introduction

The introduction tells the reader all about the type of business in which you are investing, giving the history (if you are purchasing an existing business), or an outline of the new business and its products or services. The introduction should be brief but informative. If you are describing an existing business, highlight any achievements the business has made recently.

This is the time to mention the long-and short-term goals of the business. A business should be able to project into the future and give itself guidelines and objective to strive for. If you have studied your industry carefully, you should have formulated some goals at this stage. At the same time, stress the strengths of the business, along with any identifiable weaknesses, and how these weaknesses can be overcome.

2. Company structure, ownership, and profiles

Outlined here will be the corporate structure of the business with a list of shareholders or partners. A profile of each key person involved in the business should be included. These profiles should highlight the education and expertise of the people, their business qualifications, history, and references if available. Their duties and responsibilities within the business structure should be detailed. The lenders will be looking for a business that has sound managerial experience in the key areas of sales, accounting, and operations. If there is a gap in any one of these, it will count as a strike against the business. Just remember that banks need to see sound managers in place. Competent managers are a good indication that the business will be in good hands.

3. Location

A description of the business location should relate the benefits of the building, its amenities, and its accessibility to customer traffic. Include freight routes if it is a manufacturing or wholesale business. Include traffic statistics if available from your local municipality. Detail all information about parking, area zoning, even the growth rate being experienced in the area, the cost and terms of the lease, taxes, and utilities. If you can, explain the demographics of the area, including income levels.

List any foreseeable disadvantages to your location, explaining why you chose the building you did. Detail the facilities in relationship to office space, storage facilities, and operational facilities. List any renovations or alterations that need to be completed.

4. Marketing strategy

Here is a chance to blow your horn and list all your plans for projected sales: you've put enough work into your marketing plan. If you have a strategy that is different or unique, be sure to describe it. Make sure that your marketing plans are financially viable. Include any relevant statistics or marketing studies to support your proposal.

As marketing is a key component to the success of your business, prepare this section in depth. You will have much of this information on hand after you have completed your market research (see Chapter 4) and discovered how to reach your market (see Chapter 10). What both you and the lenders need to know is:

• What is your average consumer profile (as discussed in Chapter 10)?

• How do you plan to capture your share of the market?

• What is your share of the market?

- How do you plan to sell and distribute your products/services?

- How will you price your products?

- What will your in-house customer service policies be on credit, refunds, after-sales service, and warranties?

- Who are your major competitors?

- What are you offering that the competition does not offer?

- What are the competitor's marketing strengths and weaknesses?

- What are your marketing strengths and weaknesses?

5. Industry description, potential, and future trends

Prove that you have done your homework. Describe your industry in full: how it grew in the past and where it will go. Quote some successful businesses in the same area. Quote from related articles and include facts and figures where you can. With economic trends changing so rapidly, you have to show that your type of business has longevity and can withstand these changes.

6. Product lines and revenue

List the type of products or services you will be selling. Expand on this area in detail if you are entering a relatively new field. Describe why your particular product or service is unique and revenue-generating. List any potential contracts you may be working on or already have in place. Refer to any letters of intent you may have received from prospective clients and include a copy of these in the appendix. Describe any new lines or services which you intend to sell at a later date, and why. Attach any newspaper articles relating to your type of business in the appendix. Note the expected gross profit margins and whether they will change if you diversify or expand.

7. Cost of sales and overhead

You are in business to make profits, which come from the goods you are selling. The basis of your whole business plan is your profit margins. Now is the time to detail your product costings. Show what products sell for and what the cost of raw materials, freight, packaging, wages, and any other related costs will be. Explain how the manufacturing or distribution process will operate, remembering that apart from you having to know these important facts, the lender may never have heard of your type of business before. Assume that they know nothing, so that your research will indicate that you are thoroughly conversant with the financial aspect of your business.

In a separate analysis, detail your estimated overhead costs. This section should include all expenses. (See Chapter 9 under Calculating Your Break-Even Point for a list of these expenses.) If you are using key suppliers for raw materials or key components, describe who these suppliers are, your terms of credit, and how long they have been in business. Describe any quality control methods you will be putting into place, any relevant hazards or environmental risks, and how you propose to overcome these obstacles. Mention any safety procedures at the same time.

8. Other considerations

Employees: If you intend to hire employees for your new business, list the various positions along with an appropriate job description of areas of responsibility and the expected wage to be paid to each person.

Assets and equipment: Include a list of equipment on hand and equipment to be purchased, with prices. Note whether it is new or used, how old the used equipment is and its life expectancy.

Insurance policies: Detail the cost of insurance required for liability, theft and fire, workers' compensation, and any policies that will cover key management staff. If you will have employees, mention whether you will carry extended medical benefit coverage.

Licences and permits: List any licences or permits that your business will require to operate, and how much they will cost.

9. Projections and cash flow

A projection sheet is a month-by-month calculation of your estimated revenue and expenses, covering a period of at least one to two years. These projections should include all set-up costs. The bottom line will show profits or losses for each month. A projection sheet should include the notes to substantiate the projections: it is too easy to create figures out of thin air. The figures should be supported by logic and fact. Always project lower revenue figures: conservative, rather than overly optimistic figures make a better impression on lenders.

These projections should be accompanied by a cash-flow sheet for the same period. A cash-flow sheet differs from projections. Projections show what you expect to generate in sales and pay out in expenses; a cash-flow sheet will show how soon you will receive the money from the sales and when bills must be paid.

Don't attempt to prepare these figures yourself unless you have done so before. Pay an accountant or consultant to prepare them for you, along with explanatory notes. This is not an area in which beginners should tread alone.

10. Funding requirements

This section is devoted to the amount of money you need to borrow, how you expect to repay it, and over what period of time. You should have this information available from your projections and cash-flow sheets. They will have highlighted your need for funding over a particular time and should have indicated how much the business can afford to repay each month. The loan principal and interest payments should be reflected in your cash-flow and projections. How you intend to secure the loan and with what assets should be explained here. If you are looking for an investment partner, note the share of the company you intend to trade in return for the partner's money.

Break down why you need funding. Don't ask for $60,000 as a lump sum. Separate the required money into the portion required to purchase the business, the equipment or assets, and the working capital. Your credit history should be included, and you can attach references to the appendix. Most lending institutions will require a personal statement of net worth; that is, a statement listing your personal assets and their value, as well as all your liabilities.

11. Appendix

Include any documents in the appendix that will back up the information presented in your business plan and give a clear picture to the lender that you have indeed done your homework. This section should include copies of the following:

- Up-to-date financial statements from the business you are purchasing

- A list of the assets and liabilities of each principal shareholder or partner

- Copies of letters of reference and letters of intent

- Product pictures or relevant newspaper articles

- The full resumes of key employees or partners

- Incorporation or business registration papers

- Cash flow and projection sheets

- Copies of permits, licences, trademarks, or patents

- Market surveys if available

- Equipment and assets appraisals

PREPARING YOUR PLAN FOR PRESENTATION

If you have never prepared a business plan before, gather the above information and find an accountant or consultant who will prepare it for you. This plan must be professionally presented and factual. Prices for preparation can vary from $500 to $5,000. If you feel capable of preparing such a plan yourself, use all the available reference material from libraries, the Business Development Bank of Canada and the Canada Business Centre in your area. (There is an on-line business plan available through the Canada Business Service Centre.)

Most banks have business plan information available, and some have computer discs with the template and instructions laid out, ready for you to fill in the gaps. There are many publications available on this topic: they will guide you along each step. Make the plan readable by having it well typed, with enough marginal and white space to ensure easy reading. Or type it yourself and then have it professionally edited and prepared. Finally, have your accountant review the result before submitting the final copy. Don't try to cut costs in this area; otherwise it will imply that you are cheap and sloppy.

Expect the preparation of a business plan to take time, anywhere from two weeks to two months, depending on the amount of information you have to research and prepare. In preparing this information, you may find that new questions and problems arise, and sometimes these additional problems may take time to solve. People have often prepared cash-flows and projections for their business plan only to realize the business is not a viable proposition. The time you will put into number-crunching is an invaluable investment for the healthy future of your business.

EXPLAINING PROJECTION AND CASH-FLOW SHEETS

Samples #3, #4, and #5 following show a simple example of a projection sheet, a cash flow sheet, and a reconciliation of projections for three of 12 months for a small, new retail store. If you compare the projection sheet to the cash-flow sheet, you will see that sales and expenses are projected in the month which they occur. The cash-flow sheet shows when the cash is expected in and when the bills will be paid.

This store operates on a 45 percent gross profit on retail cost and employs one person apart from the owner, who as yet can't draw a salary from the business. The sales are paid at an average of 60 percent cash, 20 percent in 30 days and 20 percent in 60 days. The owner has put $5,000 operating capital in, and has borrowed $12,500 on an unsecured line of credit for working capital to be repaid over three years. The initial inventory and some start-up costs have already been paid for. These documents show that the store's break-even point, before owner's wage, is approximately $12,500 a month in sales. Note that most of the accounts payable are paid in 30 days, with some accounts paid in the month they are due. The cash-flow sheet reflects the loan principal and interest payments, whereas the sales projections only reflect the loan expense, which is the interest portion.

SAMPLE #3

SALES AND EXPENSES PROJECTION SHEET

Cathy's Crafts N'Stuff			
Twelve Months Projected Sales and Expenses			
Description	**Month 1**	**Month 2**	**Month 3**
Sales	4,500	9,000	12,150
Cost of sales:			
Purchases	2,350	4,600	6,300
Freight in	125	350	380
	2,475	4,950	6,680
Gross profit	**2,025**	**4,050**	**5,470**
Overhead expenses:			
Accounting fees	1,500	200	200
Advertising	775	750	850
Bank charges	65	65	70
Fees & licences	230	45	0
Insurance	2,400	0	0
Loan interest	250	250	250
Office supplies	923	180	90
Promotion/marketing	400	500	450
Rent	1,100	1,100	1,100
Repairs & maint.	1,780	200	100
Telephone	410	125	125
Utilities	300	300	300
Vehicle - gas	100	100	100
Vehicle - R&M	130	130	130
WCB	65	65	65
Wages	1,800	1,800	1,800
	12,228	5,810	5,630
Profit/(loss)	**10,203)**	**(1,760)**	**(160)**
Accumulated	**(10,203)**	**(11,963)**	**(12,123)**

SAMPLE #4

CASH-FLOW PROJECTION SHEET

Cathy's Crafts N'Stuff

Twelve Months Projected Sales and Expenses

Description	Month 1	Month 2	Month 3
Cash receipts in:			
Cash sales	2,700	5,400	7,290
Receivables-30 days	0	900	1,800
Receivables-60 days	0	0	900
Loan proceeds	12,500	0	0
Total cash:	**15,200**	**6,300**	**9,990**
Cash disbursed:			
Cost of sales	0	2,475	4,950
Accounting fees	0	1,500	200
Advertising	0	775	750
Bank charges	65	65	70
Fees & licences	230	45	0
Insurance	2,400	0	0
Loan interest	0	250	250
Loan principal	0	700	700
Office expenses	450	473	180
Promotion/marketing	400	500	450
Rent & taxes	1,100	1,100	1,100
Repairs & maint.	780	200	100
Telephone	0	410	125
Utilities	0	300	300
Vehicle - gas	100	100	100
Vehicle - R&M	130	130	130
WCB	0	0	195
Wages	1,800	1,800	1,800
	7,455	10,823	11,400
Surplus/deficit:	**(7,745)**	**(4,523)**	**(1,410)**
Opening balance:	5,000	12,745	8,222
+ cash receipts	15,200	6,300	9,990
- cash disbursed	7,455	10,823	11,400
Closing balance	**12,745**	**8,222**	**6,812**

SAMPLE #5

RECONCILIATION OF PROJECTIONS WITH CASH-FLOW

Cathy's Crafts N'Stuff

Reconciliation of Projections with Cash-flow

Accounts receivable balance due:	6,660
Less accounts payable balance due:	8,095
Shortfall:	1,435
Loan due:	12,500
Contributed capital:	5,000
Current debts:	18,935
Less cash on hand after three months:	(6,812)
Reconciliation with loss:	**(12,123)**
Less loan principal repaid:	1,400

WHO WILL LEND YOU MONEY?

There are various ways in which people finance businesses. Let's face it, if you have a viable business, the ability to repay, and most important of all, security for a loan–people will lend you money, but it's all at a price. The most common ways that people finance a small business are:

1. Loans from family or friends

2. Second or increased home mortgages

3. Lines of credit from the bank

4. Credit cards

5. Redeeming RRSPs

For larger amounts, the choices more often have to come from the following:

6. Banks

7. Small business loans program

8. Finance companies and brokers

9. Government-funded programs

10. Business Development Bank of Canada

11. Venture capital and loans

1. Loans from family or friends

Having family, parents or friends who can help you is a simple way to finance a business, as long as the commitments you make to these people are honoured. Terms of interest and repayment should be made clear and always put in writing. The benefit of these loans is that family members are often flexible if repayments cannot be made on time, and usually they require little interest or low rates. Loans from friends can be trickier, and are not advised unless you do not value the friendship. There is no better way to ruin a good relationship than unpaid debts. Think carefully and decide which is more important to you: your business or your friends.

Don't ask your friends to guarantee a loan for you. This can also ultimately ruin a friendship. Falling for this once, I guaranteed a loan for a long-time friend many years ago. The person started to be late with payments, until finally the bank deducted a payment from my bank account. The friend didn't hurry to repay the debt, and this incident left me feeling quite angry and used. The friendship slowly dissipated.

2. Second or increased home mortgages

In cases where banks have refused a business loan, many people resort to placing a second mortgage on their home or increasing their first mortgage. A word of warning: It is a long-term battle to regain home equity, yet it can be easily lost with a new mortgage for a business that doesn't meet expectations. You will be left with a large mortgage payment, business debts, perhaps no immediate work prospects, and the possibility of the bank foreclosing on your home. Many marriages have dissolved for this reason. Think carefully about these risks unless your new business has guaranteed immediate income and profits.

Owning your home is paramount to your financial well-being. Would you threaten the security of your home and family for a business? Business is a gamble, even when you have a good poker hand. If you do decide to remortgage your home, remember that the business portion of the interest paid is tax-deductible, just as any form of loan interest is.

Just recently a new entrepreneur who we'll call John remortgaged his home to open a retail furniture store. John didn't plan his start-up very well. He felt he knew everything there was to know about running a store because he had managed one competently for many years. He leased a cheap building, did all the renovations and advertising, and opened the doors for business. He forgot one very important start-up step—his business licence. When the by-laws officer came by, John was told he was contravening the by-laws because the property was not zoned for retail sales. He fought hard, but the municipality would not budge, and he had to close the store.

John couldn't raise enough capital to move to another location. He returned his inventory, lost a 15 percent restocking fee of $7,500, and he lost the last month's rent on the lease. He also suffered the cost of all the renovations, advertising and signage. The final loss amounted to nearly $30,000. He will be paying this off his mortgage for the next 20 years.

3. Lines of credit from the bank

For small loans under $25,000, a line of credit is a good source of reasonably-priced financing. The interest rate will fluctuate, based on current rates, and is usually two percent higher than a mortgage. The line of credit will be repaid more quickly than a mortgage, but you must be sure that you can make the monthly payment. On a loan of $25,000 you have to find at least $750 a month for your repayment. Most banks expect a minimum of three percent of the outstanding balance to be paid each month, If your loan is secured, repayment amounts can be structured to suit your budget, and in emergency situations, you can pay the interest portion only.

4. Credit cards

They should be a last resort for financing. If you are that desperate for financing, you shouldn't be starting a business. Credit cards carry exorbitant interest rates, as high as 21 percent. For short-term financing they may come in handy, but at what price? Credit cards give you a false sense of security because they allow you to make minimum monthly payments. At the same time, the interest is compounding on the interest at an alarming rate.

Many businesses use credit cards to pay for supplies and start-up costs, so if you have to use them, keep strict control over your spending habits. Use them as a 30 day, interest-free, short-term loan to the business. Treat each purchase as a cheque which you are writing from your business account, postdating that cheque for 30 days. If your cash-flow can cover that cheque, charge it. If it cannot, don't. The principle is that if you can't afford to buy it now for cash, you can't afford to charge it. It is common sense to allow yourself 30 days credit, no more. Otherwise, you will be paying over and over again for the privilege of using the bank's money. If you have trouble controlling your plastic purchases, either cut your cards up or freeze them in a block of ice—it's called freezing your liabilities.

5. Redeeming RRSPs

Think hard before cashing in your RRSPs or any form of retirement savings because there are severe tax consequences. Depending on the amount cashed and your earned income for the year, you will have to pay between 25 percent and 50 percent of the redeemed amount in tax. Redeem them only if you know for certain that you can replace them by February of the following year. An extra tax burden is the last thing you need in your first year of business.

Sometimes redeeming an RRSP will not create a tax burden. For example, when Barry was laid off from his job in March, he was earning $4,000 a month. He received a two-month severance package, less the usual tax deductions, and one month's vacation pay. In Barry's case, $7,500 of his salaried earnings for that year plus the vacation pay were taxed at 40 percent, making $11,500 subject to 40 percent income tax.

His total earnings for the year amounted to $24,000, and Barry had $7,060 deducted in income tax.

Barry started a business in June which did not pay him a salary for that year. When Christmas was approaching, he was feeling the pinch. He redeemed an RRSP for $6,000, which brought his annual earnings to $30,000. Earnings under this amount are taxed at a lower rate; in this case Barry paid $5,860 tax. He still received a refund of $1,200, even after cashing his RRSP. Before you try a similar exercise, ask your accountant what your own tax implications will be.

6. Banks

People have many misconceptions about borrowing money from a bank. Recently a friend wanted to borrow $10,000 from a bank to finance a business investment. He felt that the bank should lend him money because he had his mortgage and all his accounts at the same bank for more than ten years. With a few details jotted down on paper, he asked for a business loan. The loan was refused, and he felt despondent. The reason for the rejection? He was totally unprepared with no business plan in hand.

Banks prefer not to finance a small business loan of less than $20,000. The amount of time spent processing the paperwork and the small amount of interest earned from the transaction doesn't provide enough profit for the bank. They are likely to steer you toward a line of credit or even remortgaging your house for smaller amounts. They also don't like to lend for working capital only, preferring to invest in tangible business assets, such as new equipment, improvements, or buildings.

No matter what kind of loan you want from the bank, you have to be well prepared and present your plan professionally. Don't go to your appointment in jeans and sneakers, unshaven, and chewing gum. You need to be financially prepared with a sound business plan, a statement of personal assets and liabilities, and proof of income earned in the last taxation year. On speaking to business loans managers, the general consensus is that the average borrower comes in unprepared. Few have business plans, or have calculated whether they have the ability to repay the loan. When you call for an appointment, ask what information will be needed, and prepare it in a professional manner.

7. Small business loans program

Your business may be eligible for a small business loan offered through the Small Business Loans Act to help new and existing businesses obtain financing from chartered banks. The funds can be used only to improve or purchase fixed assets, such as equipment or buildings. You cannot borrow to finance inventory, goodwill, franchise fees or shares: they are either intangible or expendable items. Both sole proprietorships and incorporated businesses are eligible for the program.

Under this program, you can borrow up to $250,000, which must be repaid with a maximum term of 10 years. The interest rate cannot exceed the prime lending rate by more than three percent. An administration fee of two percent of the total loan will be charged. Your local chartered bank can give you further information.

8. Finance companies and brokers

Alternative finance companies are often willing to lend money with fewer security requirements than a bank demands, but you may have to pay exorbitant interest rates. Some people have obtained second mortgages from finance companies, ultimately paying just interest without appearing to reduce the principal amount. Treat these companies as you would treat credit card financing—proceed with extreme caution and, preferably, avoid this type of financing altogether for your business.

Terry and Susan were in dire straights with their business. Terry spent money all too freely, and Susan lay awake at nights, worrying about their mounting personal and business bills. Their home was mortgaged to the hilt; the bank would not lend them more. Terry finally persuaded Susan that if they took out a private second mortgage for $50,000, the bills could be paid off. The monthly payments would be just over $400, and then Susan could sleep again.

In a moment of weakness, Susan agreed. They still had some equity in their home, but not enough for bank requirements. A private broker organized the loan, and they signed for a two-year term, paying interest only. They paid over $9,000 in interest without reducing the principal. Terry's spending habits did not change, and at the end of two years, they still owed $50,000 and had to sign for another two-year term. If you are this desperate to finance a business—think again.

9. Government-funded programs

Numerous government-funded programs are available to businesses, covering areas such as research and development, export, manufacturing, processing, environmental, agriculture, training, and management. Some are provincial and others federal. The types of loans and their criteria are always changing, so contact your local Canada Business Service Centre for more information. They will send you a list of programs for a small fee.

10. Business Development Bank of Canada

The Business Development Bank of Canada (BDBC) is a valuable resource for new and serious entrepreneurs. They have a positive attitude toward small business, offering a variety of loans to suit various needs. Some of these include in the following:

a) Term loan

If you have a profitable venture which needs financing, the BDBC can offer help in the areas of working capital; purchase of land, buildings, or equipment; and refinancing and upgrading of equipment or commercial premises. These loans are usually secured by fixed assets.

b) Working Capital For Growth loan

Small-to medium-size businesses may qualify for this loan, designed to add to financing from conventional lenders. If you have identified new areas or opportunities for growth with your business and require working capital, this loan may interest you. You must be able to provide proof of sound management, have a complete business plan prepared, prove past performance in the business, and show strong potential for profits in the future.

c) Micro Business Program

With a combination of mentoring, counselling and financing, this loan is available for start up to $25,000 and for existing businesses up to $50,000. It can be used for assets, working capital, start-up costs, research, and franchise purchases. A sound business plan is essential.

11. Venture capital and loans

Venture capital is money obtained through investors who, in return for their investment in your company, usually expect a share of your business. This share is commonly more than 50 percent, effectively giving the investors control over the financial decisions and a say in running the business. Venture capital can be hard to find, so expect to spend several months looking for this type of financing, and don't forget to prepare your business plan first. Be aware of what you are giving up in return for someone else's money. Don't bother approaching professional venture capitalists for small loans; usually they invest larger amounts ranging from $100,000 to $500,000 and more.

You could try approaching friends and associates wanting to invest small amounts of money, offering them a small share of your business in return. You would have to incorporate your business because of the share structure involved. There are probably more people willing to invest between $5,000 and $25,000 in a potentially viable proposition than you realize.

The Business Development Bank of Canada has a venture capital and venture loan program for existing companies and may be able to help you once the business is established and has shown potential for growth. Contact them for details.

HOW MUCH SHOULD YOU BORROW?

Your projections and cash-flow sheets (which you have so industriously prepared), will indicate how much money is needed to get the business rolling. Remember, you're not just taking into consideration the purchase of the business, but also the various set-up costs and some working capital. (Business start-up costs are detailed Chapter 9.)

It is risky business starting out entirely on borrowed capital. Ideally, you should be able to invest at least 25 percent to 30 percent of your own money. No one can tell you how much to borrow; however, when a loans officer is reviewing your business plan, he or she expects to see you contributing a healthy part of the capital. This proves you have made a serious commitment to the business and have faith in your ability to make it succeed. If your own capital contribution is not part of a proposal, a bank will ask you why—it will not choose to be the sole financier of any business. Only borrow what you can afford to repay. You must be sure that loan payments can be maintained, even if the business does not progress as fast as you had planned.

Chapter 7

Should you incorporate your business?

You're going to be married to your business,
so don't forget to sign the licence.

WHAT IS A PROPRIETORSHIP OR PARTNERSHIP?

A proprietorship is a business owned by one person, commonly referred to as a sole proprietor. A partnership is a business owned by two or more people. Neither type of business has been incorporated. Anyone can set themselves up as a business, register their name, and be called a proprietorship. This means that you own your business and are considered self-employed. You are not an employee of the company, as you are with an incorporated business.

For a small business which consists of just the owner, perhaps a spouse, and one or two employees, a proprietorship is usually the simplest way to start. There are no legal costs involved, just the cost of a business licence and name registration. If you are considering a partnership, it is prudent to seek legal advice and have a partnership agreement prepared.

As a sole proprietor or a partner, you are responsible for all the business debts; they are considered personal debts. You will be taxed on the profits of the business, before any wages are drawn by the proprietor. (You cannot actually draw a wage if your business is not incorporated—the money you take out of the business is called a "draw against equity.")

WHAT ARE THE ADVANTAGES OF A PARTNERSHIP?

If you find a partner who meets the criteria as set out below, a partnership can have many advantages. A combination of talents and experience will enhance your business—two heads are usually better than one. Two common problems sole proprietors experience are isolation, and no one to bounce ideas off. If you are impulsive and creative, for example, perhaps seek a partner who is level-headed and practical. This will help to keep your feet on the ground and you have the benefit of receiving input from someone who knows what you are talking about.

A partner will bring with them networking contacts, experience, information, and ideas. If you are technically minded and don't like selling, find a partner who is out-going and sales-oriented. A partner gives you the luxury of having someone to lean on and share the workload. This is beneficial when errands have to be done or you have to leave the business to visit clients. The business is not left unattended. If emergency situations arise, someone who knows the business is there to take over.

Usually, partnerships involve a financial contribution, so you are not left shouldering the full responsibility of raising start-up and working capital. In most cases, a partnership should demand an equal cash contribution and sharing of profits and responsibilities. The combined assets and incomes of two people are more desirable to banks if you are seeking loans or financing. Just be sure to have all the financial details of your partnership documented in your partnership agreement, along with defined job descriptions.

WHAT ARE THE DISADVANTAGES OF A PARTNERSHIP?

Partnerships can be a challenging way to start a business. You will spend more time with your partner than with your spouse. Think about it— you will be working together for up to 12 hours a day, five to six days a week–that's 60 hours a week for 50 weeks of the year. It almost sounds like a life sentence. You should choose your partner as selectively as you would choose your spouse. The average couple does not spend any-where near that amount of time together (excluding sleeping), and they still tend to agree to disagree regularly. Think about it.

Partnerships should be thoroughly discussed and planned before they are put into action. Many do not work because clearly documented job descriptions and divisions of responsibility are not prepared. The major cause of many marriage breakdowns is financial problems; the same is true of business partnerships. Constant arguing between partners invariably leads to one threatening to walk out (just like a bad marriage scene). If a satisfactory resolution can't be reached, the conflict usually terminates what could have been a successful business venture. A proper partnership agreement should be prepared by a lawyer to cover all contingencies.

In all the years spent in business accounting and consulting, I have not yet seen one long-term partnership succeed. One of the main problems with partnerships is that desperate entrepreneurs tend to select partners too hastily; usually they fall in love with the partner's bank account. The thought of that financial injection prevents clear and long-term thinking, such as considering the business acumen or compatibility of the partner.

When you are looking for a long-term working partner, seek out a person with the following qualities:

1. Business experience

Your partner should be able to contribute to the business to complement your expertise. There's little use having two sales people. Your partner should have skills in areas you do not.

2. Financial support

Your partner should contribute an equal capital share to the business. If the financial commitment is not in place, a partner will not be sufficiently motivated to make the business succeed. Deals such as "You put in the money, I'll put in the time" don't usually work. They will lead to arguments over who isn't doing enough, or not paying enough, in the other person's eyes. You've probably had similar arguments with your spouse.

3. Compatibility

No matter how well suited your potential partner appears to be, if you are not emotionally compatible, your partnership will face problems. You have to communicate honestly and openly, expressing your feelings when you don't agree. You should try to find someone who is honest and straightforward. Remember, don't "marry" a partner for money or brains alone.

WHAT IS AN INCORPORATED BUSINESS?

When you incorporate, your business becomes its own separate legal entity. The business consists of shareholders who purchase shares in the business and who are responsible for its operation. You can incorporate a one-owner business and own all the shares of that company. The company has a president, and if more than one person is involved, a secretary-treasurer and directors. Stricter control can be maintained with a board of directors, who help make decisions. Outrageous suggestions by one person can be blocked if company policy stipulates that any significant changes must be approved by the board.

The company owns all the assets and liabilities, and unless personal guarantees are signed, it is responsible for any debts incurred. This is called "limited liability" because it limits the shareholders from personal liability. An incorporated company is subject to stricter reporting procedures in both legal and accounting matters. Annual general meetings must be held, annual reports filed, full financial statements prepared at the fiscal year-end, and corporate taxes filed. Accounting costs are significantly higher than with a sole proprietorship.

Incorporating a business allows for better tax planning and use of profits, but this can happen only if the accounting records are kept up to date and the company's progress and tax situation is monitored closely. If you think incorporation is right for your business, consult your accountant. He or she will be able to review the potential financial and tax benefits. Use the checklist at the end of this chapter to help guide you.

WHAT ARE THE ADVANTAGES OF INCORPORATION?

1. Incorporation shows you are taking your business seriously

An incorporated business demonstrates to banks, lending institutions, suppliers, and investors that you are taking your new business seriously. It is difficult for a sole proprietor to take financial statements to a bank and obtain a loan without personal security. Lenders reviewing an incorporated business take into account the shareholders' loans, confirming that the shareholders have enough faith in the business to invest their own money. Investors prefer incorporated businesses; they are a more secure investment than proprietorships.

2. Limited liability

The debts of an incorporated company are usually not a shareholder's responsibility, should bankruptcy occur. Many people incorporate for this one reason. If the business fails, they shouldn't end up losing their home and other assets, just those of the business. People have been known to walk away from one incorporated business and start another one the next day. Some have done this repeatedly.

However, if loans are personally secured, the shareholders are still responsible for repayment. If telephone lines have been personally guaranteed, the shareholders are responsible for the debt. Any company debts that carry personal guarantees are the responsibility of the person who has signed for them. There are also certain debts that the shareholders are always responsible for, including provincial and federal taxes such as employee deductions, GST/HST and PST. One couple recently had to declare personal bankruptcy because of the huge amount of outstanding federal taxes due after the foreclosure of their incorporated business.

3. Tax planning, CPP and EI benefits

In an incorporated company the shareholders are employees of the company and may draw a regular salary during the year, with the company making Canada Pension Plan and tax deduction monthly installments. If you own less than 40 percent of the shares of the business, you may also deduct Employment Insurance (EI) payments. (Before making EI deductions, you should contact the employment office near you and ask for a ruling; each situation is different.)

The wages drawn by a shareholder become a company expense, and at year-end, a T4 is prepared. Income taxes have been paid by the company during the year, so there shouldn't be a great tax bite at year-end. If the company is in a profitable situation, your accountant may consider paying out dividends, bonuses, or extra salaries to reduce the profits. The net profits of the corporation are taxed at a lesser rate than are personal taxes.

4. Corporate tax benefits

There are a variety of corporate tax benefits available to a small business, and it would certainly pay to consult your accountant about these. There is a small business corporate tax rate available, along with many extra expense deductions, as well as certain tax credits for manufacturing, research and development, donations and political contributions, to name a few.

5. Personal tax benefits

If you purchase shares in a Canadian-controlled corporation, and you borrow money for the investment, the interest on your shareholder's loan can be used as a personal investment tax deduction. So not only does your incorporated business keep your personal taxes straight if you draw a regular wage, you could be eligible for a tax refund as well.

WHAT ARE THE DISADVANTAGES OF INCORPORATION?

1. Higher accounting costs, more paperwork

There's no doubt about it, an incorporated business does generate more paperwork. First, the incorporation papers have to be prepared. If you are a small company, you can prepare your own by purchasing a do-it-yourself incorporation guide and kit from your local bookstore or stationers. The cost to incorporate is approximately $300, depending on the jurisdiction you operate in.

Once registered, the share certificates and articles of incorporation must be completed. Policies and decisions should be recorded in the company minute book, and an annual general meeting should be held. An annual report must be filed, with a fee of approximately $35, to list any changes in directors or shareholders, or their addresses.

Scrupulous accounting records should be kept as the books could be reviewed or audited at any time. There must be a piece of paper for everything and an accounting entry to back up each transaction. Because proper financial statements must be prepared, accounting costs are more expensive than with a proprietorship. Even if the monthly accounting is recorded accurately, financial statements for a small business will cost upwards of $700, including filing the corporate taxes.

2. Payroll records are required

As an employee of the company, you will have to register with Revenue Canada for payroll remittances, draw a regular salary, keep full payroll records and submit monthly tax deductions on time. At year end, T4 slips and perhaps T4As will have to be prepared. You must make your remittances to Revenue Canada on time each month as heavy penalties and interest are charged on late filing. Because you are collecting taxes and pension monies in trust for the government, their attitude is not too friendly if payments are late. They do have the power to garnishee bank accounts to recover these funds if they are not paid in time.

WHAT IS THE DIFFERENCE BETWEEN PROPRIETORSHIPS AND INCORPORATIONS?

1. Shareholder's loan and equity

When a proprietor puts money into a business, it is called capital. When money is withdrawn by the proprietor, it reduces his or her capital. When a shareholder puts money into a business, it is called a shareholder's loan and can be repaid as the company agrees. It is considered a liability, not equity or capital, and shows this way on the financial statements.

2. Profits, losses and net earnings

When a proprietorship makes a profit or loss, it is added or subtracted from the proprietor's capital. The profit is called "net earnings" or "taxable income." When an incorporated business makes a profit or loss, it is called "retained earnings." This figure either increases or decreases each year, depending on profits or losses. A loss is called a deficit for that period.

3. Wage structure

When a proprietor takes money out of the business, it is not treated as an expense, as mentioned earlier. Withdrawals reduce the equity or capital in the business. The proprietor is still taxed on the net income of the business, regardless of how much was taken out during the year. With an incorporation, the owner's salary is considered a wage and used as a tax deduction for the business. The business then pays corporate taxes on the net profit after all wages have been calculated.

4. Legal fees for incorporation

The cost of preparing the incorporation is shown as an asset on the balance sheet, not as a deduction for legal expenses. Any legal fees incurred by a proprietor in the start-up of a business are usually considered an expense and used as a tax deduction.

5. Share issue

When a business is incorporated, a share structure is decided upon by the shareholders with the help of their accountant. A variety of share structures are available, depending on the complexity of the business and whether the long-term goals are to go public on the stock exchange. Basically, a certain number of shares are authorized for the business, and a certain number are issued to the shareholders. The number of shares issued to each shareholder will give them a proportionate percentage of the company ownership.

Two types of shares are issued, those without par value and those with par value. There are also different classes of these shares, as well as voting, non-voting, and preferred shares. Your lawyer will suggest the best form of incorporation for your business. Most small businesses use a simple share issue structure, which appears on your financial statements in the following format:

Share capital:

Authorized:	10,000 Class A common shares with no par value
	10,000 Class B common shares with no par value
Issued:	100 Class A shares at $1 each
	100 Class B shares at $1 each

COMPARING AN INCORPORATED FINANCIAL STATEMENT TO A PROPRIETORSHIP

Sample #6 following shows the same business as an incorporated business and as a sole proprietorship. Changes in format have been shown in italics. All the changes have been discussed in this chapter. You will notice quite a different format in the equity section.

SAMPLE #6
FINANCIAL STATEMENT: COMPARISON OF
INCORPORATED BUSINESS TO PROPRIETORSHIP

JASON'S GARDEN SERVICE (LTD.)
BALANCE SHEET
FROM JANUARY 1, 19XX - JUNE 30, 19XX
(Unaudited)

ASSETS

	Incorporated	Proprietorship
Current assets:		
Cash at bank	11,019	11,019
Accounts receivable	3,551	3,551
Inventories	6,245	6,245
Prepayments & Deposits	1,080	1,080
	21,895	21,895
Fixed assets:		
Automotive - trucks	65,000	65,000
Office equipment	550	550
Office furniture	850	850
	66,400	66,400
Other assets:		
Incorporation fees	*700*	*0*
TOTAL ASSETS:	**$ 88,995**	**$ 88,295**

LIABILITIES

	Incorporated	Proprietorship
Current liabilities:		
Accounts payable	10,520	10,520
PST payable	315	315
GST/HST payable	(5,342)	(5,289)
Current portion bank loan	12,000	12,000
	17,493	17,546
Long term liabilities:		
Bank loan	32,000	32,000
Loan, R. Davies	28,000	28,000
Shareholder's loan	*22,653*	*0*
	82,653	60,000
Total liabilities:	**100,146**	**77,546**

EQUITY		
Share capital:		
Authorized:		
10,000 Class A common voting		
shares with no par value		
Issued:		
100 Class A shares @ $ 1	*100*	0
Contributed capital for period:	0	*22,000*
Draws for period	0	*1,291*
Profit/loss for period:	0	*(9,960)*
Retained earnings (deficit)	*(11,251)*	0
	(11,251)	10,749
TOTAL LIABILITIES &		
EQUITY:	**$ 88,995**	**$ 88,295**

JASON'S GARDEN SERVICE (LTD.)
STATEMENT OF INCOME AND EXPENDITURE
JANUARY 1, 19XX - JUNE 30, 19XX
(Unaudited)

	Incorporated	Proprietorship
Revenue:		
By product sales & delivery	32,705	32,705
Cost of sales:		
Opening inventory	0	0
Material purchases	19,150	19,150
Wages, driver	7,200	7,200
	26,650	26,650
Less closing inventory	(6,245)	(6,245)
	20,405	20,405
Gross profit: (37.6%)	**12,300**	**12,300**
Overhead expenditure:		
Accounting fees	500	500
Advertising	2,200	2,200
Bank charges	120	120
Discounts	790	790
Fees, licences	100	100
Insurance, shop	480	480
Loan interest	2,390	2,390
Management salaries	*1,291*	0
Office stationery	1,270	1,270
Office wages	2,800	2,800
Rent	2,100	2,100
Telephone	1,280	1,280
Truck fuel	2,960	2,960
Truck R&M	1,820	1,820
Truck insurance	3,000	3,000
WCB	450	450
	23,551	22,260
Profit/loss for period:	*$ (11,251)*	*$ (9,960)*

This example demonstrates the differences between an incorporated company and a proprietorship. The difference in the GST/HST account is the GST charged on the legal fees for incorporation. With this loss situation, Jason's equity as a proprietorship has been reduced from $22,000 to $10,749. If Jason has any other form of income for the year, he can use this loss on his personal tax return to offset that income, or carry the loss forward or back to other years. The incorporated company will continue to show this loss on the statements until future profits exceed the amount of the loss, or the loss may be carried back to other years when corporate taxes were payable.

SHOULD YOU INCORPORATE YOUR BUSINESS?

The questions in Exercise #5 will help you determine whether incorporation is right for your business. If you answer yes to more than three of these questions, consider incorporation as a suitable and safer method of structuring your new business. Then make an appointment to see your accountant.

EXERCISE #5

SHOULD I INCORPORATE MY BUSINESS?

	Yes	No
I have future plans to expand and grow.	☐	☐
I will need to borrow funds for this expansion.	☐	☐
I will carry a large inventory, over $10,000.	☐	☐
I will carry accounts receivables.	☐	☐
I will carry accounts payables.	☐	☐
I will work with a partner.	☐	☐
My business is retail, wholesale or a distributorship.	☐	☐
I need my personal finances to be organized.	☐	☐
I will be hiring employees.	☐	☐
I plan to build the business and sell in a few years.	☐	☐

Chapter 8

What are you required to do by law...
and how to comply

Dot your "I"s and cross all your "T"s,
Fill out all the forms in triplicate please.

Now you have got to this stage, there is a right and a wrong way to proceed. If you step in the wrong direction now, you will be frustrated by time delays and, possibly, some major setbacks. To make things a little easier, here is the sequence of moves you should make, accompanied by some helpful hints. (A complete list of provincial telephone numbers is contained in Appendix 1.)

MUNICIPAL APPROVAL

Before you start your business, whether it be home-based, retail, or commercial, check with your local municipality for by-law and zoning requirements. There are many municipal restrictions that apply to environmental concerns, zoning regulations, and home-based businesses. Be sure your business conforms with the many regulations before making any final decisions.

Your municipality has the right to deny you a licence if its by-laws and regulations aren't met. Just recently, a new businessman opened a small store on his property, selling retail agricultural products. He didn't apply for a business licence, thinking that selling agricultural products in an agricultural area wouldn't cause any problems. Someone reported him to the municipality—perhaps an envious rival or a neighbour. Despite his best efforts to save the business, the owner did not succeed. He was selling retail products from his home and had contravened the local home-business by-laws. He had put a great deal of money into starting the store, but he was forced to close it down. Don't make a similar costly mistake.

1. Municipal licensing and inspections

Your business may have to be inspected by some or all of the following departments before a licence is issued, so check which apply to you. Your business is not ready to roll until all the individual licensing agency requirements are met. These agencies may include:

1. Fire department

2. Health department

3. Local pollution control ministry

4. Provincial motor carrier licencing

5. Property use and building inspector

6. Provincial waste management

7. Provincial motor dealer licencing

2. Home-based businesses

With the increasing numbers of home-based businesses, many municipalities are reviewing their by-laws to accommodate this growing trend. This will take time, as each municipality has its own by-laws and regulations, which are often quite different from neighbouring municipalities. As a guideline, here are some of the more common restrictions imposed by many local governments.

1. The business should be contained to the residence, and no structural alterations or additions to the residence can be made for business purposes.

2. The business should not use more than 20 percent of the residential space.

3. There should be no evidence of the business being operated from the residence, such as exterior storage or exterior operation of the business, and no sign identifying the business. (In other words, if you were to drive past the house, you shouldn't notice that a business is being operated.)

4. The home-based business is restricted to office use only. No retail sales can be made from the premises, and clients may not visit the home to purchase goods.

5. The business can be conducted by a resident or members of the family only. No one else can be employed by the business. (Note: some municipalities do allow other employees.)

6. Generating noise, electrical interference, reoccurring ground vibrations, noxious emissions, odours, or vapours, are prohibited.

7. No commercial vehicles can be operated by the home business.

8. The business may not generate special traffic beyond normal traffic volume.

Currently referred to as "accessory home occupations," the home-based businesses of today and the future are incubators for growing a business. Let's hope that progressive local governments will realize the need for updating their by-laws and encourage small businesses to start and succeed from home. Many people contravene the by-laws, thus hiding their business from the community. In these cases, there is less chance to market and expose their business, so they don't have the opportunity to succeed. Until local by-laws are reviewed and updated, don't take any chances; familiarize yourself with all the regulations and comply with them.

NAME REGISTRATION

Once you are sure your business conforms with municipal regulations, register your business name. If you are unincorporated, name registration is not necessary, but may be a good idea. If you are incorporated, name registration is required by law. If you choose a name with the words "and Associates" or "and Company," or if you are involved in a partnership, you must register your business name.

1. What are the advantages of name registration?

Registering your company name makes it easier for the public to find and remember you. Your proprietorship may grow so quickly that you need to incorporate. You could build a good, reputable business, but decide not to register your name. Another business, incorporated or not, may register your company name and have it approved. There is little you can do to prevent that. Remember: It pays to register early to protect the effort you have put into building your business and its reputation.

The process of name approval has been designed to prevent other businesses from registering a similar name. Sometimes, people will try to register a business name similar to that of another successful business, creating intentional confusion. The name-approval process ensures your name will remain distinct and give your business the protection it deserves.

2. How do you register your business name?

To register your name, choose three names in order of preference and submit them for name approval to the provincial registry. The fee ranges from $30 and up, and varies from province to province. Name approval can take from a few days to a few weeks, once again depending on what province you live in and whether you register in person, by mail, or by e-mail. Then you submit a name registration form, enclosing the prescribed fee. Registration should take only a few days.

INCORPORATION

Once your name is approved, you can proceed with incorporation. You can hire a lawyer to do the work or incorporate it yourself as discussed earlier. Do-it-yourself incorporation costs vary from province to province. In British Columbia, the fee at this writing is $300, plus $35 for the kit and guide. An incorporation prepared by a lawyer will cost $500 or more, depending on the corporate and share structure.

Incorporation papers will generally be approved in ten days to two weeks. Until then, you cannot order stationery, have licences approved, or open bank accounts, because you need the incorporation papers. Banks will not open a business account for an incorporated company until a copy of the incorporation certificate is provided. Revenue Canada also requires copies of the certificate to approve payroll, GST/HST, and provincial tax requests: allow three to four weeks for the processing of your incorporation. If you are not incorporating your business, you can pass go.

BUSINESS LICENCES

When your company name has been approved and the business is incorporated, you can apply for a business licence at your municipality and meet any other licensing requirements. Fees vary according to the type of your intended business and where you live. Usually, municipalities grant a licence straight away and will send you a copy of the licence in the mail.

BANK ACCOUNTS

Next you can open your business accounts, which will take a few days. Allow two weeks if you want to give your clients Visa or MasterCard facilities. It is better to pay for your start-up costs and all expenses by cheque; it makes for easier bookkeeping. When you pay by cash the receipts can get mislaid or lost. A cheque is a written record of each transaction. Order a two-or three-ringed cheque binder and make sure the cheque stubs are large enough to record daily deposits, expense details, computer codes, and the GST/HST transactions.

PROVINCIAL TAXES

Most provinces require that a provincial sales tax be collected on any goods purchased or imported for use or consumption. The tax is always collected by the retail outlet or the final vendor. Additional taxes are levied against items such as hotel rooms, tobacco, and motor fuels.

You may be exempt from collecting the provincial sales tax in certain circumstances; check with the provincial sales tax office listed in Appendix 1. If you are the final vendor, it will be up to you to collect this tax on all applicable sales each month, keeping proper records, and submitting the tax monthly by the date required in each province. In some provinces, you are allowed to deduct a commission for collecting this tax. It is important to have a good monthly accounting system, and be careful to submit these taxes on time—the penalties for late filing can be hefty.

Certain groups are exempt from having to pay provincial taxes; and they must quote an exemption number. Write these on your sales invoice for audit purposes.

GOODS AND SERVICES TAX/HARMONIZED SALES TAX (GST/HST)

The GST/HST is commonly disliked and confuses most people, particularly those unsure whether their gross revenue for the first year will exceed $30,000. When your business bills sales of more than $30,000 a year, you must register for the GST/HST. However, even if your first year's sales are lower than $30,000, there are benefits to registering.

In your first year of business, you incur expensive start-up costs which include GST/HST. If you register for the GST/HST, you are eligible to claim back all the tax you have paid out. For instance: you may have purchased a business or franchise and paid GST on the purchase price. For a business costing $35,000 you will pay a GST of $2,450. You will pay GST on expenses such as equipment, legal and accounting fees, telephone systems, computers, stationery, and more. If you elect to file every fiscal quarter, which is strongly advised, you may be eligible for a refund after the first three months, particularly if sales have been slow and expenses high.

1. What is the harmonized sales tax (HST)?

As of April 1, 1997, Nova Scotia, New Brunswick, and Newfoundland combined their provincial sales tax with the GST. This new value-added tax is called the harmonized sales tax. A single rate of 15 percent applies to goods previously subject to the GST. This tax consists of the seven percent GST and eight percent provincial tax. Because this is a complicated area for many business people, your best bet is to contact your local GST office for an information package and a clear explanation of just how this tax could affect your potential business.

2. How do you know when to register for GST?

Many people ask: "When do I pay GST? How do I know when I am going to reach $30,000?" The answer is quite simple. When you reach $30,000 in sales, call your nearest GST office and ask to be registered. You should start charging GST the following month. You many have the option of filing annually if you are a small business. If you earn under $30,000 a year, the GST becomes an integral part of your expenses, and does not have to be separated in accounting records.

You have to be on top of your accounting and keep good records. Tracking GST definitely increases bookkeeping time and costs. A cheque or expense which used to be entered in the books twice, now has to be broken down and entered three times. The same applies for recording all GST collected—it's a lot of extra work. Unfortunately, you don't get paid to collect government taxes, so you have to absorb additional bookkeeping costs. (See Appendix 2 for how to fill out the form.)

The average business owner has trouble paying GST installments every three months. All too often the collected tax seems to become part of the daily cash flow and is quickly spent. Businesses have been closed down for not paying their taxes. To avoid this concern, take five percent of the bank deposits (to cover GST collected and GST paid), and transfer it to a GST savings account. If you are collecting HST, add in the applicable percentage. The money will be there when you need it.

3. Is everything GST/HST taxable?

No. There are some "zero-rated goods" on which GST/HST is not charged. These include farm produce, basic groceries, most livestock, fish and seafood for human consumption, medical services, prescriptions, and exported goods. Some services are exempt from GST, and if this applies to your business, you cannot claim the tax paid nor charge it. These services include day care, most financial services, and long-term house rents. In certain circumstances, some of the following services can be exempt: legal aid, educational services, health and dental services, non-profit and charitable activities, government and certain public services. Call your local Revenue Canada office and make sure that you understand how these taxes will affect your business. When you register, an information booklet will be sent to you with your registration number.

BUSINESS NUMBERS, PAYROLL, AND REVENUE CANADA

Whenever you register with the government for GST, corporate or payroll taxes, Revenue Canada issues you a business identification number which identifies your tax accounts.

If you have employees, you must register with Revenue Canada for employee deductions. Some businesses try to avoid the complications of hiring employees by subcontracting or use casual labour instead of putting workers on a regular payroll. But you must be careful: as a rule of thumb, if a person works for you more than 40 percent of their working hours, they are considered a part-time or full-time employee and become eligible for employee benefits. These include Canada Pension Plan, employment insurance, tax deductions, statutory holidays, and vacation pay. Your employee is then protected by the provincial, and sometimes federal labour laws. As an employer, you must abide by their rules.

1. What are your responsibilities as an employer?

After you register with Revenue Canada you will be sent a start-up kit, which will include TD1 forms for the employees to fill out, information booklets, and taxation schedules. It is your responsibility to deduct the correct amount of CPP, employment insurance, and tax. You must maintain proper payroll records. Easy-to-follow payroll books are available at stationery stores.

Employees will need an individual payroll page where you enter their names, addresses, social insurance numbers, starting dates, and wages. For each pay period you must record the hours worked each day, how much was paid, and all deductions. At month-end, the total CPP, employment insurance, and tax deducted for the month is totalled, and the employer's portion is calculated. The whole amount must be submitted to Revenue Canada by the 15th of the following month.

This is how to calculate the remittance to Revenue Canada:

Employee's CPP deduction	20.00
Employer's CPP contribution	20.00
Employee's EI deduction	30.00

Employer's EI deduction (x 1.4)	42.00
Employee's tax deduction	<u>90.00</u>
Total remittance:	**$ <u>202.00</u>**

2. How much does an employee really cost?

If you hire an employee at $15 an hour, the cost is significantly more than the hourly wage. You should be aware of the extra costs involved when you are preparing projections or costings, or before hiring. As an example, let's take an employee earning $15 an hour over a period of one month.

40 hours a week x 4.33 weeks per month:	173.20 hours
173.2 hours x $15	$ 2,598.00
4 percent vacation pay	103.92
3.2 per cent Canada Pension Plan	87.64
2.7 per cent Employment Insurance x 1.4	98.19
1 statutory holiday	120.00
WCB (average rate of $3.50/$100)	<u>90.93</u>
Total monthly employee cost:	**$ <u>3,098.68</u>**

Your $15 an hour employee is actually costing $17.89 an hour to hire, or an additional $500.54 per month, or 19.26 percent of $2,598.00. (The CPP and EI rates quoted here are 1998 rates—they will undoubtedly change each year.)

3. What happens at year end?

After the final pay period for the year, each employee's wage sheet is totalled and cross-balanced for the year and a T4 is prepared. A T4 summary is filled out for the year, reporting all deductions. These are compared to the amount remitted during the year. If you have not remitted enough deductions, you must include the balance with the summary.

Usually a penalty is imposed for late remittances. A proper payroll reconciliation system should be used to monitor cumulative wages during the year. (See Appendix 2 for information on filling out these forms.)

4. What happens when an employee leaves?

When an employee leaves or is terminated, a record of employment form has to be completed within five working days. The first two copies are given to the employee, one is sent to Revenue Canada, and you keep one for your records. Revenue Canada will send you a booklet that answers all your questions on how to fill out these forms. They are available at your local Employment Canada office.

WORKERS' COMPENSATION BOARD

Any business that hires employees or subcontractors must register for workers' compensation. Some people think they don't need to register because they just operate an office or have no employees on payroll. For example, even a doctor's office has to pay compensation, although the rate is not very high.

Workers' compensation is based on industry rates determined by the risk factor involved in each industry and the number of claims filed during each year. This rate is adjusted annually, according to the performance of that industry. Registered employers are informed of the new rate before year-end.

People are often confused about the rate structure. A crane operator may be paying $6.50 for every $100 of wages paid, understandable because of the high-risk factor. A bookkeeper working in the office of the same company is covered under the same industry standard, and the employer will also have to pay the same amount. There is no division between office, sales, or operations. Be sure to include these cost factors into your cash flow because in some industries workers' compensation can be expensive.

After you have telephoned and registered, you will receive an information package and notice of your registration. You must file a return and remittance every three months. At the end of the year, an annual summary is mailed to you, which must be completed, based on final year-end payroll records and summaries of subcontract and casual wages. If you are incorporated, the shareholders' salaries are included in the payment.

If you are a proprietorship and have no employees, it is not necessary to register. However, if you employ contractors, be sure they carry their own WCB coverage. Otherwise you are responsible for their coverage. In some provinces, you can register yourself for an optional personal coverage based on your net earnings. (See Appendix 2 for more information.)

OTHER LICENCING AGENCIES

You may have to register with other agencies, depending on your type of business. The ones listed below are the most common, but each business will have to research its particular licensing requirements.

1. Ministry for the Environment

2. Ministry of Agriculture, Fisheries and Food

3. Ministry of the Attorney General

4. Ministry of Transport and Highways

5. Ministry of Health

Other areas in which you may need to contact a licensing agency are:

1. Weights and measures

2. Packaging and labelling

3. Hazardous products

4. Precious metals

5. Textiles

6. Foods

7. Patents, copyright, industrial designs, and trademarks

IS BUSINESS AS SIMPLE AS ABC AND 123?

After all that heavy, serious, and mind-boggling information, it's time to ease up the pressure and welcome you to the wonderful world of business. It should be a simple matter to earn a living in business—you sell a product or service, collect the money and make a profit, right?

Wrong. Don't think you will get away with it that easily. Big Brother is watching you and working hard to create as many headaches for you as possible.

Just look at that dense forest of acronyms: When you sell a product, you must collect the PST and remit it to the MOF, TIS, DOF, or PTC, depending which province you reside in. You must collect the GST/ HST (which replaced the FST) and record your ITCs, paying Revenue Canada the balance on a Form GST34 (E).You pay your staff twice a month, deducting CPP, EI, and tax, which is remitted monthly to Revenue Canada on a PD7A(E). At year-end, you must prepare T4s and T4As for employees, so they can complete their T1 Specials or T1 Generals, including Schedules 1 through to 100. When employees leave your business, don't forget to fill out their ROE, so they can take it to the CEC and file for EI.

All businesses must register with the WCB and, if incorporated, your accountant will prepare your year-end and fill out a T2(E) corporate return, with relevant schedules beginning at T2S(1) through to T2S(30). If you are a sole proprietorship, you just need simple a T2124A, along with all your CCA schedules.

The only way to keep track of all this paperwork efficiently is to purchase a PC, of which the depreciation is deductible on a T2S(8). The choice is whether to purchase a 300MHZ Pentium with a 12 GIG hard drive, 128MB of RAM plus a CD Rom and a CD Rom writer, or a 75MHZ Pentium 4 GIG hard drive with 16 megs of RAM, a scanner, and a mouse—or should you purchase the whole zoo? Should you buy IBM or MacIntosh? Which programs will you need? Perhaps DOS 7, Windows 98, 95, WP 8 or better? Should you get Accpac 6, 6.1, or 2000? Don't forget your 3.5-inch MF 2HD back-up disks. Besides, as this is written, the above computer terminology will probably be obsolete anyway.

When you've made all that lovely money, you should decide on investing it wisely. The choices are many. You can purchase CSBs, GICs, mutual funds, RRSPs, BCSBs, RRIFs, or RESPs for the children. The decision seems to be easy, so don't waste too much time thinking about it. Right?

Now just think of your poor accountant when you bring in all your year's paperwork. Before your GL, TB, and statements are prepared, he or she will probably take a few ASA, or a large nip of CC before tackling your T2(E)s or T1s.

We live complex lives in a complex world, and even if you don't have a natural head for numbers or technical wizardry, you need to take the time to learn the basics if you want to do better than just stay afloat.

Chapter 9

What start-up expenses will you incur?

Make sure your account is a bottomless pit,
Because when you start business, you'll use all of it!

Start-up costs escalate quickly, and you don't need any financial surprises. This is the beauty of preparing a business plan: if all your costs are researched first, you can trim or expand to suit your budget. Checklists are provided at the end of this chapter to guide you through this process.

SELECTING AND LEASING A BUILDING

1. Industrial locations

No one can predict the future, so it's difficult to project the growth rate of your business over the next few years. This can create a problem as you ponder on the building size you need, as many factors have to be considered. Leasing costs are based on square footage, with added costs for taxes and amenities. Monthly lease costs increase dramatically by adding just a few hundred square feet.

It helps to make a scale drawing of your ideal building. This plan should allow room for equipment and machinery, work and bench space, storage facilities, vehicles, lunch, washrooms and office space. This will give you a good idea of the minimum square footage needed to house your operation comfortably.

If you can afford it, allow for a 20 percent increase in growth which should occur in the first year or two. If the budget is tight, you may have to limit this luxury, keeping in mind that if the business is successful, you may have to find alternate premises. This is one of the most difficult decisions you will have to make.

The premises should be able to handle any additional power and water needs of your operation. The cost of additional plumbing or electrical work should be estimated before a lease is signed; they can be expensive. Avoid moving into a building that cannot provide sufficient utilities for your requirements.

If you need warehouse or storage space, consider its accessibility. In one case, a satellite distributorship leased premises in the upstairs of a building because the rent was cheap, but no one thought about the space needed for their product lines. The satellite dishes, even when broken down into pieces, were too wide to pass through the stairwell. The products eventually had to be lifted up to the roof, and a roof hatch was built so the goods could be stored. Apart from the inconvenience, the roof hatch was hard to make secure, and the building was broken into several times.

If the building doesn't have enough racking and shelving to store inventory, research these additional expenses. Some real bargains can be found at liquidation centres. Heating costs should be explored, and your utility company can give you monthly readouts of the building's power usage over the preceding year. This will help you with your budgeting, and you may want to consider a more effective heating method. Some buildings draw considerable power during the winter because they are not heated or insulated economically.

Sometimes buildings have windows that don't open or don't supply enough ventilation during summer. They become extremely oppressive, particularly if offices or work space is upstairs. Hot and stuffy working conditions will affect your employees' work, as will extreme cold. Investigate the performance of both heating and ventilation systems. If your business involves shipping and receiving large products, be sure that your dock and loading facilities are in working order and adequate. You will need to maximize your efficiency by having the right equipment to do the job.

Security, of course, is a major problem. Many buildings are inadequately protected from intruders. Dead bolts should be installed on all exterior doors, and a round-the-clock monitored alarm system is essential. This will help keep the building secure. It may not prevent attempted break ins, but state-of-the-art locks and an alarm system are the best preventive measures.

2. Business and retail locations

Although costs are a very important factor in leasing a building, so is location. Most people work within a limited budget, but if a retail location is the wrong one for your business, it will affect your success. Your research should have pinpointed the competition in the area. Don't set up shop too close to them just because of cheap rent: you'll spend too much money on advertising, trying to attract the competition's customers.

Be prepared to pay higher rent for a prime location. Rents are usually indicative of the location's visibility. Rent is cheap for a good reason, usually because the building is in a poor location. Retail outlets should be easily accessible to the consumer. Make sure there is ample parking; customers will go to the competition if parking there is easier. We live in the days of "life in the fast lane," and no one wants to hunt for parking spots.

Study the pattern of walk-by traffic. Note peoples' reactions when they walk past other stores. If a store makes people stop and look in the window, it's time you learned a lesson in window displays. Study the drive-by traffic as well. Drive past your potential location yourself. Does anything attract your eye? Make a note of retail outlets which catch your eye. What was it that attracted your attention? You can gather ideas for your own displays, colours, and effective methods of advertising.

Don't lease a retail location in an industrial area; success will elude you. This should be logical, but too often new retailers open shop in an industrial area for the cheap rent and then wonder why hardly anyone comes in to buy their wares. Why? People visiting industrial areas are on business and in a rush, not in the mood for shopping retail.

Leasing a small premise "just to get started" is also false economy.

Moving a business when it has outgrown its premises can cost thousands of dollars. Try to find a location to suit your needs for the first five years. Your first year or two is often a nip-and-tuck operation and will not generate the kind of profits to finance a move. No matter which location you choose, there are always extensive renovation costs involved which are not recoverable when you move.

3. Signing your lease

A lease is a legal agreement between the landlord (the lessor) and the renter (the lessee), and it should be treated as a serious document. If you have to break your lease for any reason, you are breaking a legal agreement. Read the fine print and understand what the legalese means. If the legalese baffles you, consult a lawyer.

Landlords are often quite happy to negotiate certain conditions before the lease is signed. A building may need repair work or painting, and some landlords will forego a month or two of rent in return for this work. Remember, any fixtures you attach to the building cannot be removed after you move out. Installing permanent attachments is like throwing money out the window, particularly in the case of a short-term lease.

When a lease is signed, your landlord will usually ask for the first and last month's rent in advance, so don't forget to budget for this. The last month's rent is held in trust until the lease has expired and you have moved out. This security deposit should earn interest. When negotiating a lease, estimate for how long you will need the building and ask for first refusal to renew. Be sure that all terms and conditions between you and the landlord are written on all copies of the lease, down to the smallest detail. Verbal agreements are not acceptable. For example, if a three-year lease is signed, the lease must state whether the rent will remain the same or, if not, what the rent increase will be in percentage points or in dollars, and in which month of which year.

The cost of property taxes, shared janitorial, and maintenance services should be part of the lease so you know the exact cost for each year. If you break the lease, you are responsible for the remaining rent of the lease. Be sure there is a clause that will allow you to sublet the building, just in case. Most landlords are co-operative and draw up a lease to suit both parties. They prefer contented tenants who pay on time. Occasionally you may encounter a difficult landlord. If you suspect problems, talk to your lawyer before signing the lease.

If you are leasing retail space in a shopping mall, be prepared to hand over a percentage of your gross sales to the mall property managers for their advertising fund. Generally it is around 2 percent.

BUILDING RENOVATIONS

Renovation costs can escalate rapidly if you don't watch what you are spending. Most businesses need to spend money on building renovations, alterations, and additions. Get more than one quotation from each contractor. When you are planning your cash flow, divide your building costs into priorities: the renovations that have to be done straight away, those that can wait three to six months, and those that can be deferred until the profits start rolling in. Do what is necessary to make the premises look presentable and be operational. Give your business a chance to get started before you spend much of your working capital on cosmetic facelifts to someone else's building.

Don't forget to budget for your hydro deposit. The hydro company will probably require a deposit on your account if the utilities are not included in your rent and this cost is usually based on one month's average hydro bill. You can find out the charge by calling the utility company and asking about previous usage.

COMMUNICATIONS

As this is written, it will no doubt become obsolete information as technology constantly refines our methods of communication. You'll want to keep on top of the latest technology that affects your business and assess what you need.

1. Telephones

Without a doubt, no business can exist without a sophisticated telephone system, which generally means one that includes voice-mail. Many people dislike using it, but most have learned to accept it. As the average small business can't afford a receptionist, and voice-mail is much cheaper than an answering service, most people are opting to use it for taking messages. It is an efficient way to save messages and be sure your customers and clients can get hold of you. Some systems even call to tell you that your saved messages are one week old. If you skip messages, you are reminded. Voice-mail is an efficient nag and a cheap, flexible service. For a few dollars a month, hook up and get with it.

Many other options are available for your telephone system. For example, if you subscribe to a call-waiting service, you can be "beeped" to alert you to another incoming call. If you miss it—voila! The voice-mail will take the message. Hot tip: if you are calling a business with a voice-mail direction menu and you need to talk to a real person, bypass the options by pressing zero for an operator. It usually works.

Endless services are available through your local telephone company, including call display, call forwarding and so on. For a home-based and small operation, the miracles of telephone technology are surprisingly cheap and allow you to bypass the expense of paying for a business line.

Home-based businesses can operate efficiently using a residential line, although the major disadvantage is that a residential listing is excluded from the Yellow Pages. If your business depends on this kind of advertising, order a business line (at a cost of $60 to $80 a month at the time of writing). If you have a cellular phone, you can use this number to advertise in the Yellow Pages and save yourself the cost of a business line.

A residential line can be "split," meaning that your fax machine can receive a different telephone number on the same line. The ring tone for each line is distinctly different. If you use your residential telephone line for Internet access, an incoming call under the call-waiting service may disrupt your modem and terminate your connection. You can disable call-waiting—consult your telephone company for advice. A basic home-based system should include two residential lines (one for business and one for the fax and Internet), voice-mail, call waiting, a cellular phone or a pager.

If you have business premises, you have to install one or more business lines, and your telephone service can become quite costly. Telephone costs will continue to rise when intercoms or larger systems become necessary. Be sure to factor in your rising telephone costs as you plan your operating budget.

2. Fax machines

A fax machine is standard office equipment, and again, you have many options. Computers can send and receive faxes, but unless you have a scanner, you can't send original faxes using this system. A separate fax machine line has many advantages. It can be tied into your computer for Internet access and original faxes can be transmitted without leaving your computer on day and night. Most have the facility to act as a photocopier. Thermal-paper fax machines are cheaper, but they produce thin, curly paper whose images fade after three months. If you are receiving important documents, think about using a high-quality paper for better reproduction. Name-brand, quality fax machines cost approximately $400 and upwards, depending on the number of bells and whistles.

3. Cellular phones

Cell phones are trendy and chic, but they cost an arm and a leg to operate. New cell phone owners are always stunned when the first bill arrives. It seems so easy to phone a client on a whim and talk while you drive on a boring stretch of highway. Don't forget that any call you receive costs money, and expensive "roam" charges apply for long distance when you are out of a normal reception area.

If you operate a small business, a home-based office, or cannot afford a secretary, rather than springing for an expensive cell phone service with a long-term (most often three years) contract, consider an answering service, voice-mail, or a pager. An answering service will cost you about $50 a month. Paging services are becoming extremely cheap; some are under $10 a month. But if you feel you cannot do business without a cellular phone, take care before you sign your contract. If your business doesn't succeed, you will be stuck with an expensive toy. Buy-out lease terms can cost $20 a month for each unused month.

Shop around for the best deal and air time costs; they vary greatly and the competition is aggressive. Some cellular companies offer cheap rental rates, but the air time during peak periods can be exorbitant and quickly mounts up. Corporate rates are lower per minute during peak time. If you do business at nights and weekends, add the free evenings and weekends package. You may also add a voice-mail feature which will allow you to receive calls while on the phone or are unable to take a call. These days, a long-term contract may include a free cell phone. You must pay a federal access fee of $48˚ on start-up and again each year. You may want an additional metal hydride battery (which does not develop a memory and goes flat after several charges), a leather carrying case, and a quick charger. These extras will set you back between $100 and $200.

EXTERIOR SIGNS

Unless your business is home-based (no exterior signs allowed by most municipalities) you need exterior signs. They are a costly but necessary item. Before ordering, ask the landlord whether he or she approves of your choice as landlords often place restrictions on the type and size of signs. As well, check the municipal by-laws which regulate signs as many municipalities do not allow sidewalk signs, and there are usually general size restrictions for placement on buildings.

Some people prefer to use neon-lit signs for advertising. These come with a contract for monthly sign rental which can be rather expensive, depending on the type and size of the sign. Portable flashing signs are very popular, particularly for advertising a special event or sale. These signs are highly visible and noticed by the public. I always check out the advertised specials on these signs used by many local businesses.

Before deciding on your signs or sign-writing, take another drive around your neighbourhood and look for the ones that catch your eye. Get at least three quotations before making a decision. Start with the basics— you can always add more later.

OFFICE FURNITURE AND EQUIPMENT

Every business will have different needs for its office, but certain furniture and equipment are standard requirements. If you don't have anything, starting from scratch can be expensive. It pays to shop around at the various used furniture stores, or through a "buy-and-sell" type classified newspaper. As a guideline, here is a list of some of the basics which will be needed, and their approximate price:

	Low end	High end
Office desk:	$150	$ 700
Chair for desk:	130	350
Four-drawer file vertical cabinet:	150	400
or four-drawer lateral cabinet:	500	700
Hanging frames x 4:	40	60
Fax machine:	350	600
Adding machine with tape:	80	150
Bookshelf or storage unit:	50	200
Computer station:	120	350
Chairs - metal frame, cloth seat:	20	40
Total outlay:	**$1,590**	**$ 3,550**

(This list does not include a computer system; that comes extra.)

The proliferation of warehouse office suppliers has made prices extremely competitive. It sometimes pays to buy new from an office warehouse rather than used items from a small office furniture store. If you are setting up an office store-front, you should ensure the presentation is comfortable, tidy, and inviting to your clients. This will involve added expenses for decorating and quality furniture.

COMPUTER SYSTEMS

Each business has its individual requirements when it comes to computer systems, and each person has varying levels of computer skills. To be competitive, a business should have a system that can cater to accounting requirements, word processing, some graphic abilities, a data base, and Internet access for research, e-mail, and marketing purposes.

If you are running a small service business, you might escape the traumas of becoming computer-literate, but progressive companies will ensure they are plugged in an on-line. The new millennium is all about knowledge, information, and fast communication. If you don't understand computers, part of your business education should be to attend evening classes so you can learn to love your computer and what it can do for your business.

Much has been written about computer systems and the peripherals that go with them, and technology is rapidly changing, so you should consult an expert—not a computer sales person—so you get what you really need and no more.

Computers can save you lots of time and money in the long run. If you invest in a good laser printer, many of your advertising and office forms, including your stationery and envelopes, can be designed and printed with it, saving you a small fortune in printing costs. Labels, mail-outs, and newsletters can be prepared in-house and photocopied at an instant printing store, making marketing more cost-effective. Letterhead can be printed as needed, saving money on the cost of having 500 or 1,000 printed at a commercial printer.

1. Accounting and computers

If you process a volume of sales invoices every month, you need an accounting program. With a well-designed accounting system, you have instant access to your accounting records. Sales categories can be broken down to tell you how much each product line is selling in dollar value. These figures are helpful when reordering inventory or comparing product-line profits. GST/HST and provincial tax figures are automatically available.

If you use an accounts-receivable system, your accounting system will keep a separate record for each client and give you an "aged analysis" at the end of the month, showing the age of all outstanding accounts and how much is owed. This information is invaluable for monitoring potential bad debts and for collection purposes.

Many small businesses use the programs Simply Accounting, Mind Your Own Business, or Quick Books. These programs have been designed to handle accounts-payable, accounts-receivable, invoicing, inventory, and payroll.

A word of warning to the new entrepreneur: Don't get into accounting until you know what your are doing. Your option is to hire a competent part-time bookkeeper to update the books monthly. An accounting program does not make you a competent accountant. The old saying "garbage in, garbage out" holds true when you don't understand why you debit or credit an account. Information allocated to the wrong account will give you incorrect information. Over the years, I have earned a respectable income by correcting clients' erroneous accounting practices. Usually, the owner has decided to be his or her own bookkeeper and save money by purchasing an accounting program, but without having any accounting experience. It takes three times as long to correct false entries than it does to do it right the first time.

2. Basic system requirements

Bear in mind an essential fact of life in business: The moment you have bought a state-of-the-art computer system with peripherals, it becomes obsolete. The trick is to buy a system that can remain efficient and cost-effective performing its various tasks. As a rule, a good system should last for at least three years without the need to upgrade. That goes for both the hardware and the software.

The market is extremely volatile, and prices are changing every month. The cost of a computer system will range between $3,000 and $5,000. This, mind you, is a given figure. If you want to have a state-of-the-art computer system, this price range is constant. You can spend less—what changes is the efficiency and the speed.

Nowadays, a basic computer system includes the following:

1. An IBM compatible or MacIntosh computer using the Windows operating system, with a large capacity hard drive to accommodate all your files. Keep in mind that hard drives are getting larger because the programs (software) you need to operate need more and more space. The RAM (random access memory) should be at a minimum of 16 megabytes and preferably 32 to 64 (commonly called megs). Bear in mind that an IBM compatible system allows you more software flexibility.

2. A standard colour monitor measures 15-inches, but a 17-inch monitor is much easier to read. If you plan to spend lengthy periods at the screen, spoil yourself with a 17-inch monitor with an antiglare screen.

3. A CD-ROM drive because most programs now come on CD-ROMs and are cheaper than when you buy a whole stack of floppy disks. The speed you purchase will depend on the amount of time you plan to use the computer.

4. A 600 DPI (dots-per-inch) laser printer for your quality hard copies, which should have an output of at least six pages per minute. Bubblejets and colour printers are expensive to maintain. Only buy them if colour copies are essential to your business.

5. A 24-pin dot-matrix printer, a real work horse used for accounting printouts which are necessary for hard copy and backup purposes.

6. A 56 kbps fax modem to connect you with the Internet.

When it comes to software, there are only two major players in the field in the Windows operating system (which comprises the overwhelming majority of office computer systems these days): MS Office Suite and Corel WordPerfect Office Suite. There are others, but these are the big sellers. Both office suites contains a number of programs you need to run your business. If you decide to visit the Internet, you also need to rent one of the major Internet Service Providers (ISPs). Your provider should operate enough lines that you are not waiting for access, and should back up their service with prompt, on-line technical support.

When you total everything up, expect to pay up to $5,000; if you pay more, you have picked excessively priced hardware and extraneous software. Keep your computer operations lean and efficient, and avoid hardware or software clutter. If you are a small business generating only a few invoices, 20 or 30 cheques a month, and a handful of cash, Visa, or MasterCard expenses, a computer system isn't necessary. Your accounting can all be recorded in one journal, called a combined journal.

A computer purchase can be overwhelming. If the world of computers is new to you, do as much research as you can. Talk to other business people, look out for reviews in your paper, and pick up the many free computer publications available. In them you'll find good tips on the best deals in town.

STATIONERY REQUIREMENTS

It's easy to spend too much money on fancy stationery, so be practical and design your stationery on a budget you can afford. Presentation is the key, so choose your theme and colours carefully.

You will also need to budget about $200 to $300 for those little odds and ends such as suspension files, file folders, a stapler and staples, a three-hole punch, paper clips, envelopes and stamps, bulldog clips, pens, pencils, rulers, adding machine tape, note pads, laser or photocopier paper, highlighters, pens, liquid paper, notepads, a day-timer, self-inking or rubber stamps, file trays, and so on.

1. Invoices

Unless you have a retail outlet with a cash register, you will need sales invoices for recording each sale. It is a tax auditing requirement that all sales invoices be numbered and a numerical copy kept of every invoice. If you void an invoice, don't throw it out as many people do. Mark the invoice "Void" and keep all copies in the numerical file.

You can purchase prenumbered invoice books at a stationery store for a few dollars, or have your own designed and printed. If you operate an accounts receivable or accounts payable software program, check out some of the larger national forms companies for a variety of designs that are compatible with your program. Or you can design your invoices with your office program, print the master on a laser printer, then have them printed in triplicate on NCR (carbonless) paper, at a cost of about $200 for 500 copies. If you use many invoices, have them drilled with three holes for filing in binders. Three copies allow you to give one to the customer, keep one numerical copy, and have one copy for the client's or sales files. These files are an invaluable reference source if you have clients with repeat sales.

2. Letterheads, envelopes, and business cards

Having letterhead stationery designed and printed is expensive. A neat, well-written letter will have more impact on the reader than a badly worded letter presented on embossed letterhead with gold printing. If you keep to one colour, printing costs are much lower. A textured and coloured paper stock, such as cream or parchment, can present a very professional image at an affordable cost. If you are creative and own a colour printer, you can design and print your own.

Remember when you order stationery, the shorter the print run, the higher the cost per sheet. If you have a printing outfit prepare your stationery, ask for a quotation in quantities of 500, 1,000, and 2,000. You will see a noticeable decrease in price per sheet when the print run increases. However, don't order 2,000 letterhead just because it's cheap; you will have enough stock to last for 20 years.

Business cards can cost from $45 for 1,000 to $90 for 500, depending on the number of colours used and the complexity of the artwork. Letterhead costs will vary, depending on paper stock, logos, and colours used. There is a lot of competition in the printing industry, so shop around. Recently at an office warehouse outlet in Vancouver, a stationery package with 500 sheets of letterhead, 500 envelopes and 1,000 business cards with a choice of stock logos in one-colour ink was advertised at $99.99. That price is hard to beat.

INSURANCE POLICIES

Insurance is an expensive but necessary cost. You will be told of a myriad of policies you should have, and the costs mount up quickly. You don't want to be under insured, but at the same time, be careful of being over-sold. The areas you should seriously consider are these:

1. Business and liability insurance

2. Disability insurance

3. Life insurance

1. Business and liability insurance

Businesses that operate out of leased or purchased premises obviously need insurance to cover theft and damages, but there are other areas of business insurance you should be aware of. A fire will cause terrible damage to equipment and documentation. The building and equipment can be replaced, but think of the weeks of work involved in reconstructing files, documents, and accounting records.

A business policy covers the cost of document reconstruction. It also covers window and glass breakages and theft. You could be mugged while taking a deposit to the bank. Another area for which many people fail to insure is employee theft. If you have employees, make sure you have adequate coverage.

A few years ago, I worked as a consulting controller for a company and reviewed their insurance policies. The computer equipment was woefully under-insured; equipment had been purchased without a policy upgrade. The employee theft coverage was for $5,000 only. This business employed temporary personnel, who went into other businesses on a basis of trust. The equipment insurance was upgraded, and the employee theft coverage increased to $25,000. One incidence of employee theft occurred while an employee was on assignment, and after I completed my assignment, another employee embezzled nearly $10,000. Had the policy not been upgraded, the business would have suffered a substantial loss with both of these incidences.

An insurance policy can cover a business for "errors and omissions" and liability. We all hear about clients suing businesses for malpractice, faulty products, and liability through accidents. Make sure you are well covered in these areas, and don't be too frugal. Policies can range from $750 to $3,500, depending on the type of business. A contractor's liability policy can cost up to $1,200 a year. Ask your insurance agent to guide you through establishing a comprehensive policy.

Home-based businesses must ensure sufficient insurance coverage for the office. Some people don't think of insuring their business equipment separately. Currently, most homeowner policies cover equipment in offices to a value of $2,000 only. If equipment such as a laptop computer is carried in a vehicle and is stolen or damaged, there is no coverage. The equipment is covered only while in the home. A $10,000 policy should cost less than $200, including the addition of a liability rider. Then, if a client comes to your house, trips over the dog and breaks a leg, you will be covered if he or she sues.

All other coverages available in a business policy are not currently available in a home policy extension. Insurance companies have now recognized the need to cater to the home-based sector, and many companies are now offering a home-based insurance package. Usually, they require you to insure your residence with them as well. As quoted recently by a local insurance agent, "When a person starts a home business, their first call is not to an insurance agent—when it should be."

2. Disability insurance

Sole owners of a business are not only the lifeline of the business, they are responsible for the financial security of their families. Many people fail to think about the consequences of accident, injury, or terminal illness. If something happens, the business income immediately stops and the financial security of both business and family is threatened. What protection is there for the sole business owner? Sickness benefits are not available through Employment Insurance. Workers' compensation will pay a percentage of earned wages if you are covered and if the accident or illness is work-related, but not all accidents and illnesses are. Your personal financial commitments are not insured.

One of the safest and most comprehensive protection packages available is a good disability policy. It will insure you against accidents, as well as short-and long-term illness up to 65 years of age. Not everyone qualifies for this type of policy because they are based on your age and health. To qualify for most policies, you have to have been in business for at least six months and be able to show proof of income.

Partial and total disability will require definition by your insurance broker. As an example, a serious back injury may prevent you from driving your truck, stopping you from carrying on your business. However, you may still be able to perform a desk job, so the injury would be considered a partial disability. A new policy available is called a terminal illness policy. With the stressful lives many lead these days and the higher incidence of heart attacks and cancer at a younger age, you may want to explore this option as well.

Disability policies cover contingencies in cost-of-living increases, coverage of operating overhead, immediate accident coverage (instead of waiting 30 days), and financial compensation to cover personal monthly commitments. We don't know whether, or when, we will contract a terminal or incapacitating illness or suffer a severe disability due to an accident. It is a comfort to know that enough income will be coming in to cover overhead and hiring replacement staff to operate the business. The mortgage will be paid and food put on the table. People tend to avoid personal insurance but remember: life insurance is only collectible after your death, while disability insurance is collectible by the living.

3. Life insurance

You should have some form of term life insurance to protect your family in case of your death. The coverage should be for an amount which would provide a sufficient income for your family, when invested wisely. As an example, a policy for $300,000, invested at 10 percent, would return $30,000 a year. Do your family a favour and put some form of coverage on your life. Consult a well-recommended insurance agent who will not oversell an insurance product to you. At the same time, make a proper will so your family will benefit and not the government.

The most affordable form of life insurance is term insurance, which is strictly protection in the event of the owner dying. Several factors should be taken into consideration when determining the amount of coverage needed.

• Are other family members involved or dependent on the business? If it is a husband and wife operation, and one spouse dies, the other may not have a job if the survivor cannot run the business on his or her own.

• If other family members can take over the business, then the coverage needs to be sufficient to keep the business running while the transition takes place.

• If the business is to be sold, then sufficient coverage is necessary to keep it running efficiently to ensure an realistic selling price.

• If the business is a partnership, each partner should own a policy sufficient to be able to buy out the business from the estate.

Finally, in addition to the life insurance for business purposes, ensure that your family is adequately protected, taking into consideration all living expenses. If the business is paying for the policy, the insurance payout will be taxed. If the premiums are paid personally, then taxes are not payable on the payout, under present taxation laws.

WHAT IS A BREAK-EVEN POINT?

Now that you have a good idea of your start–up costs, you can calculate your break-even point, which is the amount of dollars your business should generate monthly in gross sales to cover all your operation costs, exclusive of profits. Your business plan will give you a good indication of what those costs should be. Now it is time to calculate the break-even point for your business. When you have this information, you will know approximately weekly and monthly (even if your books aren't quite up to date) where you stand financially.

Once you know that you have to generate a certain amount of sales income each month, you can divide this figure by 4.33 to arrive at a weekly sales figure, or you can even break it down to a daily sales figure. Knowing what your sales should be to break even is motivational— because if you don't know where you are, there is no motivation to reach a goal. If sales are slow, it should motivate you to do something to boost up the figures (panic excluded). It helps you to plan your cash-flow and it motivates you to collect outstanding receivable accounts and strive for more profits.

Your starting point for this calculation is to know your approximate gross profit margin. If you are operating on a 35 percent gross profit margin, you need to generate enough profit on your retail sales to cover all overhead costs. The first step is to list your monthly expenses, as set out below in an example of a retail furniture store employing one sales person and one bookkeeper. The profit margin after the cost of pur-chases is 35 percent, or $35 profit per $100 sales.

Here's how to calculate your break-even point:

Direct overhead costs:

Wages, sales person	1,750.00
Delivery	300.00
Damaged goods	150.00
Freight in	75.00
Discounts	220.00
Total direct costs:	**2,495.00**

Overhead costs:

Accounting fees	100.00
Advertising	650.00
Bad debts	50.00
Bank charges	60.00
CPP & EI expense	260.00
Fees, licences & dues	30.00
Insurance	75.00
Loan interest	250.00
Promotion	75.00
Promotion–meals	75.00
Office supplies	150.00
Office salaries	1,500.00
Rent and taxes	850.00
Repairs–store	50.00
Repairs–equipment	30.00
Sign rental and security	65.00
Telephone, fax and cellular	260.00
Utilities	350.00
Vehicle–gas	110.00
Vehicle–repairs, insurance	200.00
WCB	35.00
Total overhead costs:	**5,225.00**
Combined overhead costs:	**7,720.00**

The combined overhead cost is $7,720 a month. This calculation does not include the cost of purchasing the furniture. That cost is taken into the 35 percent gross profit calculation. Now make the following calculation:

$7,720.00 overhead ÷ by 35 and x by 100 =
$ 22,057.14 (monthly gross sales)

Gross sales needed for month:	22,057.00
Furniture cost: (65% of retail price)	14,337.00
Gross profit: (35%)	7,720.00
Overhead costs:	7,720.00
Break even point:	**$ 22,057.00**

The furniture store has to generate $22,057 in retail sales to cover all costs. If the profit margins decrease, or expenses increase, loss will occur. These calculations don't take into account the owner's wages. You, must decide how much you need to draw from the business each month to cover your personal needs. If you need $2,500 a month for yourself, the break-even point would be as follows:

Total overhead costs:	7,720.00
Owner's wages	2,500.00
Total new overhead:	10,220.00
10,220 ÷ by 35 x 100 =	**$ 29,200.00**

To pay a $2,500 owner's salary, the store would have to generate an additional $7,143.00 in sales.

7,143.00 x 35% gross profit = $ 2,500.00

CHECKLIST OF START-UP COSTS

When you have researched and established the start-up costs for your new business, complete Exercise #6.

EXERCISE #6

ESTIMATING START-UP COSTS

Type of Expense	Estimated Cost
1. Consultation with accountant to review business purchase	$ _____
2. Consultation with lawyer to review buy-sell agreement	_____
3. Lawyer's fees to edit and prepare buy-sell agreement	_____
4. Purchase price of business	_____
5. Incorporation fees	_____
6. Business plan preparation	_____
7. Loan application and financing fees	_____
8. First and last months' rent of building	_____
9. Renovations to building	_____
10. Utility deposit on building	_____
11. Municipal business licence	_____
12. Other licences	_____
13. Telephone, fax line and Internet installation	_____
14. Cellular phone purchase and access fee	_____
15. Interior and exterior signs	_____
16. Computer system	_____
17. Printing and stationery	_____
18. Office furniture and equipment	_____
19. Advertising campaign	_____
20. Office stationery and miscellaneous	_____
21. Business insurance	_____
22. Other: _____	_____
TOTAL: $	_____

YOUR START-UP CHECKLIST

Exercise #7 provides a checklist of the steps in order of priority you should take for the setting up of your business. Use it to keep track of where you are and don't miss any important steps. If your business is home-based, some of these steps will not apply to you. Applicable telephone numbers can be found in Appendix 1.

EXERCISE #7

START-UP CHECKLIST

STEP	PROCEDURE	CHECK
1.	Decide which type of business is right for me	❏
2.	Research the market and the competition	❏
3.	Take vendor's proposal to accountant for review	❏
4.	Visit municipality to review by-laws and regulations	❏
5.	Research other licensing requirements	❏
6.	Contact lawyer to review/prepare buy-sell agreement	❏
7.	Prepare business plan and projections	❏
8.	Find suitable location for business	❏
9.	Research costs of all renovations to building	❏
10.	Contact lawyer to have lease reviewed	❏
11.	Talk to bank manager about financing requirements	❏
12.	Choose three names and register business name	❏
13.	Have incorporation papers prepared	❏
14.	Call telephone company for phone requirements	❏
15.	Order cellular phone (you will need all your phone numbers so that stationery can be ordered)	❏
16.	Apply for necessary business licences	❏
17.	Open business accounts and credit card applications	❏
18.	Apply for GST/HST registration	❏

19. Apply for provincial sales tax number ☐

20. Apply for payroll registration and information ☐

21. Register with Workers' Compensation Board ☐

22. Prepare marketing and advertising campaign ☐

23. Research computer requirements and prices ☐

24. Talk to accountant about accounting system ☐

25. Obtain quotations on exterior and interior sign work ☐

26. Obtain quotations on printing requirements ☐

27. Contact insurance broker ☐

Other: _____ ☐

_____ ☐

_____ ☐

_____ ☐

_____ ☐

_____ ☐

_____ ☐

_____ ☐

_____ ☐

Chapter 10

How do you market your business?

This is such a great idea–it'll sell itself!
Anonymous

WHAT DOES MARKETING MEAN?

You can have the best little business with wonderful potential, but if you can't market it, you don't have a business. One of the most frequently asked questions is: "How do I market my business?" The answer is: "Learn how to market yourself, because you *are* your business."

People tend to confuse the terms "marketing," "advertising," and "promotion."

Marketing means informing your potential customers about your products or service, and finding ways to establish and keep a client base. Your market is the specific group of people that consume your product or utilize your service.

Advertising refers to the various media used to convey your message, such as a printed advertisement, radio air time, television commercials, the Internet, or transit advertising. Advertising is seeing or hearing a rehearsed script, descriptive words or pictures that convey your business message to the public.

Promotion refers to the various methods by which you convey your message to the customers. You are promoting your business when you communicate with the public, telling or showing them your products or service. Many people will join business associations, play golf, or set up displays in malls and trade shows for promotional reasons.

Marketing and promotion are areas in which many people feel lost and uncomfortable. The longer you research your market, your product, and the competition, the more comfortable you will become in marketing and promoting your products or service. It will take time to learn what works for your business, and just as you think you have the answer, you will have to find new methods, because the old ones stop working effectively. To market your business, you have to use a combination of techniques which will change, depending on the time of year and the state of the economy.

Successful marketing and promotion will start to happen as you work on your personal skills to be the very best you can be. Your communication and personal skills are what will ultimately sell your business for you.

HOW DO YOU START MARKETING?

The first step is to find out who your market really is—that is, to research, define, and then target your market. Once you have achieved this step, you will become more able to focus on how to market your business. Many new entrepreneurs make the mistake of thinking they have a large market, when in actual fact, most markets are quite small.

A woman thinking of selling a line of make-up may think her market is every woman. This is not so. Narrowing it down, many women don't use or like make-up. Others have their own brands which they don't want to change. Others have a budget, and use either cheap, or conversely, expensive make-up. Some have skin allergies and have to use medicated or allergy-free products.

Sales will depend on the income level of the area in which the business is to be established. You have to understand the demographics of your consumer to narrow down and understand your true market. All this should be part of your marketing plan.

Part of marketing is to design a company name, theme, and logo that people can become familiar with and relate to a specific business. J&D. Enterprises tells people nothing about your business. Bill's Tree Topping

& Garden Services is definitely more descriptive. Work with a graphic designer so that the presentation of your business name and logo is sharp and professional. A poorly designed name and logo represents your business as being second-rate. As with a well-written letter, first impressions are vitally important.

WHAT IS A MARKETING PLAN?

A marketing plan is a map of your marketing ideas. Many entrepreneurs make the mistake of not planning this most important part of their business. Marketing is not placing an advertisement in the paper and waiting for the telephone to ring. You could have a long wait, and will waste valuable dollars with ineffectual coverage. If you take the time to research who, what, and where your market is, plan a budget and source out effective methods of advertising and promotion, your business will be off to a flying start.

Your marketing plan should include the three main components of research as detailed in Chapter Four: the status of the current and future market, product knowledge, and your competition. The next stage is to define your goals, both long-and short-term. Defining who you are targeting is next, followed by the development of your own creative strategies to attract consumers.

Your next step is to plan your media budget, coverage, and scheduling. All advertising should be carefully monitored for results. Your plan should encompass projections for one year, and actual results should be compared to your projections. A marketing plan enables you to know and monitor where you are going at all times.

Many businesses develop a mission statement, which is a statement of their beliefs and goals. An example of a mission statement from a professional business could be, "To care about all clients and their success and always be there when help is needed. To maintain ongoing support and make the word 'service' a key factor in our client relationship." Defining the reason you are in business in writing is a form of goal-setting and helps you focus on your commitment. It also looks good on promotional brochures, business cards, and handouts.

WHO IS YOUR MARKET AND WHERE ARE THEY?

An integral part of planning your business is to know who will use your services. The majority of small businesses will rely on their community for sales, so it is in your best interests to get to know everything you can about your community, or the people who will use your business. You certainly don't want to spend advertising dollars on people who don't want or need your product or service. Who are your potential consumers? Find out by answering the following questions:

- Are most of them female?

- Are most of them male?

- Are they an even mix of male and female?

- What is their average income bracket?

- Where would these consumers generally congregate?

- Do they live in apartments, houses or rural areas?

- Which radio stations would they most likely listen to?

- Which magazines are they most likely to read?

- Where would they most likely shop?

- What is their average age?

- What type of work do they do?

- What is the average family size?

- What are their interests?

- What are the physical boundaries of your business?

- Are you targeting the retail, residential, or commercial market?

Answering these questions will enable you to define the physical limitations of your business and build a profile of your average consumer. Some of the most successful businesses know exactly who they are catering to. They have narrowed down their marketing and know who their products appeal to. With this information, they can formulate marketing strategies aimed specifically at these consumers.

If you make a study of your community and break it down into the types of people who live there, you will be able to make informed marketing decisions. Knowing the income levels of your average consumer is vital. It's no use trying to sell expensive items to low-income consumers. Your study may indicate that you should choose either a better location for your business, diversify your product lines, or even choose another type of business.

Study consumers' shopping habits. Visit busy malls, strip malls, out-of-the way locations and mega-stores. Note when the stores are busy and when they are quiet. Watch which products people buy that are related to what you sell. See what they are willing to pay for a similar product. Note which days of the week are busy and know which seasonal times of the year will affect your business, either positively or adversely.

If you are a people person, design a small marketing survey and see if you can solicit some response from busy shoppers. Ask them why they buy a certain product or use a particular service, what they are prepared to pay, and the service they expect to go along with the purchase. You could offer a small thank-you for their time, perhaps a flower for a woman and a pen for a man (along with your business card of course).

Once you have a better idea of who you are targetting, you can then research the best way to advertise and promote your business. If your average consumer tends to read gardening magazines, obviously that is where you should advertise. If your consumers are living mainly in apartments, don't advertise in rural areas. Match your geographical advertising to your consumer's residential areas, and advertise through the media they are most likely to read, hear, or watch.

SERVICE IS THE KEY TO SUCCESS

With our competitive and shrinking economy, customers are becoming extremely demanding. In fact, many expect something for nothing and then they still complain. One lady who uses a brew-your-own wine store not only has the store brewing for her, she now has them doing the bottling. She then had the cheek to ask for a price discount, because the wine was advertised a few dollars cheaper somewhere else. She was receiving exceptional service, yet still asked for the impossible. This is just one example of what today's consumer expects, and it won't get any better as competition gets more formidable.

Still, without customer service, you won't have a successful business. Clients choose to use a new business expecting both service and competitive prices. They expect 100 percent performance with the best price in town. Unhappy clients can spread the word that a business is "no good" a great deal quicker than it takes to build up a good reputation. Positive word-of-mouth advertising is extremely effective in building a business, just as negative comments can deter potential business.

Customers expect guarantees with products and with services. As a business person, you should be familiar with each client's individual needs. If these needs cannot be met, tell your customers, rather than perform an inadequate service or sell them the wrong product. Remember, customers are always right, even when they are wrong. Always treat your customers as you would expect to be treated. Make a point of remembering names and faces and some family details. This will show that you are attentive and care about your clients.

Excellent service begins with your telephone manner. This is where your communication skills should be working overtime. You've done everything right and now your telephone is ringing—but you are not there to answer it. Perhaps the customer can only call on a Monday morning to ask questions about your product or service. He or she may not purchase until later in the week, but obviously you should be there every Monday morning, even if your sales are traditionally slow on that day. You should always ensure that you have open communication available to your potential customers. If your advertisements are on the radio at 7 p.m. every evening, or the talk show you just appeared on is at 8 p.m., make sure your phone is being answered at these times.

Your receptionist—and that person may be you at first—is the direct link between you and your customers. This person is your traffic controller. Customers will either come to you, or they can be diverted to the competition. It will all depend on the way they are treated in the initial telephone conversation. Along with your great service, your support staff must believe in you and your business and be willing to service your customers effectively. Train them well and treat them fairly—you'll have a much better chance of becoming successful.

Here's an example: A neighbour was having some trees cut and removed recently. Another neighbour drove by and asked the worker if he would come and quote on cutting down some overhanging branches. "You'll have to phone Bill, the boss." yelled the worker without turning off the chipper. "The phone number's on the side of the truck." This is not good for public relations. Had the employee stopped, turned off the machine and handed the neighbour a business card, it would have generated a potential sale. As it was, the neighbour had no pen and drove off feeling slighted, deciding to use another company.

Your staff are always marketing your business, and that is free advertising. Remember to thank your staff at the end of the day. Show them you appreciate their efforts, no matter what their level of employment. If you have to discipline your staff, do it privately without demeaning them in front of others. They will respect you more and will usually work even harder to promote your business.

Service is not just a matter of being nice to your clients. There are other integral factors to consider, such as contacting your customer after the sale and asking whether there were any problems. Always honour time and price commitments, even if you have made a mistake. If promised delivery dates cannot be met, telephone your client immediately and apologize. The consumer market is extremely demanding these days, and it is indeed a buyer's market. To compete, you have to sell yourself and your business first, and the sale will follow.

HOW DO YOU CREATE CUSTOMER LOYALTY?

Another sad fact of life is that, these days, very few customers are loyal. Most of their loyalties lie with their bank accounts, and you can't blame people for watching their shrinking dollars. If you have regular clients, offer them an extra incentive now and again. Thank them for coming in and remember their names. Give them an additional discount for regular business or a company coffee mug to take home. For special customers, a box of chocolates at Christmas would be well remembered.

Be good to them and they will bring you new business. Treat them as you would a good friend, especially if you meet on the street. Remember their birthdays. You can do this by starting a birthday club (explained later on in this chapter.) Make special acknowledgments to your customers if you meet them at dinner parties or during a business function; stop whatever you are doing and say hello. Even if you charge a little more than the new competitor, they'll be more loyal to you.

If a customer has sent a referral to you, take the time to send a thank-you card. These mean more to a person than you think. The fact that you took time out from your busy day to say thank you will not be forgotten. You should send these out regularly.

Think of little ways in which you can entice your customers to come back regularly. Our local shopping centre has a bakery and delicatessen combined. The bakery gives out a fresh, home-baked cookie to children, and the deli gives a free dozen crusty buns with each order of deli meat over $7. The local independent supermarket next door always has fresh, free coffee available, along with draw and suggestion boxes. The young cashiers willingly pack and wheel your groceries to the car. Senior citizens get a discount on Sundays and a free grocery delivery service once a week. My daughter and I make a ritual trip every Sunday, looking forward to our treats and the friendly service.

HOW DO YOU PRICE YOUR PRODUCTS COMPETITIVELY?

It is important to establish a pricing policy in line with your industry and one which most consumers are willing to pay. As an exercise, ask your friends and associates how much they would be willing to pay for your product or service. If they are willing to pay a hundred dollars, then perhaps if you price the product 10 percent to 20 percent cheaper, you'll sell three or four times more. Conversely, if your prices are too low, the consumer may think the item or service is not good quality. Think about how you make your own decisions when you are price shopping. Do you choose the absolute cheapest product, or one priced more middle-of-the-road?

As an example, many years ago a photographic studio chain priced a glamour make over, including makeup application, hairstyling, photography, and one 8 x 10 inch colour print for $25. The package was exceptionally hard to sell, no matter how much advertising was done. The price was raised to $55 and literally thousands of people called.

A builder constructed a townhouse complex consisting of 160 units. After a year, he had sold only three. He hired a marketing consultant and was surprised to hear that his price of $85,000 per townhouse was too low. The correct market price should have been $120,000. On the verge of bankruptcy, he had been ready to slash his price to $75,000 and bail out. He raised the price, sold out in six months and went on to build many more townhouse complexes, which of course, he priced according to the current market.

Establishing effective market pricing is one of the most crucial steps of your marketing plan. Your prices have to be competitive, yet at the same time, they must be able to generate the necessary profits to operate the business and cover all overhead expenses. If your research into the competition shows that you cannot compete with products or a service of comparable quality, perhaps this business is not a viable one for you.

PRICE COMPARISONS

As stated before, the economy is always changing, so you will have to keep on top of your pricing policies. Regularly compare the prices your competitors normally charge to the current price you are now charging. Placing a time limit on an advertised special gives consumers a sense of urgency to call now. If all your advertising has this same sense of urgency, the consumer will eventually get smart and will avoid your product or service. Let some advertising be informational and others be the clinchers that brings the consumer to your door.

It is not unusual to see price checkers strolling the supermarket aisles. Supermarkets are all about price, because some don't offer much service. You have to be prepared to keep a close eye on your competitors. Don't make the mistake of becoming complacent with your business. You should monitor the people who come into your store for advertised specials. Do they only buy the specials, or do they purchase other products? A low-priced sale isn't going to contribute much to the profits. All the lines you carry should be priced reasonably.

PLANNING YOUR ADVERTISING BUDGET

An essential part of your marketing plan should be to plot your estimated sales on paper, based on your market research. Draw a graph showing the 12 months across the bottom. On the left hand side of the graph, list the possible amount of items which could be sold in any given month. If your product relates to hours, then use this vertical column to list billable hours, or "hours sold." (See Sample #7.)

Now ask yourself, "What is the maximum work I can bill in any given month? What is the maximum amount of product available to me in any given month? How much product can I possibly sell?" You may not have the financial means to purchase all the product you need to meet all possible orders. It is a frustrating fact of business that the cash flow is often not available to stock your shelves to the maximum. Most businesses grow slowly. Keeping this fact in mind, realistically plot your maximum monthly sales by item. Total all the items for each month and plot each month's sales on your graph. Then join the dots to get your projected sales curve. (You may have a program in your computer that will prepare this information for you.)

Then take a calendar, and, starting in January, look at each day of the month, asking yourself, "What is the likelihood of anyone wanting to buy my product or service today? Is there no possibility, a little maybe, or a strong possibility?"

Some products sell well before or on Valentine's Day, Easter, spring break, Mother's Day, Father's Day, back-to-school, Halloween, Christmas and the Christmas break. Others do not sell at all. Sales curves will differ from business to business.

For example, if your product sells well on Valentine's Day, your advertising campaign should start a month before the day. Department stores start advertising Christmas as early as September. If they waited until December, they would suffer extreme financial losses.

Planning the timing for your promotional strategies is crucial. Many advertising media may not accept new advertisers when you plan to advertise; some publications have up to a six-month deadline. Most magazines have at least a one-to two-month deadline for advertising copy, while newspapers have weekly deadlines.

Now it's time to look at your projected marketing expenses. Take another large piece of paper, with the 12 months marked across the bottom, and your bar showing the dollars spent along the side. (See Sample #8.) Chart where to maximize and minimize your advertising budget. You may have some months when your advertising budget registers a zero, but this should not happen more than one or twice a year at most.

To complete your minimum marketing budget for your first year, convert your sales curve to dollars and then take 15 percent of your annual sales figure. From here, you can then plan when to spend your advertising dollars, using your sales curve as a guide. You now have your marketing budget in place. (See Sample #9, which shows a seven percent budget.)

It is unlikely that you will achieve your first year's projected sales, although your success is based on achieving this annual volume as closely as possible. Perhaps you will be one of the few who will meet or even surpass your projections. This happens to those who have the right product available at the right time and promote it the right way.

Your second year's budget should be reduced to 7 to 10 percent of this same annual sales dollar amount. By now, you will have learned more about your product, how it relates to the consumer, and which media are the most effective sources of promotion and advertising. You will still have to experiment with new advertising media or new ideas using the same media.

Your third year's budget should accurately reflect your forecast for the coming year, based on realistic judgments and using the same methods to create your sales curve, annual dollar sales, and marketing curve. By your fourth or fifth year, you may taper your advertising budget to as low as four or five percent of gross sales.

Every business will differ. Some may start with a 30 percent opening budget and end with a 15 percent budget after four or five years. The best time to start your business is two to three months before your highest sales curve. This will enable you to iron out some kinks and have your name already introduced into the marketplace. Remember, your key to successful marketing is to plan ahead.

SAMPLE #7
SALES CURVE

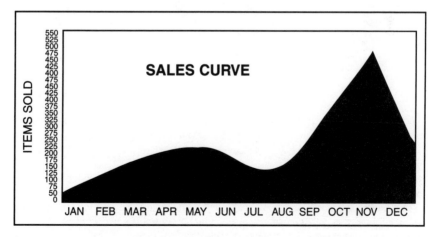

SAMPLE #8
MARKETING EXPENSE CURVE

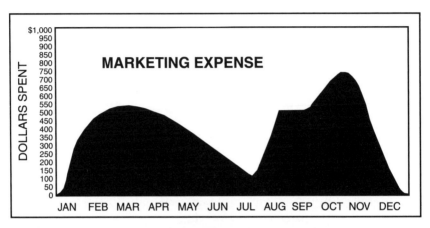

SAMPLE #9
YOUR MARKETING BUDGET

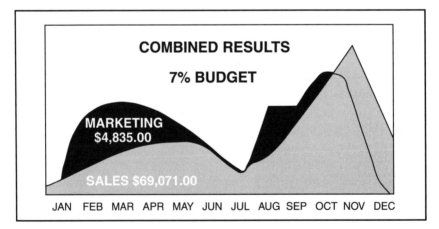

Notice that similar amounts are spent prior to Christmas season and during Spring. Sometimes it takes more advertising push to bring in business during seasonal periods. You will receive more response from your advertising dollars during peak times. Some months, advertising is futile and a waste of money.

By strategically placing your ads throughout the year you are able to maximize your return on investment. To forcast your advertising budget, look at last year's sales. Estimate your growth based on last year's sales and this year's anticipated growth (an increase of product or service lines, or a better management service to your current clients).

On opening a business, some companies will spend up to 50 percent of their estimated volume for the year on advertising. It is recommended in some university text books that a minimum of 15 percent be allocated to jump-start a business.

194

HOW DO YOU PROMOTE YOUR BUSINESS?

There are many effective methods to promote your business without spending a lot of money. You will find that many of these ideas listed below will bring you long-term and repeat business and help you to increase your confidence and communication skills.

The most successful businesses are promoted through a combination of networking, one-on-one promotional venues, and media advertising. Without a doubt, networking, combined with regular and consistent exposure to your community or market, are the best forms of promotion.

1. Networking

Many people are unsure of exactly what networking is. Networking is meeting people and having the ability to tell them who you are and what you do in a precise and interesting manner. Networking is referring people with a need to other reliable people and businesses. Networking is unselfishly helping others while you actively promote and meet new potential clients and contacts. Successful networking is increasing your potential clients and contacts and having others refer business to you. Good networkers are always looking for ways to help other people as well as themselves, because what goes around, comes around. If you network for purely selfish reasons, it will show, and the results will be far less effective.

a) How and where do you network?

Your networking success will be enhanced if you enjoy people and do not have reservations about expressing yourself. If you join Toastmasters as I mentioned before, it will be much easier to start. Your starting point should be to develop a 20-second "infomercial" about yourself and your business which can be presented to the listener in an interesting manner.

When you are introduced to a stranger, the first question one of you will ask is "What do you do?" Your mission is to have an informative answer ready. Always start your introduction with "I am" not "My name is." Here is a 20-second example.

"Hi. I am David Johnson, and my business is *Community Living Magazine*, which is now two years old and enjoyed and respected by the community. The circulation has grown from 10,000 to 35,000. We focus on community issues, biographies, and places and features of local interest. We have just started full-colour advertising at extremely competitive rates." David then presents his business card.

In 20 seconds, David has introduced himself and his business, explained in detail about his magazine, its community acceptance, and information alluding to the growth of the magazine. The listener hasn't had time to get bored with drawn-out details, yet in a short time, knows much about David's business.

The key to building relationships is to give the other person a chance to tell you about themselves and to show an interest in what they do. If they don't present their business card, ask for it, mentioning that you would like it in case you know of someone requiring his or her type of service. You are now a perfect audience, and have made the first step toward building a relationship. If you think you have met someone you would like to keep in touch with, call him or her the next day and say know how much you enjoyed the conversation.

You can network everywhere – at meetings, trade shows, social occasions, and in a bank lineup. The opportunities are endless, although some tact and diplomacy should come into place at certain times. You can't be all about business, but you can be looking to help others, at the same time letting people know who you are and what you do.

Ideally, you should join at least one or two specific networking groups. These range in structure from women's networks, to leads contacts, to morning gatherings. There are a variety of networking organizations springing up. There is sure to be one or two which will meet your needs and time commitments. Ask your local chamber of commerce for details, as they are usually aware of any well-established groups within your community or area. Networking group members usually turn to each other when they require information or products.

b) Join the chamber of commerce

The chamber of commerce is in business to be the voice of business and the community. As a member, you have the opportunity of many benefits and discounts. Unfortunately, many people join and do nothing, so nothing happens. You should attend dinners and special events, such as business-after-business events and trade shows. Go to some of the seminars of interest and attend special speaker events.

Offer your services to one of their committees, as many chambers are run mostly by volunteers. Give of your time to your community and they will in turn give back to you. You will expand your knowledge, meet many people, and feel satisfied with your contribution to the community. Join the Rotary Club for the same reasons. They help many deserving community groups, and the rewards are most satisfying.

c) Attend regular trade shows

There is no better way to advertise your business than to display it at a trade show. Many people have the wrong expectations of these events, expecting people to flock to their table and place multiple orders. Trade shows do not work like this. They are an excellent opportunity for you to meet potential clients face-to-face and start building a relationship. When your service or product is needed, you will probably be called.

When people visit your table, don't ram your business down their throat. Be polite and informative, ask them what they do, have a competition or prize box on hand for business cards, and make sure they leave with a brochure, card or handout. It doesn't stop there. Follow up all interested people with a polite phone call, telling them how much you enjoyed meeting, and that you would be pleased to help, should the need arise.

2. Evaluations and testimonials

Evaluations and testimonials are under-utilized by many business owners. If you are new in business or have a new product or service, ask satisfied clients if they would mind writing a testimonial. Thank them with a little gift. People believe in the written word, and testimonials are a wonderful business reference. They are invaluable. Collect them and put them into a "brag book." Show this book to other clients, along with photos of your work or products.

If you are introducing a new product or service, find reputable companies or clients who would like to test your product for you or offer it at a cost price in return for an evaluation or testimonial. Ask for written permission to use these results in any promotional literature. Most people are impressed with testimonials—aren't they one of the main features of a book that influences your purchase?

3. Press releases

The press is a powerful tool that once again, is not used by enough people. Your local paper is always looking for items of interest to print. Find a way to create a unique approach to your business and send out press releases. You may have a new product that is environmentally friendly, or be holding a workshop. If you like writing, submit articles to magazines within your field of interest. Once again, the written published word carries much weight. This is another reason why it is so important to become an expert in your field.

For example, a one-day workshop being held for small businesses was promoted in a variety of ways. Press releases were sent to eight newspapers, and it was promoted through networks, radio, and the chamber of commerce. Of the people registered, 59 percent read about it through press releases and newsletters, 9 percent heard through the radio, and 32 percent through one-on-one networking.

4. Personal appearances

As your confidence grows, think about increasing your skills as a speaker. You can use these skills over time to build your reputation as an expert in your field. Offer to teach adult education classes, design workshops, speak at chamber of commerce events, networking groups, and anywhere you can get up in front of a group. Once you are in front of an audience, you are considered the expert. Business will follow, and your name will become well-known over time, not just in your own community, but further afield.

5. Conferences and seminars

Never stop learning. Too many new business owners think they don't have the time or the money to spend on education. This is a grave mistake. Not only will you learn more about your chosen field, you will meet new people and make new contacts, sometimes with the opportunity of setting up a small display table.

The one-day seminar mentioned above was designed to help home-based operators learn about four key areas of small business management. It was heavily advertised throughout the province, including one of two newspapers which are circulated throughout the province, which in turn supports hundreds of thousands of small businesses. Only 22 people attended, and of those 22, the evaluations were excellent. Thank-you cards and phone calls followed in abundance. What happened to all the other small businesses? Were they too busy to grow their businesses? Don't make the mistake of thinking you know it all.

The above methods of promotion require excellent communication and people skills. As your knowledge and confidence grows, try these methods discussed in this section. They are proven successful and involve very little cash outlay compared to media advertising. However, they do require you to spend time on marketing and promoting your business. You should schedule time in each day to follow up, promote, and market your business. It cannot grow by itself.

WHICH ADVERTISING MEDIA SHOULD YOU USE?

Finding the advertising media that works best for you is going to be a difficult task, involving a certain degree of trial and error. You will have to test the market by trying different methods and monitoring the responses. When customers call, or walk into your store, always find time to ask them, "Where did you hear about us?" Make sure you have a sheet of paper with a heading for the various forms of advertising, and mark their response down under the applicable heading. Now your advertising results are being monitored.

When you start your advertising campaign, study each medium carefully and take the time to monitor your results. Sign up for just one issue in a magazine, one week of radio air time, or two days in the local newspaper. Browse through the Yellow Pages and study your competitors' advertising techniques. If most have placed a large advertisement, then obviously the Yellow Pages are working well for them.

By the same token, a smaller advertisement can work just as well if you are using other methods of promotion. Your clients need to find you, but you don't need horrendous advertising bills tied into annual contracts. Place an advertisement that you can afford; don't deplete your entire budget. Your advertising costs will be billed with your monthly telephone account. Compare the monthly cost to the overall response.

The most successful businesses not only take advantage of the most obvious form of advertising, such as directories, they also create a demand and subsequent need in the consumer for their products through effective advertising and promotional campaigns. Listed below are various forms of advertising and promotional media and their benefits.

1. Point-of-purchase material

Posters, banners, table tents, brochures, displays, balloons, and in-store coupons displayed next to your product are all point-of-purchase materials that can really make a difference to your product's visibility. Take advantage of the audience that walks by your service or product and make that product stand out from the rest. How many times have you impulsively grabbed a product at the checkout or in the aisles because it was prominently displayed?

If you are painting a house, place a sign telling the neighbours which quality company this neighbour chose. This is similar in concept to point-of-purchase material, but is directed more to service-oriented businesses. Your sign may even go a step further and contain a brochure holder, so passers-by can take a promotional brochure home with them.

2. Radio

Radio advertising is usually recommended for advertising highly consumable items and to establish consumer awareness. If you don't have a large inventory, several outlets, or fast selling items such as hamburgers, audio or computer equipment, then printed material will most likely be the medium you should use to relay your message to the consumer. If you can afford radio air time, combine it with printed media. Radio advertising used by itself will not generate business as it is too short-lived to leave a lasting impression on the consumer. You have to back it up with other promotional methods.

3. Television

Television commercials are out of the question for the average new entrepreneur. It takes a very large budget to pay for enough frequency to make people aware of your business. Unless you have a highly consumable item which is readily available at many outlets, or you are offering a high volume mail-order product, you will not generate enough business volume to cover your costs.

4. Transit advertising

If you live in a city or town that has an active bus or train service, you may want to consider transit advertising. The advertisements placed on the back or side of a bus are extremely visible. If you have sat behind a bus in traffic, you have probably read many of them. Smaller advertisements placed inside a train or bus are effective too—the bored and tired commuters often have nothing better to read. You can also place large advertisements on the back of bus seats or inside bus shelters. If you advertise this way, be sure your product or service will appeal to the general public in your geographical area.

5. The Internet

Many books have been written—and are currently being written—about marketing on the Internet, so the wheel is not going to be reinvented here. It should go without saying however, that the most competitive businesses will keep up with technology and be accessible via e-mail and the Internet. Many new businesses rely solely on the Internet for their sales, with new cyberspace businesses starting every day.

For a local business that deals specifically with a local market, Internet accessibility could enhance business, particularly ones such as restaurants or florists, where orders could be placed over the Internet. It is another form of media exposure to those consumers who love playing with their keyboards or who don't have time in their busy day to pick up the phone.

A business that has services or products appealing to provincial, national, or international consumers would be well advised to consider a Web page. Many tourist resorts and bed and breakfast accommodations have solicited international business from their Web pages. If you specialize in any type of product, for example, collector dolls or other similar items, a Web page and ordering system based out of the Internet will be an asset to the business.

Because results are still unknown and cyberspace is evolving so rapidly, you may want to be conservative in the amount of money spent on a Web page, then monitor the results closely. If orders start coming in, you can expand the page and perhaps make it more powerful. As with most things, you pay for what you get. A professional Web page can range from $1,000 to $5,000, depending on its size and features.

Surfers are generally looking for specific information, turning to the Internet to research a subject and increase their knowledge. The businesses that are getting more visits to their sites are those offering information in their area of expertise. For example, a business consultant could prepare information similar to seminar handouts, covering topics of interest, such as " Ten Hot Tips For Saving On Your Taxes."

If you do have a Web page, splash you e-mail and Web page address on every piece of paper, advertising, business card and brochure. Another tip for local businesses, such as a truck accessory company, is to put a small classified in a "buy and sell" newspaper, suggesting readers visit your Web site. On-line consumers will make a point of visiting your site before purchasing products.

Depending on the amount of time you have to spend on advertising through the Internet, you could think about making yourself a cyberspace expert with these informational services. You never know where it may lead. You have three choices with advertising on the Internet: you can do nothing, you can put up a Web page and update it periodically, or you can go all out and spend time finding creative ways to market your business using a variety of Web techniques. The choice can only be yours.

6. Specials

Offering specials is another form of advertising. Where possible, calculate your retail prices so you can offer regular specials. People love a deal and can't resist words like "sale," "special," "70 percent off," or "inventory clearance." Offering to pay the GST/HST for the first 20 customers can be effective, particularly on high-priced items. Specials are necessary to clear out slow-moving inventory, maintain cash flow, and to bring new customers to your store.

7. Mix and match

You will always receive more response from one source of advertising than another. You have probably been told that the more often your advertising is used, the more effective it becomes, or that your first advertisement may not work for you, and don't expect too much from the first-time run.

The truth is, every advertisement should work for you if it is designed and priced properly. The more times it is used, the more effective the results. Your response rate should increase gradually, so don't expect the telephone to be ringing off the hook after the third advertisement.

Rather than waiting three months to see your advertising work for you, use the same strategy, only in shorter time periods. You will make profits with a strategic advertising plan. Two or three marketing techniques, combined in the same time period, will make more money faster for you and with fewer losses. Remember, you cannot afford to wait for your market group to get to know you. You must make your business known in a relatively short time period.

Place an advertisement for consumer awareness and informational purposes in a medium such as a magazine, radio, or both. Then send out a flyer or coupon with an advertising envelope or coupon book. Your magazine and radio advertising is not expected to draw people in to call you, whereas your coupon or flyer will. Your market is now surrounded by the information you have imparted. You are informing the public of the benefits of your product or service with one form of advertising, and asking them to come in with another. Both forms of advertising should be carried out within the same time frame.

You do not have to deplete your advertising budget to do this. If you are buying radio time, then either buy the same day, all day, every week using the same time slot, or use the same time slot every day on the same days every week. Your magazine and coupon advertising may only be black and red instead of full colour. Full colour for your product or service may not be necessary, unless you are selling something very colourful. So save your money and buy a little at a time.

PROMOTING YOUR BUSINESS ON A SHOESTRING BUDGET

There are so many advertising media open to you it is difficult to know which will work best for your business. You will be bombarded by advertisers vying for your business, and each one will seem to have their own merits. Try to identify which methods are the most effective at the minimum cost. The aim is to get your name known as quickly as possible without depleting your bank account. This can happen quickly if you don't set up an advertising budget. As a rule of thumb, once you are established, you should not spend more than 4 percent to 5 percent of your gross sales a month on advertising. Your start-up advertising budget will be higher. Not all advertising will work effectively for your business. Here is a list of some suggested advertising and the approximate cost if you are on a shoestring budget.

1. Newspaper advertising

It pays to keep your name in the local community paper, and the classified section is a good place to start. The rates are cheaper than display advertisements, and the longer you run the advertisement, the cheaper your rate becomes. A three-line ad for a ten week period in a local paper will cost between $7 and $10 an insertion. A one-inch display column will cost between $30 and $40. Some newspapers have special display pages, such as professional listings or home improvement pages, and will offer you a cheaper rate if you advertise for a 12 week period or longer.

Avoid large advertisements; they cost hundreds of dollars and people tend not to read their local paper thoroughly. Some are so loaded with junk mail and flyers that the consumer shakes the flyers out in order to find the paper. Consumers are on media-overload and have no time to read all this advertising. You may receive only one or two calls from your expensive display. For example, a women's network with sponsored advertising places a quarter page advertisement in the local paper once a month. Over a period of eight months, it was surprising to find out how many women stated that they have never even noticed the advertisement, which is valued at over $400 per insertion.

Many community newspapers are becoming aware of the limited budgets of small businesses and are changing their advertisements accordingly. If you are home-based, many papers are now carrying home-based small display advertisements, which are quite cheap. If you are advertising in a newspaper, design your advertisement with a coupon which has a time limit, so you can monitor the results through the coupons received.

2. Coupon books

Coupon books give your product or service a longer shelf (or drawer) life. The recent cost of a coupon book distributed to 30,000 homes was $450 plus GST. This works out to 1.5 cents a copy. The books are usually delivered with household mail or the local newspaper. This can be an extremely effective and cheap method of distribution.

Once again, you are targeting a mass market. You may receive only a few phone calls, because you have to be reaching the consumer at the right time, with the right product, at a time when they can afford it, and have time to shop. Don't use coupon books for cheaply priced, small items, unless you offer a service such as dry cleaning where usually a page of specials are offered. They are better used for a more expensive service, such as vehicle or household repairs. Time limitations are important to monitor your response to this type of advertising. Don't forget to include a clip-out coupon so you know where your customers are coming from.

3. Flyers

Flyers can solicit business, but the returns are lower than you would expect. As with all advertising, your flyer will be circulated to hundreds or thousands of people along with other junk mail. You should think about seasonal peaks and ebbs. Any form of advertising taking place in August will have an extremely low return unless your product is associated with summer leisure. Most of the country is on vacation, either physically or mentally, and the household coffers are empty afterwards as the children go back to school. For example, a flyer circulation of 1,300 sent out during August had a response rate of only three calls, a return of only 0.23 percent. A coupon book run of 30,000 had a response rate of only five calls, or 0.02 percent.

Flyers can be designed on your computer and photocopied at the printer for about five to eight cents a copy for one colour. Don't distribute them indiscriminately–keep them for trade shows or distribute them to specific areas which you have identified as being potentially lucrative. If you have a product, offer, or event of local interest, try delivering one or two hundred around the neighbourhood and monitor the response.

4. Brochures and handouts

A professionally prepared brochure is invaluable for networking events, trade shows, mail-outs and promotions. Don't prepare your own. Find a good graphic artist to design an appealing layout. Keep lots of white space, and don't try to cram too much information into it. Your brochure is a teaser. It will give enough information, but the rest will be obtained when a potential client calls you. If you require an expensive coloured brochure, you may have to look at a large print run to make it cost-effective. But don't over-order, as businesses often change direction or address, and you don't want to be left with a pile of useless paper.

Take the time to prepare informational handouts. People love information. Make your handouts informative, without blatantly advertising your business. Handouts can be used at any networking event, trade show, or seminar, and they show you as being the expert in your field. If your business is garbage disposal, prepare some handouts on how to recycle garbage, or the effects of bacteria in household situations. If you have an accounting business, prepare information on home-based tax deductions, or a sheet of tax tips. The information on these handouts can also be used as topical pieces for your Web page.

5. Delivery of promotional material

Door-knocking is for the well-trained professional sales person who can handle regular rejection without getting a complex. You do get the advantage of talking to people, and the results can be effective, but it is extremely time-consuming. Local newspapers will offer a flyer delivery service. Circulation runs are broken down into areas, and there is usually a minimum delivery requirement of 2,000 flyers, although each newspaper will have its own minimum requirements. The approximate cost for this is $45 per 1,000, or 4.5 cents each. The flyers are delivered with a bunch of other junk mail, and yours may get overlooked in the pile.

Canada Post offers a flyer delivery service. If you use their premium rate, you pay approximately 10 cents per piece. Your flyer is delivered with the mail, and you can choose the days you require delivery. Canada Post aims to have all flyers delivered within three working days. If you are smart, you will pick the delivery days when the local paper with all its flyers is not delivered, preferably near the end of the week. People have more time to read their papers and mail at the end of the week and are more liable to call you on the weekend or first thing Monday morning.

6. Target marketing

If you are performing a residential service such as driveway-paving or tree-pruning, prepare a flyer on your computer, preferably one that will fit two to a page. Have it photocopied and cut to size. Deliver 50 to 100 flyers to homes close to where you will be working, noting on the flyer that "We are in your neighbourhood," or "Drive by 34534 Willow Drive and see us at work." Talk to as many people as you can while delivering the flyers. This is one of the most effective methods of promotion in residential areas. Neighbours tend to be curious. They also want what their neighbours have, particularly if it looks better than what they have. It's called "keeping up with the Joneses." This is an extremely cheap method of promotion, and if you keep the master copy in your computer, you just change the address as required.

7. Thank-you, Christmas, birthday, and discount cards

If you perform residential services, return to your clients with a little thank you—perhaps a plant or something for them to remember you by. Offer a referral fee if they recommend you to friends and neighbours. If any of your clients refer other clients to you, take the time to send them a thank-you card. Your efforts will be remembered.

If you have a retail outlet, display forms near the cash register for customers' names and addresses for your birthday club. Send your customers a discount coupon to be used during their birthday month, along with a birthday card. This is a very effective method of promoting sales. People love to receive these cards, and will often return to your store before their month is over to buy something with their discount coupon.

Some stores offer a discount club, where they will supply the customer with a small card. Each time the customer purchases an item over a certain value, they punch or stamp the card. After 10 visits, the customer receives a free item or a discount off their next purchase. Dry cleaners, bookstores, photo developing stores, and coffee houses often do this. People use these cards even though they clutter billfolds or wallets because they are an incentive to save money.

Where possible, get your customers' names and addresses, phone numbers, and postal codes. Send them a Christmas card and personally sign it. People appreciate being remembered. It will also remind them who you are and that you cared enough to go that one step further. I look forward to a Christmas card each year from the local Cantonese restaurant and the family real estate agent. Many small businesses use newsletters to keep in touch with their customers, and if there is a special event happening, you can prepare a mail-out to clients.

8. Word-of-mouth advertising

You will no doubt do your very best to please your customers, so if you ask your customers politely to spread the good word for you, they will. Give each two or three business cards or brochures. As you sow you shall reap. Word-of-mouth advertising spreads twice as fast as conventional advertising methods. Do you want your customers to keep this wonderful service a secret, known only to themselves? Many businesses have built a solid client base using the referral method, which is very cheap and effective. Don't forget to thank any customer who has passed on a referral.

This is just a small chip off the advertising block. Most of the above suggestions involve little cash outlay but take some time. They are the special, personal touches which clients like and remember—and often tell others about. There are many more ways to promote your business, and you should read some marketing books for some fresh and innovative ideas or talk to a professional marketing consultant. Statistics are available, and they can show you proven methods which apply to your particular type of business. Always be aware of and note what attracts you to a business, and analyze their marketing methods. Remember, you need to use a mix of all the above methods to effectively promote your business.

Chapter 11

How do you organize your accounting and paperwork?

She filed bills under "B" and letters under "L,"
Where the rest of it went, who can really tell?

No doubt about it, you have to be organized to keep on top of your paperwork. As soon as you start a business, you will receive a mountain of correspondence from various federal and provincial agencies and an assortment of advertising mail which may or may not be of value to you. If you organize your office properly from the beginning, the paperwork won't bog you down. Too many people let their papers pile up, leaving mail unopened for days and weeks at a time. Finally, they go through it all in a hurry without paying attention to what they read. That sloppy method can lead to missing important information. Organization is an essential ingredient to a successful business operation.

YOUR 30-SECOND FILING CABINET

First you will need a four-drawer filing cabinet. Allow lots of room for files, because the more crowded your files become, the less organized you will be. Buy suspension frames for each drawer, and legal-sized hanging files and file folders. Add tabs to the file folders for visibility. Use different coloured file folders and hanging files for easy identification. The files you will use the most should be put into the top drawer. Now establish a hanging file and file folder for the following papers:

1. Incorporation papers and related correspondence

2. GST/HST file: one folder for remittances and one for information pamphlets

3. Revenue Canada payroll file: one for payroll schedules, one for payroll records

4. Provincial sales tax file for remittances and information

5. Workers' compensation file

6. Files for other licensing agencies

7. Telephone contract file for cellular and business line contracts

8. Accounts to be paid file for all unpaid accounts. Organize alphabetically

9. Paid accounts files: one for each regular supplier, such as hydro, telephone, and two for miscellaneous accounts

10. Bank account file for details of bank account and Visa merchant documents

11. Cheque and deposit book file: keep spare cheques in here as well

12. Bank statement file for reconciled bank statements and cancelled cheques

13. Cash expense file for expenses you paid personally

14. Petty cash file for petty cash receipts

15. Sales invoice file for completed sales invoices or invoice books, but use a three-ring binder for copious amounts of invoices

16. Posting file for all work ready to be entered into the accounting records

17. Advertising file for advertising information and rates

18. Asset file for purchases exceeding $200: file invoices here as an asset register

19. Vehicle file for information and bills relevant to the business vehicle

20. Expense report file for completed expense reports and spare expense sheets

21. Quotation file for quotations on work you have pending

22. Quotation file for quotations on purchases you make

23. Financial file for monthly accounting papers and year-end documents

24. Job costing file for completed job costings

25. Correspondence files for letters sent to clients

26. Business start-up costs file

27. Insurance file for all policies

28. Contacts and follow-up file

You may add to this list, as each business has different requirements, but this system will keep you well organized. In the top drawer, put files with which you will work regularly, such as accounts to be paid, paid accounts, invoices, payroll, provincial taxes, workers' compensation, and banking. One drawer down put the business information you use less often. Two drawers down: correspondence, advertising, completed invoices, and papers used infrequently.

Documents can be filed in three different ways:

1. Numerically: Sales invoices only. Always put the latest number to the front, so they are filed in historical order. This should be done after the invoices are posted (entered) to your books.

2. Alphabetically: Paid account files. For each supplier, put the last paid invoice to the front. The most recent purchases are at your finger-tips in monthly order.

3. Chronologically: All other files. File the latest correspondence in front.

This efficient filing system lets you find any paper in 30 seconds or less. Papers do not get lost, and at year-end, after your financial statement has been completed, you can remove the last 12 months' paperwork from each file, put it in a storage box, and reuse the files for another year. However, keep important information, such as incorporation papers or asset purchases. This is a good opportunity to sift through each file and discard papers you no longer need, such as advertising, old quotations, and completed correspondence. Keep your accounting records for seven years.

HOW DO YOU ORGANIZE YOUR PAPERWORK?

1. Each day

As soon as your mail arrives, open it. Make piles for accounts to be paid, cheques to be deposited, government and provincial mail, advertising, and other important items. Tackle one pile at a time. Check supplier accounts for correct pricing. Make a note in your day-timer or calendar of the payment date, and file them away in your accounts-to-be-paid file.

Match each cheque to be deposited with an invoice number, making sure the full amount has been paid. Make a note of any discounts taken, short payments, and the invoice number being paid. Put the cheques in your deposit book, and prepare to write up the deposit. Read all the government correspondence, such as your payroll, GST/HST or provincial tax remittances, noting when their payment is due, and file them. Scan your advertising mail and file it either in your advertising file or the recycling bin. Attend to the important things at once, or you will probably forget.

2. Each week

The key to keeping on top of the mountains of paperwork is to dispense with it as soon as possible. Keeping a weekly routine is necessary to achieving this goal. If you are a service industry, or bill clients during the month, prepare your billings at the end of the week. Then put a copy of the invoice in your posting file for entering to your books.

Review and pay your bills regularly. When you pay a supplier, take out the accounts-to-be-paid file, remove those you need to pay, write the cheque (writing the GST amount on your cheque stub), write the cheque number, date, and amount paid across the invoice. This gives you a cross-reference in case there is a dispute over payment. File the account. If you have time, subtract the GST from the cheque amount, and write this sum on your cheque stub with a short description of the type of expense (e.g., office supplies). This will save your bookkeeper time later, and the expense will be allocated to the right account.

Empty your wallet or purse at least once a week, extracting the cash receipts for gasoline, lunches, stamps, and miscellaneous supplies. Put them into your posting file, clipped together. Do the same if you run a petty cash float. Balance the float at least once a week, stapling all the expenses together, with a piece of paper stapled on top, detailing the amount, the cheque number, and the date. If receipts are not clear, write on them what they are for. Put this into your posting file. Keep credit card receipts in a separate file so they can be matched to the statement later.

3. Each month

After the month is completed, go to your posting file and sort through it, putting the papers into the following order for either yourself or your bookkeeper. If your bookkeeper does the accounting more regularly, you have the pleasure of performing this task regularly.

1. Sales invoices: Batch the sales invoices numerically, starting with the oldest invoice. Find any missing invoice numbers. Attach a tape showing the addition of the completed invoices for the month. They are now ready to be entered in the books and you know how much you billed for the month.

2. Cheque stubs: Remove the month's cheque stubs from your binder and carry your balance forward to the next cheque. Clip the stubs together and check each one, making sure each stub is clearly marked with the type of expense and the GST amount. Fill in any missing information and put them into the posting file.

3. Cash expenses: Sort your cash expenses into categories, such as gasoline and stationery. Staple them together with a tape of each total and mark them cash-out-of-pocket expenses. They will be entered in your books.

4. Bank deposits: If you can order a bank deposit book in triplicate, take each daily deposit from the book, staple them together in date order, and put them into the posting file. If you enter from your deposit book, list the deposits for the month on a tape and staple this total to the last deposit for the month.

5. Miscellaneous: Anything else of importance for the bookkeeper should be noted in the posting file.

6. Credit card statements: If you use your credit cards for personal and business expenses, go through each statement when it arrives, using a high-lighter to mark the business expenses. Take your pile of credit card receipts and the supplier's invoice and attach them to the statement in the order the charges appear. Your bookkeeper cannot work just from a statement; for audit purposes, each charge must have an accompanying invoice. A common mistake made is to include only the credit card voucher. If you don't attach the invoice from the purchase, how can your bookkeeper, or you, know the type of expense, and the taxes paid?

4. Start a priority list

The bain of most self-employed people's existence is motivation and organization. Which priority should you prioritize first? Sometimes, it is simply overwhelming and you feel lost at sea. If being organized is not your strong point, try using the priority list system. Take an eight-column pad and list all the things to do on the left-hand side. Across the top, make columns for the deadline date, A+, A, B, and C priorities. Decide on a deadline date for each task, then go down your list and allocate a checkmark to note the priority for each job. Next, start working on the A+ priorities, starting at the earliest deadline date, crossing them off the list with a highlighter when the job is completed. Sample #10 shows an example of such a priority list.

SAMPLE #10

WEEKLY PRIORITY LIST

THINGS TO DO: WEEKENDING JUNE 15, XXXX					
THINGS TO DO	DEADLINE	A+	A	B	C
Bill clients	June 3	✔			
Pay monthly accounts	June 7	✔			
Order business cards	June 15			✔	
Write thank-you cards	June 10		✔		
Clean filing cabinet	June 30				✔
Follow-up phone calls	June 4	✔			
Quotation for Mrs. Baxter	June 9		✔		

Review the list each week or two and add new priorities. You will be surprised just how many C priorities can be simply crossed off without any action being taken. Rewrite the list, reviewing the A, B and C priorities, and move them to a new column where required. There is a certain amount of satisfaction at seeing work crossed off the list, which is also a constant reminder not to forget anything important. This efficient system really works if you use it.

WHICH ACCOUNTING SYSTEM SHOULD YOU USE?

Every business has varying accounting requirements depending on its size and the volume of transactions. A small, one-person business may use one journal for all the monthly accounting. Once your business starts generating more paperwork, think about using a software program. It's a good exercise for a small business to start with a manual system, so that the basic concept of accounting is well ingrained before changing to a computerized system. Any changeover should be done with the help of your accountant to make a smoother transition.

Accounting is the weakest area in most small businesses. All too often, I am presented with shoe-boxes crammed with papers one week before the April tax deadline. The owners don't have a clue where their businesses stand financially. Accounting has also arrived in Ziplock bags, fruit boxes, and grocery bags (both paper and plastic). The most repulsive ever presented was a well-used, gravy-stained, family-sized, cardboard fried chicken tub, complete with dried coleslaw on the bottom. This filing method says a great deal about the owner.

Late arrivals like this usually create an income tax problem, particularly for sole proprietors who pay tax on the net profit of the business. A sudden tax bill of many thousands of dollars, coupled with late GST/ HST payments, soon puts them in deep financial waters. Some people never learn and just get deeper and deeper into the financial hole, until bankruptcy is the only alternative.

Others have a mental barrier about using their accountant for advice. They also have a mental block about paying their bills on time. Your accountant deserves respect; he or she has your best interest at heart. Spend some money on learning how to run your accounting system and keeping it up to date—the future of your business relies heavily on you monitoring your progress through the accounting records.

WHAT ACCOUNTING RECORDS DO YOU NEED?

Without accurate information, you are floating at sea. There are many pieces which make your accounting puzzle fit together. Whether you use a manual or a computer system, a full set of accounting books consists of the following:

1. **Sales journal**: records sales and taxes

2. **Cash receipts journal**: records all money coming into the business

3. **Cheque register (or synoptic journal)**: records cheques written and charges against your bank statement

4. **Cash expenses journal**: records out-of-pocket and petty cash expenses

5. **Accounts payable journal**: records unpaid supplier accounts

6. **General journal**: records adjustments made to your books, usually made by your accountant

7. **General ledger**: combines the above books, ready for the preparation of the financial statement

8. **Trial balance**: a listing of your financial accounts to show that the books balance

9. **Financial statements**: A compilation of all of the above which shows the financial situation of the business

If you opt for a manual system, you need to use the first seven journals, which for small business, can be combined into one simple book. A computerized accounting system combines all the above functions into one program, eliminating the need for column additions, cross-additions, and posting the first six journals to the general ledger, which then has to have each page totalled and cross-balanced.

A computer program will only take a pile of numbers and put them where you tell it to. If you enter a wrong account number, the information will go to the wrong place, and your financial information will be wrong. The importance of organized and controlled paperwork cannot be stressed enough. The lack of it causes the demise of many businesses.

Even data entry takes meticulous manual preparation. Entries should be posted in batches, which at month-end are balanced to an accounting control. Accounting means that every figure has to be entered in the books twice. That is how the term double-entry bookkeeping saw the light. One entry acts as a control—either to the bank account, accounts receivable or payable records—the other is descriptive and tells you what the amount is for.

What is a chart of accounts?

A chart of accounts is a directory of your business financial accounts. Each account is allocated a number, and the chart is listed in the order of the financial statement accounts. Each business will have a slightly different chart of accounts designed to give you the information you require from your business. Listed here is the chart of accounts for Jason's Garden Service. The following pages show Jason's financial accounts and accounting journals with explanations to help you organize your own system. (See samples #11, #12, #13, #14, #15, and #16).

SAMPLE #11

CHART OF ACCOUNTS: JASON'S GARDEN SERVICE

Current assets:

1000 Bank account
1020 Accounts receivable
1030 Inventory
1040 Prepaid expenses

Fixed assets:

1200 Automotive equipment
1220 Office equipment
1230 Office furniture

Income:

4000 Sales - supplies
4010 Sales, delivery
4020 Other income

Expenses:

5000 Accounting fees
5010 Advertising
5020 Bank charges
5030 Discounts
5040 Fees, licences & dues
5050 Insurance
5060 Loan interest

Current liabilities:

2000 Accounts payable
2010 Provincial tax payable
2020 GST/HST collected
2030 GST/HST paid
2040 Bank loan payable
2050 Wages payable
2100 Loan payable - R.Davies

Equity:

3000 Owner's capital
3010 Owner's draws
3030 Retained earnings (profit)

Cost of sales:

4500 Material purchases
4510 Truck fuel
4520 Truck repairs
4530 Truck insurance
4540 Driver's wages

5080 Office supplies & printing
5090 Promotion–meals
5100 Rent & property taxes
5120 Telephone and cellular
5130 Travel & accommodation
5140 Utilities
5150 Workers' compensation

1. The sales journal (monthly sales invoices)

A sales journal records every invoice or all cash charged to your customers each month. It is a valuable source of sales information used to compile your accounts receivable records. Sales information should be organized so it can give you informative figures.

Jason divided his sales into different categories such as bark mulch, gravel, topsoil, sand, and delivery charges. Every month his sales journal gives him a dollar value of products sold (see sample #12). This information will help when he re-orders supplies and will indicate seasonal trends. Provincial taxes and the GST are recorded at the same time.

SAMPLE #12

SALES JOURNAL: JASON'S GARDEN SERVICE

Sales Journal: September XXXX										
DATE	NAME	INV. **#**	TOTAL **Dr +**	SAND **Cr -**	MULCH **Cr -**	SOIL **Cr -**	GRAVEL **Cr -**	DEL. **Cr -**	PST **Cr -**	GST **Cr-**
09/01	J.Smith	2346	171.00	35.00	35.00	50.00		30.00	10.50	10.50
09/03	B.Jones	2347	969.00	150.00	200.00	200.00	200.00	100.00	59.50	59.50
09/15	I.Reid	2348	513.00				400.00	50.00	31.50	31.50
09/27	S.Bull	2349	214.00			165.00		35.00	7.00	7.00
TOTAL			**1,867.00**	**185.00**	**235.00**	**415.00**	**600.00**	**215.00**	**108.50**	**108.50**
			=	+	+	+	+	+	+	+

Jason can now look at his monthly sales and see which products sold well. His taxes are calculated, and he completes his provincial sales tax return and files it on time. He files his GST quarterly and has the three months' sales figures ready for when the return is due.

The *Dr+ and Cr -* signs under the headings denote debit and credit. When the columns are added across the page, the total of the debits should equal credits. If you calculate the totals on an adding machine tape, the balance will be zero. The plus + and minus - signs are there to help those among you who do not understand debits and credits. The accounting rule is this: add all debits and subtract all credits to balance your books.

Jason now can convert sales figures into percentages. This is a common accounting practice. It makes for easier costing and budget preparation. For example, gravel is 36.4 percent of his total sales, before tax. You can calculate your percentages quite easily using this formula:

Gravel sales   <u>600.00</u> x 100 (%)

Total sales   1,650.00 = 36.4%

2. The cash receipts journal (daily bank deposits)

Your cash receipts journal records everything deposited to your bank account while keeping a record of the money's origin. Not all money deposited is from sales. If you maintain more than one bank account, enter each bank account separately each month, either on another page or underneath the first completed one. Never enter two bank accounts together—your books will be a nightmare to correct! The key to an accurate cash receipts journal is to keep your bank deposits clearly itemized. Before making a bank deposit follow these steps:

1. Be sure that each cheque is matched to a paid invoice number and that all discounts or short-payments are noted. (You should have made these notes when sorting the mail.)

2. Put the cheques in alphabetical order and enter each one in the deposit book. Next to the cheque, or on the page opposite your deposit, write the invoice number being paid. If cash is deposited, write down the invoices being paid.

3. If other funds are deposited—such as capital from owners, loans, or rebates on expenses, note in your deposit book from where the money came and what it is for. All entries in your deposit book should be identified in detail.

The next step is to enter each daily deposit in the cash receipts journal (see Sample #13):

1. Date: Always put the date of the bank deposit in this column.

2. Invoice No: Note the individual invoice numbers being paid with each cheque.

3. Total Bank: Put the total of the daily bank deposit in this column. It should equal the total of each cheque listed in "bank in" column.

4. Bank In: A line-by-line breakdown of each cheque which equals the "total bank" column

5. Discount: Show the amount of discount taken in this column. The total of the cheques deposited, plus the discount, should equal the total of the invoice being paid.

6. Accounts receivable: The total of the invoice being paid, including any allowable discounts taken by the customer.

7. Account No: The account number from the chart of accounts, used to identify any other type of bank deposit.

8. Amount: This column records the amount of that deposit.

9. Description: Make a note here of where the money came from.

SAMPLE #13

CASH RECEIPTS JOURNAL: JASON'S GARDEN SERVICE

Cash Receipts Journal: September XXXX

DATE	NAME	INV. #	TOTAL BANK	BANK IN Dr +	DISC- Dr +	A/REC. Cr -	A/C #	AMT Cr -	DESCR.
09/07	J. Smith	2346		167.58	3.42	71.00			
09/07	B.Jones	2347		949.62	19.38	969.00			
09/07	S.Swan	2333	1,667.20	550.00		550.00			
09/10	J.Davies		1,000.00	1,000.00			(3000)	1,000.00	Capital
09/15	I.Reid	2348		513.00		513.00			
09/15	R.Davies		2,513.00	2,000.00			(2100)	2,000.00	Loan
09/27	S.Ball	2349		209.72	4.28	214.00			
09/27	J.Toms	2327	539.72	330.00		330.00			
TOTALS:			**5,719.92**	**5,719.92**	**27.08**	**2,747.00**		**3,000.00**	
			=	=	+	=		+	
						-		-	

Jason's cash receipt journal is now completed for the month. The book should not be closed off until the bank statement is received and each daily deposit in the "total bank" column is checked against the bank statement. Sometimes you can make mistakes in your additions, or the bank will issue you a credit memo which must be entered in your cash receipts journal. You may receive interest from your account, and that too should be entered.

3. The cash disbursements journal (cheques written)

The cash disbursements journal is probably the one you will use the most. This book will record each cheque, including all monthly payments you may have automatically deducted from your bank account, such as loan or car insurance, bank charges, and any other money the bank decides to deduct from your account. If you don't record a cheque, your books won't reconcile.

Your cheque stubs are, of course, well itemized with the total expense, the GST and the actual expense amount net of GST. If you are using a computerized accounting system, all cheques should be added on a tape at month-end, the bank reconciled, then each cheque entered in the accounting system. The cheque stub should have the correct account number from the chart of accounts noted on it. When everything is entered, the accounting program's bank balance should match your manual reconciliation.

In a manual system, each cheque is entered in the cash disbursements journal and the bank reconciliation is completed at month-end using the cash receipts and cash disbursements journal. A 20-column book is ample. The columns should be set out according to the expenses you use most every month. Those you incur infrequently can be entered into the miscellaneous column with a short description of the expense. Jason's main expenses are the purchase of materials, GST, truck costs, and wages. Some of his expense columns are set out here as shown in Sample #14.

SAMPLE #14

CASH DISBURSEMENTS JOURNAL: JASON'S GARDEN SERVICE

Cash Disbursements Journal: September XXXX

DATE	NAME	C/NO	BANK OUT(Cr)	GST Dr.	MATERIAL Dr.	WAGES Dr.	TRUCK Dr.	DRAW Dr.	MISC Dr.
09/01	Leasit Co.	024	749.00	49.00					700.00 Rent
09/01	FuelUp	025	995.10	65.10			930.00		
09/03	Office Co.	026	69.55	4.55					65.00 Office
09/03	Gravelpit	027	856.00	56.00	800.00				
09/08	Sandpile	028	428.00	28.00	400.00				
09/15	S.Jones	029	525.00			525.00			
09/15	D.Spence	030	650.00			650.00			
09/15	Rev.Can.	031	730.00			730.00			
09/15	Min.Finan	032	350.00						350.00 S/Tax
09/27	SupplyCo	033	1125.00	73.60	1,051.40				
09/30	J.Davies	034	500.00					500.00	
09/30	S.Jones	035	525.00			525.00			
09/30	D.Spence	036	600.00			600.00			
09/30	Loan	—	450.00						450.00 B/loan
09/30	Charges	—	35.00						35.00 S/chges
TOTALS:			8,587.65 =	276.25 +	2,251.40 +	3,030.00 +	930.00 +	500.00 +	1,600.00 +

4. Bank reconciliation (balancing the bank account each month)

Balancing your bank account monthly should be a number one priority, as it's the main control for your bookkeeping. It's too easy to miss entries, transpose figures, or forget an automatic deduction from the bank account. A reconciliation assures you that what you have written in your cash receipts journal and cash disbursement journal balances to your bank statement: all your entries are correct. It does not mean you have allocated them to the right expense column, but at least your bank columns are correct.

When your bank statement arrives for the previous month, make sure that your books are ready for month-end close-off by performing the following checks:

1. All cheques should be written in numerical order.

2. Voided cheques should have the number recorded and marked "Void".

3. Make sure each expense is entered in the correct column.

4. Do not close off either book until the bank is reconciled.

5. Make sure all deposits are entered.

Next, take your cash receipts journal and check each daily deposit total against the bank statement using a check mark. Correct any wrong deposits and enter any deposits or bank credit memos you have missed. Total your bank deposits for the month, making sure your total agrees with the bank statement deposits.

Change to your cash disbursements journal and sort the cancelled cheques from your bank statement according to their numerical order. Then read down the bank statement "debit" column, checking off each cheque on your statement to your cash disbursements journal. Circle those entries on your bank statement not in your journal—such as service charges, loan payments, and NSF cheques—and enter these as well. Mark cheques entered in your journal but not yet shown on the statement, with a "U/P" (unpresented) for your reconciliation. Then total the "bank out" column for the month.

Now it's time to prepare your reconciliation. Jason's reconciliation is shown in Sample #15.

SAMPLE #15

BANK RECONCILIATION: JASON'S GARDEN SERVICE

Bank Reconciliation: September 30, XXXX	
1. Balance end of August:	4,296.53
2. September deposits from cash receipts journal:	5,718.92
	10,015.45
3. September cheques from disbursements journal:	(8,587.65)
4. Balance September 30: (per Jason's books)	**$ 1,427.80**
5. Bank statement balance September 30:	3,677.80
Less unpresented cheques: 033	(1,255.00)
035	(525.00)
036	(600.00)
6. **Balance as per bank statement:**	**$ 1,427.80**

Correct the balance in your cheque book if it differs from your reconciliation. If one of the unpresented cheques is not listed on the bank statement the following month, carry it forward on your reconciliation as unpresented, and phone the recipient. If the cheque has not been received, put a stop payment on it and issue another one. Reverse the old cheque out of your books by entering it in parentheses ($600.00) across the page, and deduct this amount from your monthly totals.

5. Petty cash and out-of-pocket expenses

One journal can record both your petty cash expenses and those out of your pocket. Don't forget to keep every receipt and record the expense. The journal is set up similar to the cash disbursements journal: the expense columns are set up to suit your business. Jason kept a petty-cash float and spent some of his own money on business expenses (see sample #16).

SAMPLE #16

PETTY CASH JOURNAL: JASON'S GARDEN SERVICE

Petty Cash Journal: September 30, XXXX

DATE	PAID TO	PETTY CASH Cr -	CAPITAL IN Cr -	GST PAID Dr+	OFFICE Dr+	MATERIAL Dr +	GAS Dr .+	OTHER Dr.+
09/02	Gasup	53.50		3.50			50.00	
09/04	Office World		48.15	3.15	45.00			
09/07	Harry's Place		26.75	1.75				25.00 Bus.Lunch
09/09	Haulit	32.10		2.10				30.00 Delivery
09/11	Rockpit	64.20		4.20		60.00		
09/15	Drugmart	46.01		3.01	43.00			
09/18	Gasup		21.40	1.40			20.00	
09/22	Spark' N Shine	16.05		1.05				15.00 Windows
09/27	Telemart	37.45		2.45				35.00 Phone
TOTALS		249.31	96.30	22.61	88.00	60.00	70.00	105.00
		=	=	+	+	+	+	+

229

6. Other journals

If you maintain these four journals and reconcile your bank account each month, you will have most of your accounting information in excellent order. If you need a financial statement in a hurry, your accountant can prepare one from your figures. Most small businesses do not need an accounts payable journal. This system is used more by larger companies with a full accounts payable system.

The general journal records transactions not recorded in your other journals. Usually these entries are prepared by your accountant at year-end, or when a financial statement is needed. These types of transactions include information such as depreciation, prepaid expenses, the business portion of home office and vehicle costs, corporate taxes due, and inventory changes. Leave these details to your accountant—that's why you pay him or her.

The general ledger compiles information from all the separate journals in order of the account numbers in your chart of accounts. This contains all information needed to prepare your financial statement. Computer accounting packages enable accountants to take the journals you have prepared, enter the monthly totals and other details into their own program, and record the information in the general ledger. This is much quicker than spending hours, or even days, preparing the information manually.

A combined journal suits small businesses with minimum paperwork. Your accountant can easily set one up and show you how it works. The combined journal is called that because the sales, cash receipts, cash disbursements, and cash expenses can be combined into one book. If you need a detailed record of sales and expenses, one journal will not work. You need a separate sales journal, plus a combined journal, because journals with more than 20 columns are awkward to work with.

PREPARING FOR FINANCIAL STATEMENTS

Because a financial statement is a snapshot of your business taken at a particular date, there can be no loose ends. To make that picture as accurate as possible, here is the "things to do" list your accountant will give you:

1. Sales invoices and taxes collected for the period to be recorded

2. Bank deposits recorded and allocated correctly

3. A list of outstanding accounts receivable, balanced with your books

4. Cheques recorded and allocated to the correct expense column

5. Bank accounts reconciled

6. A list of unpaid accounts (accounts payable), and what they are for

7. Petty cash and proprietor's cash expenses

8. Statements from lenders of outstanding loan balances

9. Outstanding payroll taxes and other tax accounts balanced

10. Prepaid expenses (your accountant will check this for you)

11. A correct physical inventory figure

12. General journal entries you have made

Lucky for you the accountant will ask all the right questions to be sure that the information is on hand before a statement is prepared. However, a few areas could render your statements incorrect, and your accountant has no control over these. They are your responsibility. Here's why:

1. Your inventory could be costed incorrectly

2. Sales invoices may not have been entered

3. Late supplier accounts in the mail are not yet recorded

4. You have entered expenses to the wrong account

MISTAKES EVERY AMATEUR BOOKKEEPER MAKES

There are countless errors to make in bookkeeping, and I can attest to repeatedly making every one possible. After all, we are only human, no one is perfect, and we get tired and lose concentration. Let's face it, bookkeeping is a tedious chore. These are my excuses—you will create your own as you stumble through this new learning experience. Attending an evening class in bookkeeping will turn on some light bulbs and convert this foreign language into something less formidable.

When your books don't balance, its best to use a slow and methodical process of elimination to find the mistakes. Here are some of the most common bookkeeping mistakes:

1. A sales invoice, cheque or bank deposit is added incorrectly. Check the extensions across the page, line by line, to make sure every line cross-balances.

2. Figures are transposed. Here's a hot tip: If the unbalanced amount is divisible by 9, check all your figures until you find the transposed amount. For instance, if $325 is written as $352, the difference is 27. This is divisible by 9. Try this with any set of figures; it always works.

3. You have added a column incorrectly. Re-add all the columns.

4. You have added a credit balance, or subtracted a debit balance. Re-add your page totals.

5. You have carried your page totals forward to the next page incorrectly.

HOW DO YOU COST INVENTORY?

Counting and costing inventory is probably the worst part of owning a business. If you don't quite understand how to cost your inventory correctly, your financial figures will be way out. Inventory is just like having cash in the bank, only it is transformed into material items, so it is obviously important to take a correct physical count and cost every item at the right price.

Even if you maintain a theoretical inventory on your computer, once a year, this dastardly chore has to be performed. A retail company carrying a $150,000 inventory did not physically count it for many years. When it was finally done, the computer showed figures of $30,000 more than the physical count. The business immediately lost $30,000.

Here is the correct way to prepare your inventory:

1. Ask two people to count each item together. It's too easy to make a mistake doing this task alone.

2. Prepare inventory sheets listing each item, quantity, price, and the extension total.

3. Count off every item in the store or plant purchased for resale or manufacturing. Don't include fixed assets such as furniture or stationery.

4. If you manufacture or assemble goods and they are partially completed, estimate their value, including labour, at their current stage. These goods are called "work in progress."

5. Make a list of damaged products or slow-moving inventory that should be devalued and put the inventory out for sale on clearance or dispose of it. If it can't be disposed off, tell your accountant the value of these goods.

6. When pricing the items, price them at your cost, not retail price.

7. Extend all calculations and have a second person check your work, ensuring that all written calculations are very clear to read.

An error in inventory can make a vast difference to your profits. An example: A food manufacturing company used an expensive concentrated mix for their drink products. The bags weighed 45 pounds each. When the inventory was being extended, the weight was listed at 90.50 pounds at $27.45 a pound. The decimal point was misread due to sloppy writing. This was not noticed until the financial statements were prepared and the company showed a large loss. The correct weight was in fact 905.0 pounds. This made a difference of $22,358.02 to the profits. The financial statements had to be recalculated at the company's expense.

What is a "landed cost?"

A landed cost is the total cost of purchasing, assembling or manufacturing a product. You need to know this information for determining your selling prices and to monitor your gross profits and production costs. When you cost imported products, include all costs incurred to "land" the product. If you are importing parts to build garden umbrellas and have a stock of shafts complete with hardware, your costings should include the following calculations:

Umbrella shafts, 2 feet long	.90 each
Umbrella shafts, 3 feet long	1.30 each
Metal tapers	.50 each
Hinges	<u>.40 each</u>
	3.10 each
Duty on shafts	.35 each
Duty on hinges & tapers	.25 each
Freight on all components	<u>.45 each</u>
Landed cost:	**4.15 each**
Assembly	<u>1.30 each</u>
Completed cost of shaft:	**$ <u>5.45 each</u>**

HOW DO YOU RECORD VEHICLE EXPENSES?

Vehicles are an accountant's nightmare. Most proprietors use their personal vehicle for both business and personal use, getting in a mess when it comes to tax time. Recording vehicle expenses is done in several ways, depending on the status of the business. How your vehicle expenses are calculated will depend on these factors:

1. Whether your business is a proprietorship (or partnership)

2. If incorporated, whether the business owns the vehicle

3. If incorporated, whether you own the vehicle

1. A proprietorship, vehicle owned by you

You operate a small business and you use your vehicle for the business and for personal use. What do you do to track expenses? First, purchase an auto mileage log from the stationery store. Keep it in your vehicle and note the starting reading on your odometer (for example, 120,000 kms).

Every time you use the vehicle for any business-related trip, note the date, where you went, and the number of business-related kilometres. At the end of your business year, note the ending kilometres. During this period, be sure to keep all receipts related to the running costs of the vehicle. The expenses you can claim are:

• Gasoline

• Repairs and maintenance

• Insurance

• Loan interest (restricted)

• Leasing costs (restricted)

• Depreciation (restricted)

At year-end, your accountant will need to know the total of all these costs, and will prepare the following calculation:

Gasoline receipts for year	1,350
Repairs and maintenance	850
Insurance	1,220
Loan interest	730
Depreciation ($18,000 cost)	5,400
Total costs:	**$ 9,550**
Starting kilometres:	120,000
Ending	140,225
Total kilometres for year:	20,225
Business usage from log:	14,375 = 71.07%

Allowable claim: $ 9,550 x 71.07% = $6,787.18

Every receipt you lose means you will pay more tax. A $20 lost gas receipt could increase your taxes by $5. The same applies for business mileage not logged. Revenue Canada demands a log be kept for audit purposes or your vehicle claim could be denied. Keep it up to date religiously, whether going to the bank, the stationers, or the garage for a repair. It mounts up surprisingly quickly. Log every trip relevant to your business, including research and start-up travel.

2. An incorporated company owns the vehicle

If your incorporated company owns the vehicle, expenses are paid by the business. There are limitations to the amount of depreciation, loan interest, and leasing costs which can be claimed. Your accountant will give you these figures. Revenue Canada seems to have a dislike for people driving Mercedes-Benz cars and writing off all the costs against their business. Make the most of the depreciation allowance and be sensible in your vehicle selection.

3. An incorporated company, you own the vehicle

If you own a vehicle and use it for business in an incorporated company, a mileage allowance should be paid to you. The current rate is approximately 35 cents a kilometre. This allowance is designed to cover all vehicle running costs, including depreciation. You need to keep a log and submit a regular expense sheet to the company so you can be compensated for your expenses.

WHAT EXPENSES ARE TAX DEDUCTIBLE?

Most expenses incurred to start and operate a business are tax deductible. There are limits to some, and others are not allowable. As a guide, here is a list of the most common business expenses:

1. Research costs

All research costs including literature, vehicle expenses, training sessions, start-up kits, travel to and expenses related to out-of-town conferences and seminars, consultations with professionals, educational courses.

2. Start-up costs

Repairs to buildings, fees and licences; legal, accounting, business plan, loan application and financing fees; first month's rent, telephone line additions, printing and stationery, advertising costs, free samples, and promotions.

3. Operational costs

All costs involved in the manufacture or purchase of products for resale.

- Raw materials
- Freight
- Customs, duty, and brokerage fees
- Inventory purchases
- Equipment repairs and maintenance
- Wages to assemble or manufacture products
- Wastage or damaged inventory

4. Direct costs

Direct costs are those related directly to selling. These include:

- Sales wages and commissions
- Referral fees
- Displays and samples
- Delivery expenses
- Discounts, rebates, and coupons

5. Overhead costs

Overhead costs are those incurred in the day-to-day running of the business:

- Accounting, legal, consulting, and professional fees
- Advertising, marketing, and promotion
- Bad debts

- Bank and credit card service charges

- CPP and EI expense, extended health, and employee benefits

- Depreciation and amortization

- Fees, licences, and subscriptions

- Insurance *

- Interest on business loans

- Management salaries, bonuses, and dividends (if incorporated)

- Office supplies and all printing

- Promotion—business meals *

- Rent, property taxes, mortgage interest

- Repairs and maintenance to premises and equipment

- Security monitoring, sign rental

- Seminars, conferences, * and trade shows

- Sub contractors and casual labour *

- Telephone, pager, cellular phone, Internet, Web pages

- Theft *

- Travel and accommodation *

- Utilities

- Vehicle fuel, oil, repairs and maintenance, insurance

- Workers' compensation

Note: * These expenses are limited in the type of deductions available to you. Business insurance is fully deductible, but personal insurance and disability policies are not, unless your business is incorporated and the business is the benefactor of the policies. Business meals are only 50 percent deductible. You are allowed to attend two conferences a year, including travel costs.

Subcontract and casual labour is tax deductible only if you have a receipt from the contractor. Don't fall for the trap of people asking for "cash under the table." Every time you pay cash without getting a receipt, you are not only losing out on your tax deduction, you are understating business expenses. Leave the tax liability to the subcontractor—it's their choice to be honest or not. If you incur theft of cash or products, you can claim the portion not compensated by your insurance company.

If you are still reading this, congratulations on sticking with it. You have probably decided that by now the only way to avoid all this tedious, time-consuming, brain-draining paper-shuffling and chicken-scratching is to hire a bookkeeper. That's not a bad idea—make yourself a short-term goal to build your business to a point where you can do just that. Then you'll have more time to make it even more successful. Until then, learn to do it yourself. A good manager understands the inner workings of the business and never completely relinquishes financial control to someone else.

To end this chapter on a lighter note, here is a story from the other side—from an accountant's perspective. Think about these poor people as you industriously prepare your year-end accounting, and do the very best job you possible can.

BE NICE TO YOUR ACCOUNTANT

Accountants are mostly very nice people. It's not their fault they sometimes appear a little stoic or dry. Think about it: if you spent seven years or more studying this profession, you'd probably become a little dry and staid yourself. It's a lot for the brain to digest, and accountants have a huge responsibility to their clients. Their life consists of number-crunching and shoe-box-sorting, one hand attached permanently to the adding machine, the other on the keyboard or telephone. Accountants have to be serious. Would you appreciate your accountant cracking a joke when you are being told you are going bankrupt?

As every January approaches, accountants prepare themselves for the four-month onslaught of paperwork which must be assembled, processed to perfection, and depleted by the April 30th tax deadline. Do you, the taxpayer, ever stop to think about how much trauma these poor people go through? As the deadline approaches, the latecomers line up in droves, clutching their piles of miscellaneous mountains of triplicate T3s, T4s, T5s, and all that other official paraphernalia.

When all is said and done, accountants are only human, although they are expected to create god-like miracles with tax returns, wondrously changing taxes due into healthy refunds. If there are taxes to pay, of course it is the accountant's fault, don't you agree? There also seems to be a serious misconception here that accountants can survive on no sleep for four months, work eight days a week, 30 hours a day, and not make mistakes—all for a small and reasonable fee.

You may notice that as the tax deadline approaches, you could well be greeted by smiles forced through gritted teeth, accompanied by monosyllabic type conversations and outsized sighs of despair. If you have acute hearing, you will probably hear some under-the-breath, rambling mutterings as you leave the office. Other signs of ATTSS (Accountant's Tax-Time Stress Syndrome), are the slamming of telephones in client's ears after 10 p.m. phone calls from late filers. This is not to be confused with office doors slamming after late clients leave, or messages on the accountant's answering machine, informing clients that they are in Tahiti when they call at 11 p.m. on a Sunday evening.

Trembling hands, black, baggy eyes, nicotine-stained fingers, coffee dribbles on clothing, and nervous twitches are all identifying signs of accountants who suffer from this annual affliction. Most of these symptoms are a direct result of clients leaving their year-end until the last minute, then presenting the whole shooting match in the proverbial grocery bag—unsorted of course—and demanding a refund.

Accountants survive on a different diet than do Ordinary People. A Real Accountant needs five to six pots of coffee a day, half a bottle of Stress pills and assorted vitamins, two cartons of cigarettes, a two-for-one pizza order, and at least half a bottle of premium scotch followed by Valium chasers. If these important daily dietary requirements are not met, your accountant will not survive this crucial time of year. There is no available time allocated in the daily agenda for sleep as this process is extremely time consuming and the stand-down pay is lousy.

You can easily identify an accountant on May 1st. Take a trip to the airport and study the departure areas for destinations such as Alaska, Iceland, Tahiti, Barbados, the Caribbean, Tibet, or Australia. You will notice a long line-up of hunched and ragged robotic-type excuses for humans stumbling to the check-out counter. Fifty-five percent of all passengers are accountants. Then check the bookings for the most desolate and isolated fishing or health resorts in the interior. Fifteen percent of the accountants will be heading for a hideaway in the bush.

Twenty percent of the accountants fly to Reno or Las Vegas, preparing to gamble away your accounting fees with great delight and fiendish glints in their eyes.

Sadly though, if you check the admissions to private and mental health institutions, five percent of the accountants will be newly registered. Last but not least, the obituary column will reveal the whereabouts of the final five percent of this loyal, devoted, and sometimes dying breed.

But you—yes you—can help change these sad statistics. Visit your friendly accountant in early January with all your paperwork in neat, organized, and legible order. Stop our Canadian dollar being so heavily invested into other countries on accountants' recuperative vacations. Reduce mental health costs, and stop the unnecessary trauma of accountants' funerals and family grief. Make your New Year's resolution now—always be nice to your accountant, get your taxes in early, and don't gripe about your accounting bill.

Chapter 12

Your home office – heaven or hell?

Home is where the heart (i.e. computer, fax, photocopier, answering machine, telephone and dirty laundry) is.

This is where all the action will be—the hive of industry—your 10' x 12' home office. Even architects and builders recognize the growing long-term trend to home-based self-employment and are designing and building homes and multi-dwelling complexes with this purpose in mind. Having worked in a store-front office for many years before moving my business home for the past 13, I couldn't entertain the thought of working anywhere else. There is no substitute for living on a small acreage on a quiet and friendly street, surrounded by birds, horses, animals, trees, peace, and quiet. This atmosphere allows for the luxury of concentrated work without photocopier sales reps and uninvited guests dropping by.

Having this long-term SOHO (sole operator home-office) experience, I have had the opportunity to encounter just about every possible positive and negative situation. You will have to evaluate for yourself whether a home-based office is the ideal situation for your needs, because working from home is not for everyone. Most people think it will be a wonderful existence, until reality sets in and they experience the isolation and inherent home-office problems. Read on and decide for yourself whether you are cut out for this often lonely and hectic lifestyle.

WHAT ARE THE ADVANTAGES?

There are many advantages to working from home, the main ones being:

1. Low overhead

2. Home-office tax deductions

3. Flexibility of hours

4. Security, peace, and quiet

5. Safety in inclement weather

1. Low overhead

A home-based office eliminates much of the overhead expense of a business. Even a small office incurs high monthly overhead. Leases, business telephone lines, fancy office furniture and decorations, hydro, signs, and reception costs are expensive. First impressions are extremely important when clients come into your office. They expect to find well-furnished, comfortable, and clean surroundings, preferably with some nice additional touches. A cheaply furnished office doesn't make a good impression, and this is what counts. You have to generate a high-dollar volume just to cover office overhead costs. What a waste of profits. Wouldn't you prefer they go in your pocket rather than to the landlords?

Then the office has to be staffed from nine to five. It is expected. Nothing irritates a customer more than a sign reading "closed for lunch—back in half an hour." A walk-in customer may not come back. Haven't you experienced this same frustration? If you are a solo operation, your choice is brown-bagging your lunch, hiring part-time help, or closing up shop for at least an hour a day while you rush to do your errands. You don't have this problem with a home-based office.

2. Home-office tax deductions

Your home incurs expensive operating costs just like any business. The beauty of a home-based office is that a portion of these costs can be claimed on your income taxes (see below for further discussion). You pay these costs anyway, so it's a bonus to be able to claim them as a tax deduction. You can only claim a home-based office if it is the head office of your business. You cannot claim an office in a leased building as well as your office at home where you work nights and weekends. This is just one of Revenue Canada's little rules by which we must all abide.

3. Flexibility of hours

The flexibility gained in a home-based business makes them very attractive to parents of young children. You can take the children to school, and if you get a flat tire, you don't have to worry about being at the office by nine o'clock. If you are too ill to work, you rely on your voice-mail or take the portable phone to bed and rest. Although your work won't get completed, you will be able to rest. If you lose time during the day, can't meet a deadline, or the computer crashes, you can burn the midnight oil, wearing pyjamas and slippers if you so desire. If the school phones to say your daughter is ill or has broken her arm, you can pick her up and nurse her instead of feeling guilty because the office is unattended. My daughter was ill for two weeks out of three, including spring break. Although her demanding presence was somewhat trying as I worked, being at home was a blessing.

You can organize client appointments to suit your schedule. If you are a late riser or a night owl, you can book appointments for a time convenient to you. If you think new clients may feel uncomfortable visiting a home-based office; make them feel at ease right off the bat. When making the first appointment, ask them whether they prefer tea or coffee and let them know a muffin is waiting. This strategy seems to break the ice. If you don't have a consulting room, keep one room comfortable and spotless, and meet there. My clients like to sit in the bright and cheery family room, where they can watch the horses through the sliding doors and see an attractive garden. A comfortable setting will usually relax first-time clients.

Lunch at home? You can use leftovers in the refrigerator instead of having to pay for a calorie-enriched lunch. You can return phone calls, read the newspaper, watch the news on TV, or open your mail. You can take a walk around the garden or around the block and get some exercise and stress-relief. My horse always neighs for his lunch at noon, so there is no option but to stop work, break out the hay, and have lunch.

4. Security, peace, and quiet

There is a certain feeling of control and comfort derived from working at home. Your home is secure because you are there. You know there won't be a burglary, as so often happens when people are away at work. If something goes wrong, you can deal with it as it happens. I have dealt with disasters ranging from freezing and flooding to famine (couldn't get to the store because of heavy snow). Other disasters include a broken washing machine, dryer, refrigerator, toilet, garage doors, microwave, burst pipes, overflowing gutters, a flooding property with marooned horses, sick animals and children, lost puppies, stray cows, and an aged mother with various illnesses, including broken bones. As inconvenient as it is at the time to your work, it is good to be home when disaster strikes. Emergencies can be dealt with immediately. Although when your spouse arrives home and asks "Did you have a nice day dear?" the answer is not always "Yes."

When you are not expecting visitors or clients, you can dress casually, instead of donning the expected business attire, saving on your wardrobe costs. It does pays to dress neatly however—someone will eventually catch you out if you work in your dressing gown until eleven in the morning.

Portable telephones make your working life easier: you can be in the garden or the washroom without using your voice-mail. If clients need to see you after hours or at a weekend, you will have to train your family to co-operate and have the home looking presentable. Your clients will appreciate this special service. Now this all sounds peaches and cream, but in reality, developing the necessary discipline can take years to get down to a fine art and involves a great deal of in-house training.

5. Safety in inclement weather

I was in the final stages of writing the first edition of this book when an unexpected 12 inches of snow was dumped across the Lower Mainland of British Columbia. Before the snow had a chance to melt, the cold weather turned the streets into skating rinks. Needless to say, I didn't leave the house for several days, feeling extremely sympathetic towards those brave entrepreneurs who had the responsibility of opening their doors at nine o'clock in the morning.

You have all probably experienced freezing rain, black ice, white-outs, blizzards, flooding, wind and ice storms, and heavy snowfalls. Driving in these conditions is potentially life-threatening and hazardous to your health. It is with great relief that you can continue working through these conditions without having to take one step outside into the danger zone.

WHAT ARE THE DISADVANTAGES?

So now you have the bright side of a home office, let's look at the other side. A majority of home-based businesses don't fly because of lack of structure, discipline, and self-motivation. It's not easy being stuck in a small office by yourself—particularly if you have come from a corporate environment. Here are some of the problems you will experience working at home.

1. Business is not taken seriously

2. Family do not respect the home office

3. Neighbours do not understand you are working

4. Home chores can get in the way of office work

5. Isolation from consumers and the business world

6. Motivation is difficult

7. Good weather can tempt you to play

8. Difficult to keep to a schedule and routine

9. You eat, sleep, and breathe work

10. Business grows but facilities don't

1. Business is not taken seriously

It is up to you, and you only, to set your goals and decide whether you are going to get serious about your business. Many people putter along at home without having goals, business plans, or any structure. You are on your own, so you should make a point of joining business organizations and networks to bounce your ideas off other people. Take a business course, become knowledgeable about how to administer a business, and set defined goals. If you heed the advice in this book on organization, marketing and planning, you should have a good idea by now about how serious you are about your business.

2. Family

Because your family is very special to you, it can be difficult to ignore their demands. You will have to train them to respect the fact you are working, and this is no easy chore. This starts with you taking yourself seriously and demanding the family's respect. Younger children in particular find it hard to comprehend, because you will always be their parent first and a worker last.

If you use the method of taking set days for work and others for the family, let them know that on your "at-home" days, you are available for them and their interests. Even on work days, always make quality time for your children afterwards. You will get more productive work accomplished by thus structuring your week, and you won't feel guilty of ignoring the children.

If you plan to work past school hours, organize a babysitter or after-school care for your children. Otherwise you will lose valuable work time. If you just want to work part time, work two or three full days and take the other days off. During those work days, make every hour productive. If your days are constantly broken into pieces, you will never feel any sense of accomplishment.

It may be worthwhile to hold a family meeting to stress to your spouse and children that your work at home is serious. Ask them to respect the ground rules—and be patient. It may take everyone time to adjust to the new situation. Once you set the rules, don't bend them, or you will lose the family's respect.

One of the most important rules should be to teach your children telephone etiquette. One way to achieve this is to install the "smart ring" option, where one ring denotes a business call and the other a personal call. Don't give your friends the business number. You then have the choice of not answering the home line while you are working. Instruct your children never to pick up the telephone when it rings for the business.

At the same time, children are always tempted to pick up the telephone, so teach them to be a polite receptionist and answer with the business name. My eight year-old daughter has often been complimented on her telephone manners, even with personal calls. She has learned that between the hours of nine to five, she does not answer the phone, but some clients do call after hours. With the many choices of modern communication and technology, there are many inexpensive options to help solve the home/office competition.

3. Neighbours

If you live in a community where your neighbours are a friendly bunch, you will have to train them too. The hardest ones to train are those who don't work. They can't relate to a structured home-office environment. They have a habit of dropping by for a quick cup of coffee and staying forever.

When the door bell rings and it's a neighbour, answer the door wearing glasses, holding a pen and a pile of papers. If the portable phone is handy, grab that too. This ruse works extremely well, accompanied by: "Oh, hi Julie, did you come to help me meet my deadline? What a hectic day! I envy you not having to work!"

There's an art to dealing with tedious phone calls from neighbours. When they call and say "How are you?" you have to tell them "I'm up to my ears in paperwork, can I call you after supper? or "I have a deadline to meet, I work Fridays, you know." After much practice you will get these lines down pat and the message will eventually get through. Learn to be tough. Good luck!

4. Home chores

It can be difficult to "turn off" all the chores calling at you when you work from a home office. You may be tempted to load the laundry while you are working—but don't do it! You don't need these distractions. On a work day, abandon all thoughts of housework. If you can't complete the chores before nine in the morning, leave them until after five. Just make sure the house or office is presentable if clients are expected. The rest can, and must, wait. If you don't put a value on your time and learn to keep to a schedule, working at home will become a lost cause. The only way to succeed is to be self-disciplined, work to rules, and make sure that everyone respects them.

5. Isolation

Isolation is one of the hardest problems to overcome when working from home, and it takes a real effort to become visible to the consumer and business community. It's easy to entrench yourself at home, but while you are doing this, no one knows who, what, or where you are. Marketing is difficult enough for any business, but it's even harder from a home-based office. To stay in touch with the business world, and to find and network with potential clients, you have to become involved in your community.

As suggested in Chapter 10, join associations, networks, attend trade shows, join the chamber of commerce or Rotary and become visible and a voice in your community. There are many other organizations you can join. Choose at least one that interests you, so you can also enjoy a social life. It's easier to network among friends and acquaintances than in a room full of strangers.

6. Motivation

Now you are the boss, you are the only person who can decide on the future of your business. Motivation is synonymous with goal setting, passion, organization, confidence, and communication. No one will care whether you are making your business work or not—that is your job. An organized and structured routine, knowing where you are going with your business plan, and having a passion for your work are all motivational factors that should inspire you to move forward.

Here are some words which should be deleted from your working vocabulary: later, lethargy, apathy, I can't, tomorrow, I'm scared, no time, and it can wait. Keeping that positive attitude is so necessary. Instead, add these words to your vocabulary: drive, positive, organization, incentive, inspirational, initiative, ambitious, now, priorities, I can, and now.

7. Good weather

As silly as it sounds, fine summer weather makes working at home difficult. If your office or work space becomes stuffy, your concentration level drops and thoughts of going outside become urgent. If the temptation is too great, plan to work to a certain time and take a couple of hours off to enjoy the sun. You will achieve more by motivating yourself to finish in time. If you feel guilty after taking a break, you will probably work even harder to catch up.

The alternative is to start work earlier, take a sun break, and work in the evenings. During summer I sometimes ride my horse in the cool of the morning on quiet days. I achieve more this way by not feeling deprived of this ultimate pleasure. If you can combine work and play success-fully, do it. You will feel motivated, exercised, relaxed, and ready to toil again.

8. Hard to keep to routines

Working in your home office requires strict self-discipline. Many peo-ple don't succeed because they don't know how to be organized. There are enough helpful tips in this book to show you how to resolve this problem. Businesses remain mediocre without a disciplined mind; work-ing at home compounds the problem. Pretend you are going to a regular office every day and adjust your routine to that schedule. Take regular mini-breaks, a lunch break, and an afternoon energy break. Don't finish your day until five o'clock. It may sound like going to school—the rou-tine and discipline principles are no different. When you work at home, something will always interrupt your work; deal with unscheduled di-lemmas as they occur. You should put in at least six productive hours a day, make your phone calls, and attend to your paperwork.

9. Eat, sleep, and breathe work

You may close your office door, but switching off your work thoughts is not so easy. Clients often forget that you have another life besides work and will call you at all hours unless you train them well. Most people make the mistake of allowing clients to call after hours rather than tak-ing the chance of offending them and losing business. We have all been guilty of that.

Don't accept business calls after hours, excluding emergencies. Inform new clients that your working hours are nine to five, Monday to Friday. Let them know that family time is a priority. Most people will respect that. If clients call at inopportune moments, evenings or weekends, tell them you are busy and will return their call in the morning.

You need to have some kind of leisure activities in your life to switch your brain from work to family. Where possible, plan some form of physical activity every day, a little gardening or a short walk. Spend time reading stories to your children, or join a club which interests you. Pursue some interests in the home which are strictly yours, such as painting, reading, carpentry, or working out in your home gym. Pursue both an outside and inside interest, because the weather may affect some hobbies.

If you have to work at night, try to stop by nine and relax for an hour or two before bedtime. Otherwise you will be working all night in your head and awaken feeling tired, listless, and undermotivated. There is life after work, but only you are responsible for making it happen.

10. Business growth

Growth doesn't sound like a problem, but for many, it becomes a big headache. Your business may eventually require more space; the office or workshop becomes crammed with stuff you need, and there is nowhere in the home to expand to. You are not yet large enough to move out of your "incubator" and into larger, leased premises. Your work can become hampered by a disorganized work space.

When people reach this stage, they often impulsively run out and rent a commercial space without being financially ready for this huge step. This is where planning your future goals and cash-flow projections for the business are an asset. In your planning stages, determine the maximum space you will need to reach your projected sales working from home. Determine by the projected sales figures when you will need larger premises, and research these costs thoroughly beforehand. You will then know if those sales can support the extra overhead. If they can't, think how you could reorganize your home space, or research other alternatives.

WHAT HOME-OFFICE TAX DEDUCTIONS ARE AVAILABLE?

Your home-based office replaces a leased or purchased building, and therefore most costs relating to that space are tax-deductible, proportionate to the size of the work space. Deductions are calculated based on the number of square feet your business occupies in the home. This square footage includes storage sheds or outbuildings used for business purposes. First measure the square footage of the home, including the outbuildings. Then, calculate the square footage of the business portion.

For example, if your office is 12' x 14', and you use a 15' x 12' garage, the business portion of your home is 348 square feet. If your home is 1,750 square feet, your business portion is calculated as a percentage of the whole home, in this case 19.89 percent.

Keep all your home-related expenses in a file for year-end so your accountant can add them to your business return. Deductible expenses are:

1. Mortgage interest

2. Property taxes

3. Rent

4. Hydro, gas, oil heating, garbage disposal, water

5. Repairs and maintenance

6. House insurance

7. Business long-distance calls charged to residential lines

In our example, if these expenses amounted to $13,000 for the year, the business portion would be $2,585.70, or 17.89 percent. If you do specific renovations, alterations, or repairs to your work space, keep these costs separate; most are deductible.

If you have a major repair, such as replacing a roof, the cost will be amortized over a number of years. The full cost cannot be written off in a one-year period. The same will apply to major renovations necessary to house the business, such as an extension to your office space. Your accountant will depreciate these costs gradually.

Home maintenance costs can mount up quickly. You have to be on top of all costs and keep good records. Small items such as vacuum bags, cleaners, and coffee for clients constitute part of your home expenses. If you maintain your garden nicely, keep all the receipts. Most people pay for these expenses out of personal funds or with credit cards, so keep track of them in a home-expense file.

Add to this file hydro bills, mortgage statements, and house insurance. If you don't have a business telephone line, you can't claim the basic monthly telephone rental. If you have additional services, such as call waiting or voice mail for the business, they are deductible, including long-distance business calls. When the telephone bill arrives, it is a good idea to separate the business portion, pay that portion of the bill with a business cheque and pay the personal portion with a personal cheque.

At year-end, total these individual costs for your accountant, and make a complete list of all home expenses, including the square footage information. This will save your accountant time and you money.

There are exceptions to home-based office usage. One example is a child care business operated at home, which is calculated on a different formula:

1,350 sq.feet x 12 hours x 5 days x 50 weeks x $7,000 = $ 1,802.88

1,800 sq.feet   24 hours   7 days   52 weeks

This formula takes the number of rooms used for child care, over the total square footage, multiplied by the number of hours in a day the home is used for business, multiplied by the number days a week the business is open, multiplied by the number of weeks in a year it is operated, multiplied by the total home expenses! It's probably easier not to open a child-care business because the calculations are rather complicated. For that you hire an accountant. Be aware that if you use over 50 percent of your primary residence for a business, as some daycare operations do, when you sell the home, the business portion will be subject to capitals gains tax.

If you decide to work at home, consider all this information carefully. It will take you time to find your pace, so don't expect miracles in the first few months. Like any new skill, being a SOHO takes practice. Work on building a network of friends, associates, and mentors. Don't isolate yourself because business won't come to you—you have to go out there and make it happen. This book is your companion and guide to get you started—the rest is up to you. Always remember, *you* are your business. Once you are on a roll, the rewards are many and the savings enormous.

Chapter 13

What will your story be?

*Now make your dream a reality, because you know where
you are going and what you are doing.*

There's a lot of information in this guide which will take you time to digest. You'll probably want to read some sections a few times to absorb the messages. If you follow the advice closely, and if your choice of business is sound, you can be on your way to success and a new way of life. Don't expect it to be easy because it takes hard work and commitment. You will be master of your destiny and proud of your achievements. You will grow as you learn and be enriched with new knowledge and skills.

Now you know the right way to start your new venture, here are two stories of newly minted entrepreneurs. One is about a couple, Steven and Susan, who did everything the right way, and one is about another couple named Frank and Fiona, who didn't. I trust your story is going to be one of success like that of Steven and Susan.

WHY STEVEN AND SUSAN SUCCEEDED:
A SUCCESS STORY

Susan had always loved flowers, often dreaming about opening her own flower shop one day. Meanwhile, Steven and Susan worked hard to secure their future. Susan worked a few days a week as a physiotherapist and

Steven held a secure job with the government. Their mortgage was nearly paid off, and life was going well for them.

Susan's dream came a little closer to reality the day she saw a chain of three flower shops for sale in the local paper. Discussing her idea with Steven, they decided to pursue the advertisement and phoned for an appointment. Susan knew immediately which of the three locations she preferred. The shops were located in her town, a large, sprawling country area which was quickly changing into suburbia. The prime location was near a busy intersection, but had ample, accessible parking. For these reasons, this store was priced higher than the others.

The owners tried to encourage Steven and Susan to buy one of the other locations, but Susan had done her homework and was not to be swayed by a cheaper purchase price. The store she wanted was priced at $60,000. The other two were priced at $50,000.

Susan asked for all available information and was given a list of equipment, some sales figures, and a combined financial statement for the three stores. She contacted her accountant to review the figures. They sat down and Susan presented all the information she had gathered.

She had been very thorough, researching the terms of the lease, garbage collection, telephone lines, and other overhead expenses. Unfortunately, the financial statements didn't give her much specific information on the performance of her chosen location. She had been given a statement of sales figures, broken down into months, and from that her accountant pointed out the seasonal trends the store experienced. It was obvious that February was a rosy month because of Valentine's Day, May was bursting with profits because of Mother's Day, and December blossomed because of Christmas. The other months showed average sales.

The list of equipment was valued at $11,500, and included coolers, furniture, and fittings. The inventory would be calculated at the date of takeover and would cost approximately $3,500. This meant the goodwill was valued at $45,000.

The financial statements did not reflect this value overall as one of the flower shops had been losing money. Susan's accountant asked for the name of the vendor's accountant and called him with a list of questions. She requested separate financial statements for the one store, advising

Susan and Steven to wait until the figures arrived. The other accountant admitted the figures were not quite up to date and that separate figures were not readily available.

When the information finally arrived, Susan's accountant reviewed everything carefully. The assets of each store were separated. From this information she found out that the equipment, valued at $11,500 on the sale agreement, was only worth $6,500 on the books. The equipment was old and had been well depreciated.

The statement of income and expenditure had been combined for the three stores, and that made analysis difficult. Susan's accountant studied the cost of sales section to arrive at gross profit margins. One thing was certain: healthy gross profits could be made with flowers. The problems had arisen in the overhead section of the financial statements. For some reason, the store's overhead was extremely high, particularly the telephone, advertising and vehicle costs. She suggested to Susan she find out why.

Susan knew that the other two stores were not located in prime areas, therefore advertising costs had been high. The business carried expenses for three vehicles, and a lot of long-distance calls were made, which had substantially added to the telephone costs. She concluded that she could operate the business more efficiently. Susan's accountant suggested they prepare a month-by-month analysis of what the store could really do if it were operated efficiently, based on the information they had on hand.

Susan had researched the operating costs, including staff wages. Her accountant took the monthly sales figures, applied the cost of flowers and accessories using the percentages from the financial statements, and arrived at a monthly gross profit. The monthly expenses were added, and they agreed that the business should be quite profitable. Her accountant felt the goodwill was not worth $45,000. She suggested a total purchase price of $45,000, including the equipment, goodwill, and inventory.

Susan haggled and bartered with the vendors for a week, quoting facts and figures from her accountant. She finally purchased the business for $47,000, saving $13,000 off the asking price. Steven was going to keep his secure job and Susan intended to follow her other career for two or three days a week, using hired staff to fill in when she was unavailable.

This way, they maintained a guaranteed income. They increased their mortgage to buy the store, but the payments were in range of their combined incomes.

As soon as Susan had opened the store she returned to her accountant loaded with papers and pages of questions. They consulted regularly for the next four months until Susan knew how to enter and maintain her books, reconcile the bank accounts, look after the Visa and MasterCard accounts, and calculate the payroll, GST, and provincial sales tax. She insisted on preparing the books herself, and every two months her accountant reviewed her progress, correcting mistakes, and teaching Susan a little more about bookkeeping. Soon she became proficient at her accounting, realizing why the books were organized the way they were. She used her Visa to purchase the flowers and supplies because it was convenient. She paid the balance monthly without incurring interest charges, giving her 30 days to turn flowers into hard cash.

Susan and her accountant decided that because of the three peak seasonal trends, a snapshot financial statement would be prepared every four months. This allowed them to monitor profits and review Susan's income tax situation. In Susan's first year of operation, paying two staff members while she continued part-time with her other job, Susan's store made a profit of $27,000. Had she worked in the store full-time, the profits would have been even higher. They made enough money to trade in their old van for a new one after the first 18 months, as well as invest in some RRSPs for the future and take a well-earned trip overseas.

Susan's dream became a reality because she was willing to research, listen, learn, and work hard. The store is a success and will increase in value as the years progress. This couple did everything right, taking no chances and learning how to manage and monitor their business carefully. They still continue to reap the benefits of their hard work.

WHY FRANK AND FIONA FAILED:
A NOT SO SUCCESSFUL STORY

Fiona loved to draw and paint. It was so relaxing to lose herself in a canvas creation and to produce beautiful paintings from tubes of oils. She had raised a family and hadn't worked full time for many years. Her children were now teenagers and seemed to need her less. Fiona was bored and desperately needed to feel a sense of purpose. She started working part time for an art gallery nearby, thoroughly enjoying the atmosphere and people. She could talk knowledgeably with the customers and looked forward to her job each day.

Becoming restless, she suggested to Frank that she would like to have her own store one day. Frank agreed it was a "nice idea" and the seed was planted, until it became an obsession with Fiona. She just had to have her own art and hobby supplies store. The dream of owning her own business and being with all those nice artsy people each day became the focus of discussions. Tired of her constant whining and nagging, Frank finally relented, telling Fiona to "check things out."

Fiona started looking for a small store to rent and enquired about stock inventory prices from suppliers. She didn't think about a business plan, profit margins, overhead, or competition—and especially not where the money would come from. She just envisioned the store in her mind— the rest would happen on its own, or Frank would take care of it. She knew her art materials very well and decided she would hold painting classes at the store for additional income and exposure.

She found a small retail store with a strip mall across the road: a lot of traffic seemed to pass by. She was close to a restaurant and bookstore, so she was sure that customers would come to see her. It wasn't a very big store, and the rent was $1,000 a month. Well, she would have to cut back in other areas, because this was the location she wanted.

The store needed extensive renovations to accommodate her inventory, so Frank said he would cash in an RRSP, and they could use their Visa to meet other expenses. Fiona didn't check for competition nearby. A large hobby store was located on the other side of town. The only other real competition was far away, so she expected to attract local trade. Fiona forgot that people are mobile and travel around to shop. The couple purchased a basic inventory but the store still looked a little empty, so they purchased more, using their credit cards. The inventory grew to nearly $25,000, and finally the store looked ready. Frank, luckily, kept his full-time job.

Fiona made a 50 percent profit margin on her retail prices. She offered a 10 percent discount to her regular customers, and the slow-moving inventory was put into the mark-down bins. Many customers took advantage of her Visa and MasterCard facilities. She started the painting classes, paying the instructors most of the class fees. This way, she still made a small profit and the students purchased some supplies from her. She didn't advertise, as the money was tight. In her mind, the word-of-mouth seemed to be working.

In the first year, the store grossed $50,000 in sales, with the expected 50 percent gross profit after material costs. Fiona had her books prepared by a bookkeeper but hadn't been happy with the service. She took her books to another accountant who had been recommended to her. The accountant looked at the general ledger in horror. Using a high-lighter he made notes, line-by-line, of the incorrect allocations of many expenses by the bookkeeper. By the time the financial statements were finished, Frank and Fiona had incurred an additional $500 in accounting fees to correct the books, on top of the normal year-end fee to prepare the statements and taxes.

Their accountant was quite concerned at the sad story the financial figures reflected. The business had lost $10,000 in the first year, without Fiona making any income. He prepared a break-even point for the business and reviewed the financial statements with Frank and Fiona, explaining what the store should do to cover the overhead costs. He also knew the competition in town and the size of the inventories they carried. One competitor carried at least $80,000 worth of inventory, the other more than double that amount.

The review of the financial statements highlighted many problems, the main one being lack of sales. The store was only averaging $4,500 in sales a month, hardly enough to cover the rent and a few expenses. Obviously people were travelling to the competitors' stores for better inventory selection and lower prices. Fiona had not advertised or marketed her business; she seemed to expect everyone to know she was there. The store needed to make a monthly volume of at least $8,000 in sales to cover the present overhead and put $500 into Fiona's pocket.

Fiona's generous discounts ate up 10 percent of the retail sales, or $5,000 a year. The monthly rent was 24 percent of sales, and the material costs were 50 percent. Instructors' fees and some casual labour accounted for 17 percent, leaving only 1 percent to cover all other operating costs such as accounting, bank charges, telephone and utilities, vehicle costs, trade shows, promotion, shop supplies, repairs and maintenance, credit card interest, and office supplies. The store was not going to make it without drastic changes to the operation.

After a long and serious discussion with their accountant, Frank and Fiona returned to the store, somewhat deflated. They weren't sure how to tackle this problem, but started by reducing some discounts to their clients.

A few months later, they returned to their accountant, advising him that they needed a financial statement; they would sell the store. The sales for six months were averaging $5,500, and the store was still losing money. The financial statements didn't look very healthy at all, and they couldn't find a buyer. A few months later they closed the store, disposed of the inventory at reduced prices, and showed a $13,000 loss for the nine-month period.

There were tax benefits for Frank, as his losses offset his regular income, and Fiona will have enough carry forward losses to offset her income for quite a while. But this did not compensate for the $40,000 they invested in the store, the lost RRSP savings, and the huge credit card debts which would have to be paid down slowly at exorbitant interest rates.

Frank and Fiona made many mistakes common to the new entrepreneur who start a business wearing blinders. They hadn't sought professional advice before start up. Had they done so, they would have been advised not to start the business in the first place. They didn't research competition or market trends. Their rent was too high in proportion to the amount of inventory they carried. They did not promote the business and were overly generous with their discounts and the instructors' wages. They used expensive credit and endangered their future security by redeeming their RRSP savings. Frank and Fiona lost $40,000 in this very expensive exercise.

Because you know better, don't let this be your story.

Appendix 1

Provincial fingertip telephone directory
Small business Web sites

This directory contains the telephone numbers of several agencies you will need to contact for your business. For provinces with multiple branches, contact the main branch as listed, and they will be able to supply you with the number you need. With the ever-changing government tax structures, some information may be subject to change. Revenue Canada has consolidated many of their offices into central taxation centres, so call the numbers listed for all payroll, forms, and GST/HST information. Telephone numbers are listed alphabetically by province.

The Web sites contain valuable information for starting a business, including interactive business planners, statistical information, start-up and business management tips, and other resources. Both Canadian and U.S. sites are listed. Site addresses are subject to change.

ALBERTA

	Telephone	Fax

Canada Business Service Centre
The Business Link, Business Service Centre

	Telephone	Fax
	(403) 422-7722	(403) 422-0055

Business registration and incorporation
Alberta Registries, Corporate Registry

	Telephone	Fax
	(403) 427-2311	(403) 422-0055

Revenue Canada Taxation Centres

	Telephone	Fax
Calgary	(403) 221-8970	(403) 691-6676
Edmonton	(403) 495-3200	(403) 495-6407
Lethbridge	(403) 382-3049	(403) 382-3052
Red Deer	(403) 341-7047	(403) 341-7053

Provincial sales tax office

	Telephone	Fax
Edmonton	(403) 427-3044	(403) 427-0348

Workers' Compensation Board

	Telephone	Fax
Edmonton	(403) 498-4000	(403) 498-7865

Business Development Bank of Canada

	Telephone
Calgary	(403) 292-5000
Lethbridge	(403) 382-3000
Red Deer	(403) 340-4203
Edmonton	(403) 495-2277
Grand Prairie	(403) 532-8875

BRITISH COLUMBIA

Canada Business Service Centre
Canada/BC Business Service Centre

	Telephone	Fax
	(604) 775-5525	(604) 775-5520

	Telephone	**Fax**

Business registration and incorporation
Ministry of Finance and Corporate Relations

	Telephone	**Fax**
	(604) 356-2893	(604) 356-1428

Revenue Canada Taxation Centres

	Telephone	**Fax**
Vancouver	(604) 669-2990	(604) 691-4446
Burnaby	(604) 669-2990	(604) 666-1234
Kelowna	(250) 470-6600	(250) 862-4744
Penticton	(250) 492-9470	(250) 492-9518
Victoria	(250) 363-0500	(250) 363-8188
Prince George	(250) 561-7800	(250) 561-7869

Provincial sales tax office

	Telephone	**Fax**
Vancouver	(604) 660-4524	(604) 660-1104

Workers' Compensation Board

	Telephone	**Fax**
Richmond	(604) 273-2266	(604) 276-3151

Business Development Bank of Canada

	Telephone
Campbell River	(250) 286-5800
Cranbrook	(250) 417-2200
Fort St. John	(250) 787-0622
Kamloops	(250) 851-4900
Kelowna	(250) 470-4812
Langley	(604) 532-5150
Nanaimo	(250) 754-0250
North Vancouver	(604) 666-7703
Prince George	(250) 561-5323
Surrey	(604) 586-2400
Terrace	(250) 615-5300
Vancouver	(604) 666-0345
Victoria	(250) 363-0161
Williams Lake	(250) 398-8233

MANITOBA

	Telephone	Fax
Canada Business Service Centre		
Winnipeg	(204) 984-2272	(204) 983-3852
Business registration and incorporation		
Manitoba Consumer and Corporate Affairs		
	(204) 945-2500	(204) 945-1459
Revenue Canada Taxation Centres		
Winnipeg	(204) 983-3918	(204) 984-6752
Brandon	(204) 726-7669	(204) 726-7868
Provincial sales tax office		
Taxation Division, Department of Finance		
	(204) 945-6444	(204) 948-2087
Workers' Compensation Board		
Winnipeg	(204) 954-4321	(204) 954-4968
Business Development Bank of Canada		
Winnipeg	(204) 983-7900	(204) 983-0870
Brandon	(204) 726-7570	(204) 726-7555

NEW BRUNSWICK

	Telephone	Fax
Canada Business Service Centre		
Fredericton	(506) 444-6140	(506) 444-6172
Business registration and incorporation		
Ministry of Corporate Affairs	(506) 453-2703	(506) 453-2613
Revenue Canada Taxation Centres		
Bathurst	(506) 548-6744	(506) 548-9905
Saint John	(506) 636-4909	(506) 636-5718
Moncton	(506) 851-3727	(506) 851-7018

	Telephone	Fax

Provincial sales tax office
Education and Inquiries Revenue Division

	(506) 453-2404	(506) 453-3044

Workers' Compensation Board

Saint John	(506) 632-2200	(506) 632-4999

Business Development Bank of Canada

Bathurst	(506) 548-7360	
Edmundston	(506) 739-8311	
Fredericton	(506) 452-3030	
Moncton	(506) 851-6120	
Saint John	(506) 636-4751	

NEWFOUNDLAND AND LABRADOR

Canada Business Service Centre

St. John's, NB	(709) 772-6022	(709) 772-6090

Business registration and incorporation
Department of Government Services and Lands

	(709) 729-3315	(709) 729-0232

Revenue Canada Taxation Centres

St. John's, NB	(709) 772-2610	

Provincial sales tax office

Tax Administration Branch	(709) 729-3831	(709) 729-2856

Workers' Compensation Board

St. John's	(709) 778-1000	(709) 738-1714

Business Development Bank of Canada

Corner Brook	(709) 637-4515	
Grand Falls/Windsor	(709) 489-2181	
St. John's	(709) 772-5505	

NORTHWEST TERRITORIES

	Telephone	Fax
Canada Business Service Centre		
Yellowknife	(867) 873-7958	(867) 873-0101
Business registration and incorporation		
Registrar of Companies, Department of Justice		
	(867) 873-7490	(867) 873-0243
Revenue Canada Taxation Centres		
Yellowknife	(867) 920-6650	
Territorial sales tax office		
Ministry of Finance	(867) 920-3470	(867) 873-0325
Workers' Compensation Board		
Yellowknife	(867) 920-3888	(867) 873-4596
Business Development Bank of Canada		
Yellowknife	(403) 873-3565	

NOVA SCOTIA

Canada Business Service Centre		
Halifax	(902) 426-8604	(902) 426-6530
Business registration and incorporation		
Registry of Join Stock Companies		
	(902) 424-7770	
Revenue Canada Taxation Centres		
Halifax	(902) 426-5300	(902) 426-7170
Sydney	(902) 564-7099	(902) 564-3095
Provincial sales tax office		
Retail sales:		
Tax Information Section	(902) 424-6300	(902) 424-0702

	Telephone	Fax
Workers' Compensation Board		
Halifax	(902) 491-8000	(902) 491-8002

Business Development Bank of Canada

Bridgewater	(902) 527-5501
Halifax	(902) 426-7850
Sydney	(902) 564-7700
Truro	(902) 895-6377

ONTARIO

Canada Business Service Centre

Toronto	(416) 954-4636	(416) 954-8597

Business registration and incorporation*

* Call the Canada Business Service Centre for all other local listings

Toronto	(416) 314-8880	(416) 314-0102

Revenue Canada Taxation Centres

*For local offices not listed, call any Revenue Canada office for information

Barrie	(705) 739-6000	(705) 721-0056
Belleville	(613) 962-2563	(613) 969-7845
Hamilton	(905) 570-7260	(905) 572-2338
Kingston	(613) 547-7590	(905) 545-5570
Kitchener	(519) 579-0490	(519) 579-4532
London	(519) 645-4223	(519) 645-5026
Mississauga	(905) 566-6702	(905) 615-2453
North York	(416) 221-5695	(416) 218-4820
Ottawa	(613) 957-8109	(613) 957-8130
Peterborough	(705) 876-7319	(705) 876-6422
St. Catharines	(905) 688-3523	(905) 688-5996
Sault Ste. Marie	(705) 941-5218	(705) 941-5387
Scarborough	(416) 954-0212	(416) 954-5787
Sudbury	(705) 671-0541	(705) 671-0405
Toronto	(416) 954-3400	(416) 954-5294
Thunder Bay	(807) 623-3039	(807) 622-8512
Windsor	(519) 252-5829	(519) 252-1836

	Telephone	Fax
Provincial sales tax office		
Fuel and tobacco:		
Taxpayer Services Branch	(905) 433-6393	(905) 436-4507
Retail sales:		
Retail Sales Taxpayer Services	(905) 432-3332	(905) 435-3535
Workers' Compensation Board		
Toronto	(416) 344-1000	(416) 344-3999
Business Development Bank of Canada		
Barrie	(705) 739-0444	
Hamilton	(905) 572-2954	
Kenora	(807) 467-3535	
Kingston	(613) 545-8636	
Kitchener - Waterloo	(519) 571-6676	
London	(519) 675-3101	
Mississauga	(905) 566-6417	
North Bay	(705) 495-5700	
Oshawa	(905) 725-3366	
Ottawa	(613) 995-0234	
Peterborough	(705) 750-4800	
St. Catharines	(905) 988-2874	
Sault Ste. Marie	(705) 941-3030	
Scarborough	(416) 954-0709	
Stratford	(519) 271-5650	
Sudbury	(705) 670-6482	
Thunder Bay	(807) 346-1780	
Timmins	(705) 267-6416	
Toronto	(416) 973-0341	
Toronto-North	(905) 264-2100	
Windsor	(519) 257-6808	

PRINCE EDWARD ISLAND

Canada Business Service Centre

Charlottetown	(902) 368-0771	(902) 566-7377

	Telephone	Fax
Business registration and incorporation		
Department of Provincial Affairs		
	(902) 368-4550	(902) 368-5283

Revenue Canada Taxation Centre

Charlottetown	(902) 628-4244	(902) 368-0248

Provincial sales tax office

Taxation and Property Records Division

	(902) 368-4171	(902) 368-6164

Workers' Compensation Board

Charlottetown	(902) 368-5680	(902) 368-5705

Business Development Bank of Canada

Charlottetown	(902) 566-7454	

QUEBEC

Canada Business Service Centre

Montreal	(514) 496-4636	(514) 496-5934

Business registration and incorporation

Inspecteur général des institutions financières

Québec	(418) 643-3625	(418) 646-9660
Montreal	(514) 873-5324	(514) 873-6431

Revenue Canada Taxation Centres

Chicoutimi	(418) 698-5780	(418) 698-5544
Hull	(819) 994-4045	(819) 994-1103
Laval	(514) 956-9120	(514) 956-6915
Montreal	(514) 283-5585	(514) 496-8143
Québec	(418) 648-5809	(418) 648-4251
Rouyn-Noranda	(819) 764-3474	(819) 797-8366
Sherbrooke	(819) 821-4008	(819) 564-4226
Trois-Rivières	(819) 373-8783	(819) 371-2744

	Telephone	Fax
Provincial sales tax office		
Revenue Québec	1-800-567-4692	
Workers' Compensation Board		
Québec	(418) 643-5850	(418) 643-2236
Québec Administration Centre:		
Montreal	(514) 873-7183	(514) 873-7007
Business Development Bank of Canada		
Chicoutimi	(418) 698-5599	
De Maisonneuve	(514) 283-5858	
Drummondville	(819) 478-4951	
Granby	(514) 372-5202	
Hull	(819) 997-4434	
Laval	(514) 973-6868	
Longueuil	(514) 928-4120	
Québec	(418) 648-3972	
Rimouski	(418) 722-3300	
Rouyn-Noranda	(819) 764-6701	
Saint-Laurent	(514) 496-7500	
Saint-Léonard	(514) 251-2818	
Sherbrooke	(819) 564-5700	
Trois-Rivières	(819) 371-5215	

SASKATCHEWAN

Canada Business Service Centre

Saskatoon	(306) 956-2323	(306) 956-2328

Business registration and incorporation

Saskatchewan Justice Corporations Branch

	(306) 787-2962	(306) 787-8999

Revenue Canada Taxation Centres

Regina	(306) 780-7279	(306) 757-1412
Saskatoon	(306) 975-5692	(306) 652-3211

	Telephone	Fax
Provincial sales tax office		
Taxpayer Services, Revenue Div.		
	(306) 787-6645	(306) 787-9644

Workers' Compensation Board
Regina   (306) 787-4370   (306) 787-0213

Business Development Bank of Canada
Regina   (306) 780-6478
Saskatoon   (306) 975-4822

YUKON

Canada Business Service Centre
Whitehorse   (867) 633-6257   (867) 667-2001

Business registration and incorporation
Department of Justice, Corporate Affairs
                          (867) 667-5442   (867) 393-6257

Revenue Canada Taxation Centre
Whitehorse   (867) 667-8154

Provincial sales tax office
Revenue Services, Department of Finance
                          (867) 667-5345   (867) 393-6217

Workers' Compensation Board
Whitehorse   (867) 667-5645   (867) 393-6279

Business Development Bank of Canada
Whitehorse   (403) 633-7510

SMALL BUSINESS WEB SITES

CANADA

Business Development Bank of Canada
   http://www.bdc.ca

Canada Business Service Centres
   http://www.cbsc.org/main.html

Community Futures Development Corp.
   www.communityfutures.com

Eastleigh Management Services
   http://www.smallbizpro.com

Home Base Business Resource
   http://advgroup.com

InnoVisons Canada & The Canadian Telework Association
   www.ivc.ca

Interactive Business Planner
   http://www.cbsc.org:4000

Microsoft Small Business Information
   http://www.microsoft.com/canada/smallbiz

Ontario Community Futures
www.cbsc.org/ontario/bis/1889.html

Ontario Association of Community Development Corp.
www.oacdc.com/reference.html

Strategis Main Menu
http://strategis.ic.gc.ca

Welcome to Statistics Canada
http://www.statcan.ca

Western Economic Diversification
www.wd.gc.ca

Yahoo! Canada
http://www.yahoo.ca (click on: Business and Economy)

UNITED STATES

Entrepreneur Magazine
http://www.entrepreneurmag.com

Microsoft
http://www.microsoft.com/smallbiz

Small Business 2000
http://www.sb2000.com

Small Business Administration
    http://www.sbaonline.sba.gov

Small Business Resources
    http://www.smartbiz.com

Start-Up Do-It-Yourself Resources
    http://www.startupbiz.com

US Chamber of Commerce
    http://www.usccsbi.com

World Business Solution
    http//thesolution.com

Year 2000
    www.2000.com

Appendix 2

How do you fill out those forms?

---

1. Quarterly GST/HST Report

2. Provincial Sales Tax Remittance

3. Workers' Compensation

4. Revenue Canada Payroll Remittance:

5. Year-end T4 Preparation

6. Year-end T4 Summary

QUARTERLY GST/HST REPORT: INSTRUCTIONS

Your quarterly GST/HST report will be sent to you in plenty of time to complete. You have one month after the quarter ends to file your return. Listed below are the line-by-line instructions.

Line 101: Total your gross sales for the three-month period, before any taxes. Put this amount in Box 101.

Line 103: Total the amount of GST/HST charged on all sales. Cross-check this amount by multiplying the gross sales by 7. The two amounts should agree. Put this amount in Box 103.

Line 104: Enter any GST/HST collected on income not applicable to the three-month period. Enter to Box 104.

Line 105: Total all GST/HST due for this reporting period and enter to Box 105.

Line 106: Enter all the GST you have paid on purchases for the same three-month period, enter to Box 106.

Line 107: Enter any GST paid adjustments here, such as GST paid in previous periods and not reported.

Line 108: Total all GST paid for the period and enter to Box 108.

Line 109: Net tax: Deduct the GST paid (Line 108)from the GST/HST collected (Line 105) and enter to Box 109.

Line 110: Deduct any installments paid, if you file annually.

Line 111: Deduct any applicable rebates and enter to Box 111.

Line 112: Total Lines 110 and 111, enter the total to Box 112.

Line 113: Enter the balance payable or balance due to Box 113.

Line 114: If a refund is claimed, enter the amount to Box 114.

Line 115: If a balance is payable, enter the amount in Box 115.

This top portion is your working copy, and should be kept in your GST/HST file. Write the cheque number on the copy, and then enter the totals onto the remittance slip at the bottom of the page. Send the remittance slip and your cheque to Revenue Canada.

QUARTERLY GST/HST REPORT: SAMPLE

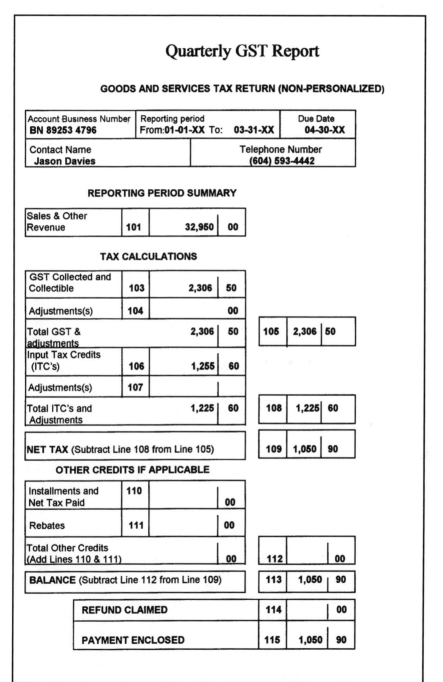

Quarterly GST Report

GOODS AND SERVICES TAX RETURN (NON-PERSONALIZED)

Account Business Number **BN 89253 4796**	Reporting period From:**01-01-XX** To: **03-31-XX**	Due Date **04-30-XX**
Contact Name **Jason Davies**	Telephone Number **(604) 593-4442**	

REPORTING PERIOD SUMMARY

Sales & Other Revenue	101	32,950	00

TAX CALCULATIONS

GST Collected and Collectible	103	2,306	50			
Adjustments(s)	104		00			
Total GST & adjustments		2,306	50	105	2,306	50
Input Tax Credits (ITC's)	106	1,255	60			
Adjustments(s)	107					
Total ITC's and Adjustments		1,225	60	108	1,225	60
NET TAX (Subtract Line 108 from Line 105)				109	1,050	90

OTHER CREDITS IF APPLICABLE

Installments and Net Tax Paid	110		00			
Rebates	111		00			
Total Other Credits (Add Lines 110 & 111)			00	112		00
BALANCE (Subtract Line 112 from Line 109)				113	1,050	90
REFUND CLAIMED				114		00
PAYMENT ENCLOSED				115	1,050	90

PROVINCIAL SALES TAX REMITTANCE: INSTRUCTIONS

Each province has their own form available for the completion of provincial taxes collected. The one reproduced here is for British Columbia. The principle of reporting is the same for each province. You must remit the provincial taxes collected each month, based on the monthly gross sales. Some provinces allow a commission for collecting the taxes.

The remittance instructions are as follows:

1. Total your sales for the month, less any provincial or Federal taxes. Enter this amount in Box 1.

2. Calculate the applicable tax on this amount (e.g., 7 percent in British Columbia). This amount should come directly from your sales records. Enter this amount in Box 2. Make sure the percentage is correct.

3. Deduct any commissions due and enter this amount in Box 3. Rates of commission will be found on the sales tax form.

4. Deduct the commission from the total tax collected, and enter in Box 4.

5. If you have used any goods from your inventory for personal use, enter the purchase price of these goods in Box 5.

6. Calculate the sales tax payable on this sum and enter into Box 6.

7. Add Box 4 to Box 6, and enter the total into Box 7.

8. Enter any further adjustments here. Consult your form for detailed explanations.

9. Enter the net sales tax payable in Box 9.

Make sure your remittance is made in time, as penalties and interest charged on late filing are extremely heavy, and you will also lose your vendor's commission.

PROVINCIAL SALES TAX REMITTANCE:
SAMPLE (BRITISH COLUMBIA)

Each province has their own form available for the completion of provincial taxes collected. The one reproduced here is for British Columbia. The principle of reporting is the same for each province. You must remit the provincial taxes collected each month, based on the monthly gross sales. Some provinces allow a commission for collecting the taxes.

Province of British Columbia	Ministry of Finance and Corporate Relations REVENUE DIVISION	**TAX REMITTANCE ADVICE** *Pursuant to the* *SOCIAL SERVICES TAX ACT*

1. TOTAL SALES	10,950	00
2. TAX COLLECTABLE ON SALES	766	50
3. DEDUCT VENDOR'S COMMISSION (see reverse)	25	29
4. NET TAX DUE ON SALES	741	21
5. PURCHASE PRICE OF TAXABLE GOODS USED FOR VENDOR'S CONSUMPTION	350	00
6. TAX DUE ON PURCHASES % OF ITEM 5	24	50
7. TAX PAYABLE BEFORE ADJUSTMENT (Item 4 plus Item 6)	765	71
8. ADJUSTMENTS IF ELIGIBLE (see reverse + or -)		00
9. TOTAL AMOUNT DUE (Item 7 plus or minus Item 8)	765	71

PAYABLE AT MOST CANADIAN FINANCIAL INSTITUTIONS

WORKERS' COMPENSATION: INSTRUCTIONS

Workers' compensation is payable in all provinces, but industry rates will vary from province to province, as will the wages subject to compensation. In some provinces, shareholder's salaries are optional. In this example, all wages have been calculated, including shareholders, subcontractors and all employees on payroll.

Workers' compensation is paid by employers in all provinces as a form of accident insurance covering all employees. Although coverage and methods of calculation will differ from province to province, each worker must have coverage which is paid by the employer, based on their industry rate as determined by the Workers' Compensation Board in their particular province.

In some provinces, the shareholder's salaries are optional coverage; in other provinces, all shareholders' salaries must be insured. Each worker usually has an annual salary limitation for insurance purposes. Subcontractors, if not carrying their own coverage, must be included in these calculations.

Some provinces will carry a personal optional insurance plan for self-employed proprietors or partners, which will be based on their annual earnings. Coverage is calculated as below:

A. Shareholder's earnings: Calculate the gross shareholder's earnings for the period as listed on the return. Do not use net figures. Take the gross earnings from the payroll records and enter to Box A.

B. Wages and salaries: Calculate all gross wages earned by all employees on payroll, taking this amount from the payroll records. Enter to Box B.

C. Subcontractor's earnings: If you have hired any casual or subcontract labourers who are not covered by their own Workers' Compensation coverage, total these amounts and enter to Box C.

D. Personal optional coverage: If an amount has been entered in this box, then the proprietor has elected for personal coverage. This amount will be pre-determined and entered in Box D.

E. Total earnings: Total all earnings in Boxes A, B, C and D and enter the cumulative total in Box E.

WORKERS' COMPENSATION: SAMPLE

Workers' Compensation is payable in all provinces, but industry rates will vary from province to province, as will the wages subject to compensation. In some provinces, shareholders' saleries are optional. In this example, all wages have been calculated, including shareholders, subcontractors and all employees on payroll.

WORKERS' COMPENSATION BOARD

19XX EMPLOYER'S REMITTANCE FORM
Assessment Department

Jason's Garden Service Ltd.,
14355 Willowbend Avenue
Countrytown, B.C.
V2X 1Y1

PERIOD COVERED	January 1,19XX March 31, 19XX
REGISTRATION #	W43649382
DUE DATE	April 20, 19XX

	KIND OF INDUSTRY	KIND OF INDUSTRY
A. SHAREHOLDER'S EARNINGS (Limited companies only)	15,000.00	
B. WAGES AND SALARIES	37,500.00	
C. SUBCONTRACTOR'S EARNINGS	2,900.00	
D. PERSONAL OPTIONAL PROTECTION		
E. TOTAL EARNINGS (A + B + C)	55,400.00	
F. ASSESSMENT RATE	3.50%	%
G. ASSESSMENT (E X F)	1,939.00	

*MAXIMUM ASSESSABLE EARNINGS FOR 19XX PER WORKER IS $55,000

TOTAL ASSESSMENT	1,939.00
DEDUCT ASSESSMENTS PAID OR BILLED	00
ASSESSMENT DUE	1,939.00

F. Assessment rate: The industry assessment rate per $100 will be printed in this box.

G. Assessment: Multiply the earnings in Box E by the assessment rate in Box F, as a percentage. This is the amount due and payable for the period.

Total assessment: Enter the total assessment for the period in this box.

Deduct assessments paid or billed: Deduct any payments made during the year, and pay the balance by entering it in the Assessment Due box.

Workers' compensation is usually calculated on a cumulative basis for each period. The payments made during the year are then deducted from the total, and the balance due is payable. Be sure to familiarize yourself with the maximum insured earnings for each worker. At year-end, an annual summary will be sent, and all over-payments and adjustments can be made on this form.

Once again, don't be late with your payments, as penalties and interest mount up quickly. In some provinces which require shareholders to contribute, there is a minimum coverage which must be paid for each shareholder, whether they actually draw the wages or not.

REVENUE CANADA PAYROLL REMITTANCE:
INSTRUCTIONS

Deductions made at source from employees' payroll cheques are to be remitted to Revenue Canada by the 15th of the following month. You will receive a Form PD7A(E) in the mail each month, with room on the front to show your monthly calculations. This piece is kept for your own records. The remittance stub is mailed in with your cheque.

Maintaining your payroll involves ensuring that your individual payroll records are reconciled each month, totalled on a cumulative basis, (ready for your T4s at year end), a monthly reconciliation prepared and your Revenue Canada remittance prepared.

Your payroll records should also agree with your general ledger payroll accounts. If you are not sure how to do this properly, ask your accountant to show you. To prepare the monthly payroll remittance, follow these steps:

1. Total the gross wages, Canada Pension Plan, Employment Insurance and tax columns for the month on each employee's payroll sheet. Make sure the columns balance to the net amount of the cheques issued.

2. List each employee's totals for the month on a payroll reconciliation sheet:

3. Calculate your Revenue Canada remittance by using the following equation:

CPP deducted for month:	$ 145.00
Employer's portion:	145.00
EI deducted for month:	220.00
Employer's portion x 1.4 =	308.00
Tax deducted:	1,415.00
Remittance due:	2,233.00

4. Transfer these amounts to the payroll remittance for your records.

5. Fill in these amounts on the front of the remittance marked "2" and attach your cheque for payment.

6. Make sure the cheque is paid, not mailed, by the 15th of the month.

7. Keep all your remittance copies for year-end reconciliation purposes.

REVENUE CANADA PAYROLL REMITTANCE: SAMPLE

Deductions made at source from employees' payroll cheques are to be remitted to Revenue Canada by the fifteenth of the following month. You will receive a Form PD7A(E) in the mail each month, with room on the back to show your monthly calculations. This peice is kept for your own records. The remittance stub is mailed in with your cheque.

Revenue Revenu
Canada Canada

STATEMENT OF ACCOUNT FOR CURRENT SOURCE DEDUCTIONS

1 Statement of account as of:
November 15, 19XX

Account number
87429 9555 RP

Employer name
Jason's Garden Service Ltd.

Balances on last statement		Current balances	
Amount paid for 19XX	Assessed amount owing	Amount paid for 19XX	Assessed amount owing
6,016.80	00.00	7,691.50	00.00

EXPLANATION OF CHANGES

Date	Description	Amount
October 15, 19XX	Payment Oct.19XX	1,674.70 Cr

Thank you for your payment. Please use part 2 to make your next remittance

---

2 Revenue Revenu
Canada Canada

CURRENT SOURCE DEDUCTIONS REMITTANCE VOUCHER

Account number **Dept.use only**
87429 9555 RP

Amount of payment   1 7 2 3 ¦ 6 3

Jason's Garden Service Ltd,
14355 Willowbend Ave,
Countrytown, BC
V2X 1Y1

Month for which   Year X X   Month 1 1
deductions were withheld

Gross monthly payroll   8 6 4 5 ¦ 0 0

Number of employees
in last pay period   0 4

Reverse side:

CPP contributions	El premiums	Tax deductions
317.26	232.68	1,173.69
Current payment	Gross monthly payroll	No. of employees-last period
1,723.63	8,645.00	04

YEAR-END T4 PREPARATION: INSTRUCTIONS

If you balance your payroll monthly and keep the totals cumulative, your year-end work is minimal when preparing T4s. At the end of the year, follow these steps:

1. Total each employee's payroll sheet, including gross wages, CPP, EI, tax deductions, and net wages. The totals of all the deduction columns should add across to equal the gross wages.

2. Refer to your employment guide from Revenue Canada to find the minimum insurable earnings for your particular pay period, as each pay period differs. If you did not enter this amount when each payroll was prepared, now is the time to do so.

3. Go down the gross wage column, and check that each gross wage entry qualifies for insurable earnings. If the wages do not, subtract them from the gross wages for the year to arrive at your insurable earnings amount for the year.

4. Now transfer the annual payroll totals to a reconciliation sheet as set out above, adding columns for address, social insurance number, and insurable earnings, plus any other relevant figures required, such as registered pension plan contributions, pension adjustments, union dues, and donations paid. You will need a spreadsheet to prepare this information. You should now have all employees' information on a master sheet.

5. Enter each employee's details across the page. When all employees are entered, add each column down and then cross-check the final balances to make sure that your additions agree.

6. Check the wage totals with your general ledger to make sure your accounting records and payroll both agree.

7. Enter each employee's details onto a T4, putting the relevant information into the right boxes. Do not forget to include such amounts as employment commissions and other taxable benefits.

8. On a basic T4, the following boxes should have entries:

Box 14:   Employment income before deductions: enter gross wages.

Box 16:   Employee's CPP contributions: enter the annual CPP deducted from payroll.

Box 17: Employee's QPP contributions: enter the annual QPP deducted from payroll.

Box 18: Employee's EI premiums: enter the annual EI deducted from payroll.

Box 20: Registered pension plan contributions: enter the amount of your company pension plan deductions.

Box 22: Income tax deducted: enter the annual amount of income tax deducted.

Box 24: EI insurable earnings: enter the amount calculated in your payroll records, up to the annual limit, which can be found in the payroll guide.

Box 28: Exempt CPP & EI: Certain people are exempt from CPP, being those under the age of 18 and those over the age of 65. Shareholders are exempt from EI if they own more than 40 percent of a business. If these cases apply for an employee, mark the box with an X. If you don't, Revenue Canada will send a request for payment for the unpaid CPP or EI.

Boxes 30 to 42:

These amounts should be included in the gross earnings in Box 14. Enter each individual amount where applicable.

Box 44: Union dues: If you have deducted union dues from your employees, enter the amount here.

Box 46: Charitable donations: If you have deducted donations from employees,enter the amount here.

Box 50: Pension plan or DPSP registration number: Enter your pension plan number here.

Box 52: Pension adjustment: If you have a company pension plan, enter the amount of the pension adjustment here. Refer to your guide for further details.

Box 10: Enter the province of employment for the employee.

Box 12:   Enter the employee's social security number here.

Employer's name:

Enter the registered business name in full.

Box 56:   Employee's number: enter the employee's payroll number

Box 54:   Enter your Revenue Canada payroll number here.

Don't forget to write the employee's name with the surname first, then his or her full address.

9. When all T4s have been completed, total all the boxes to ensure they equal your records from your master sheet. Start by totalling the gross wages first. They should agree with the gross wages on your spreadsheet. Then do the same for CPP, EI, tax and any other deductions. If the records do not agree, start checking off the amounts on your tape against the master record to find your errors. If the T4 cannot be corrected neatly, void it and prepare another one.

10. When all the records agree, separate the T4s: the top copy goes to Revenue Canada with the T4 summary, the second and third copies go to the employees, and the fourth copy is kept by the employer.

Revenue Canada has available a T4 short form, which eliminates many of the information boxes which smaller businesses will never use. Boxes 30 to 40 are deleted, and the format of the T4 has changed. Don't let this change scare you. The box numbers correspond with the old T4 format, and the new T4 should be completed in exactly the same manner as the standard form.

YEAR-END T4 SUMMARY: INSTRUCTIONS

Once your T4s have been completed, your last job is to fill in the T4 summary. In Box 68, enter the number of T4s you are filing. Then continue to complete all other information. To calculate whether you have paid enough in annual deductions to Revenue Canada, complete the following calculation:

Total CPP deducted for year:	1,000.00
Total employer's portion of CPP:	1,000.00
Total EI deducted for year:	1,300.00
Employer's portion x 1.4	1,820.00
Total tax deducted for year:	12,500.00
ANNUAL REMITTANCE:	$ 17,620.00

Compare this amount to the amount shown as received on your last Revenue Canada remittance, which you would receive in late January. The two figures should agree. If you have underpaid, you will have to remit the balance on your T4 summary, and will be subject to penalties and interest. If you have overpaid, Revenue Canada will credit your next year's account, or, you can request a refund.

Now it is time to fill in all those little boxes.

Box 14: Enter the gross wages for the year.

Box 20: Enter the amount of registered pension plan contributions from employees.

Box 52: Enter the total pension adjustment amount.

Box 24: Enter the total EI insurable earnings of all employees for the year.

Box 16: Enter the total employee's CPP deductions for the year from your calculation above.

Box 27: Enter the employer's CPP contributions, which equal Box 16.

Box 18:   Enter the employee's EI deductions for the year from your calculation above.

Box 19:   Enter the employer's EI contributions for the year, totalling 1.4 times the employee's deductions, from your calculation above.

Box 22:   Enter the total income tax deducted for the year from your calculation above.

Box 80:   Total all deductions reported in Boxes 16, 27, 18, 19 and 22.

Box 82:   Enter the amount of your Revenue Canada remittances for the year, as stated on your January remittance summary .

Boxes 84 and 86:

If you have underpaid, enter the amount in Box 86. If you have overpaid, enter the amount in Box 84.

Fill in the required information in Boxes 71 through 78, sign and certify your return. Keep the last copy for your payroll records, attach your T4 copies for future reference.

ABOUT THE AUTHOR

Frances McGuckin has worked in the management field of small to large businesses for 16 years in both Australia and Canada, and has been a business consultant for 15 years. Her seminars and workshops on small business start-up and management are extremely popular, as was the first edition of Business For Beginners. She has earned a YWCA Women of Distinction Entrepreneurial nomination in Vancouver, British Columbia in 1998, as well as nominations for business excellence awards in her community.

She writes a weekly business column, various articles for newspapers and magazines, and is a feature writer and editor of a community magazine. Frances is a founding member and Co-ordinator of a large women's network, a director of the Langley Chamber of Commerce, and sits on various advisory committees related to small business, self-employment programs, and community affairs. She speaks on many topics related to small business to chambers of commerce, associations, colleges, multilevel and network marketing groups, and special business and educational events.

For more information on speaking engagements, author interviews, special events, or this book, please contact:

Eastleigh Publications, a division of Eastleigh Management Services
21944 6th Avenue,
Langley, British Columbia
V2Z 1R6

Telephone: (604) 530-3601
Web page: www.smallbizpro.com
e-mail: info@smallbizpro.com